McGraw-Hill Series in Speech

CLARENCE T. SIMON, *Consulting Editor*

Basic Voice Training for Speech

McGraw-Hill Series in Speech

CLARENCE T. SIMON, *Consulting Editor*

Basic Voice Training
for Speech

ELISE HAHN   CHARLES W. LOMAS

DONALD E. HARGIS   DANIEL VANDRAEGEN

University of California at Los Angeles

McGRAW-HILL BOOK COMPANY, INC.

NEW YORK   TORONTO   LONDON

1952

BASIC VOICE TRAINING FOR SPEECH

Library of Congress Catalog Card Number: 51-13585

Preface

Basic Voice Training for Speech grew out of a need felt by the authors for a text in voice training which would integrate a moderate body of content, drawn from voice science, with usable drill material for voice improvement. Too often the course in voice becomes either content or drill, to the virtual exclusion of the other, or perhaps two unrelated courses taught simultaneously. We felt that on the college level a knowledge of the basic physiology of voice production and the elementary physics of sound would help students to understand their own voices, and would therefore make drill an intelligent process instead of a mere routine prescribed by the instructor. On the other hand, we also believed that experimentation with the vocal mechanism would help to make the knowledge of vocal physiology vital instead of abstract and formal. For this reason, except in the opening chapters, drill material has not been left to the end of the chapter, but follows immediately the factual data upon which it is based.

Throughout the book, all drills have been pegged to the basic concept that the student must first hear and analyze his own voice before he can improve it. Chapter 1 develops this thesis and sets the student to work on preliminary analysis; in each of the subsequent chapters, the reader is advised to listen and analyze before he begins to drill. Most of the drill material is devised, first, to isolate the skill to be developed; second, to incorporate it in simple texts; third, to utilize it in appropriate reading matter; and finally, to make it function in original speaking. This sequence is important to the learning process and should be retained in practice.

The book is so organized that many individuals, properly motivated to improve their voices, should be able to follow the exercises and develop in vocal skill without help from an instructor, particularly if they have access to recording equipment. Most students, however, will profit by the instructor's guidance. In the first place, it is desirable to have every student make a recording of his voice early in the course, preferably in the first two weeks. The material to be recorded should include standardized reading matter, a brief informal interview giving personal data, and a short extempore speech. The student should retain possession of the record and be able to play it on his own phonograph, if he has one, or on a playback machine in the speech laboratory. With the instructor's help, he should then analyze what he hears on the record and set up a plan for his personal development. During the interview, the instructor may well make an additional wire or tape recording, preferably without the student's knowledge, to reinforce the evidence of the formal record. The instructor should point out to the student what parts of the book will be especially helpful to him, and may often suggest reading of some sections in advance of class assignment. It is best, however, to plan a definite sequence of drills which will keep the emphasis on only one or two skills at a time.

Additional conferences with the instructor should be encouraged. A few students with special problems may well be assigned by the instructor to work in the speech clinic with advanced students. Paired and group drills are also helpful. When formal speaking or reading assignments are made, the instructor may sometimes retain half the class for group drills while the other half is dismissed to work in pairs, helping each other to prepare the formal assignment for class delivery. If recording machines can be made available to students for at least a part of their practice period, the quality of their work will be better.

The problem of grading in a voice course is more difficult when both content and improvement in skill must be considered. In our teaching, we try to weigh the grade approximately equally on knowledge and skill. We give both a written and an oral final examination. Sometimes a part of the written final follows our consistent emphasis on listening, and includes analysis of the voices of other students who are giving their oral final. The oral final consists of part reading and part original speaking, blended into a single theme. A final recording on the same disk with the initial one may be used to judge oral progress, also. The standardized material on this recording should be identical with that on the first record to facilitate comparison.

This book was written to be used in a one-semester course, and is so used on the U.C.L.A. campus. By extending the amount of time devoted to drills and having more formal reading and speaking assignments, however, the material may be used in a two-semester course. Under this plan, the best place to divide the material would be at the end of Chapter 7, reserving the chapters on articulation for the second half of the course. If this is done, we recommend the use of a good dictionary as a supplementary text. The introduction and guide to pronunciation in Webster's Collegiate Dictionary is particularly helpful. We like the American College Dictionary for its recognition of unstressed forms in General American speech. For a phonetic dictionary, we recommend Kenyon and Knott's Pronouncing Dictionary of American English.

Appendix II is not designed as a comprehensive anthology of reading selections. It does, however, offer some material, both formal and informal, for practice. Frequent references to Appendix II in the text point up selections which are best adapted to developing skill in a particular area. Both student and instructor, however, will have additional selections which they wish to use. These should be chosen purposefully, with particular attention to the skill being developed at the time the selection is read in class.

We wish to express our gratitude to Lee J. Wexler, the artist who prepared many of the illustrations used in the text; to Dr. Ralph Richardson, for reading some of the chapters and making helpful suggestions; to Dr. John Moncur and Dr. Wesley Lewis, who have taught from the book in its earlier forms; and to our publishers and the editors and readers whose helpful comments have materially improved the book over three years of revision.

ELISE HAHN
CHARLES W. LOMAS
DONALD E. HARGIS
DANIEL VANDRAEGEN

LOS ANGELES, CALIF.
April, 1952

Contents

1

Critical Listening and Self-analysis

But if you mouth it, as many of your players do, I had as lief the town-crier spoke my lines.—SHAKESPEARE

To Shakespeare's Hamlet, the town crier was the personification of unintelligent, indifferent, and meaningless speech. The monotony of his voice and its lack of clear and understandable articulation were symbols of his indifference to his material and his disinterest in his hearers. But we do not need to be town criers—or players—to have "town-crier" voices.

Take a look at Bill Jones, a three-sport letter man. In football he played the hardest hitting game at end in three student generations, and he was spectacular at catching passes. Everyone said he was a certain All-American. He was All-American on campus, too—he made the best fraternity in the university and he was a good student, well above average without being brilliant—in short, he met your expectations as a Big Man on Campus.

Yet, when you heard him speak, you took a second look. Somehow he didn't sound quite as you had anticipated. Instead of the deep, resonant voice you expected to hear coming from his big frame, you heard a high-pitched, thin tone. Moreover, his words came out at a tumbling, rapid rate that made them difficult to understand, because many of the small syllables and words were omitted.

Bill was able to compensate for his vocal problems. You soon forgot his weak and colorless voice because you continued to admire his good qualities. But there are other people in the world who are less fortunate. Their bad voices are the dominant features of their personalities. They are the Mr. Milquetoasts of society. Their associates discount their ideas. They are ignored at social gatherings. The nasal whine, crudely slurred articulation, or timid whisper may easily become the key to social or business oblivion.

You constantly make judgments about people on the basis of their personal traits, and of these, one of the most important is the voice. Voices give you cues to many things about individuals: where they have been brought up, what education they have had, and what racial and socioeconomic groups have influenced them. From his voice you may detect how a speaker feels about himself: assured, uncertain, proud, self-effacing. In the same way you may know how he feels toward others: friendly, defensive, sympathetic, aggressive, indifferent. Moreover, at the moment of speaking he may be displaying or hiding his emotions about the subject under discussion; you judge him on this, too.

But you yourself are judged by other people, and by the same standards you apply to them. You may have acquired considerable skill in the use of your voice through the process of unconscious imitation and of trial and error. Yet you may be aware that you sometimes have a "town-crier" voice—that you are not always equally effective in communicating your ideas and feelings to others. Many an average speaker will say, "I can argue with a friend. Why can't I convince a *group* of people that I believe in what I am saying?" or, "I sound interested and enthusiastic when I talk at home. Why can't I always sound that way?" or again, "I'm sure I can read aloud with meaning or act a scene when I am alone. Why can't I make an audience respond to me?" or in still another situation, "My voice sounds strong and vital when I practice my speeches. What happens to it when I deliver my speech to the class?"

Of course there may be many answers. The influence of your emotions may distort your speech; habits of speech which served you well in one situation may not be adapted to a new occasion; you may be using a pattern of speech appropriate to an earlier level of growth, but no longer suitable to your age and education.

If you wish to improve your communication, you must know what your present speaking skills are, how you can vary them to suit specific purposes and situations, and what faults or emotional obstacles stand in the way of your further development as a speaker. These suggestions may sound reasonable as you read them, but there are serious barriers to undertaking this analysis.

BARRIERS TO OBJECTIVE ANALYSIS

Habit

What stands in the way of an objective scrutiny of your own speech? As a small child you listened intently to the voices of people about you. You became aware that your voice was a tool by which you could control the actions of people near you, and you constantly experimented with your voice in an effort to make sounds exactly like those made by the members of your family. When you reached the point where your wants could be satisfied easily by the use of voice, this process of listening and adjustment slowed up, and perhaps stopped altogether. Your habits were relatively fixed. Not until you came in contact with other voices radically different from your own, or until you became aware of weaknesses in your pattern of speech which prevented you from attaining desired ends, did you begin to listen again.

Self-justification

But there is an even more important, though somewhat irrational, reason why you fail to hear your own voice objectively. If someone tells you that your voice is unpleasant, you bristle, "If you don't like it, don't listen." Or you may rationalize, "I was tired; I didn't like the people; I didn't feel like talking, anyway." In this way you protect yourself from both criticism and improvement. You think of your voice and articulation, quite correctly, as being an intimate part of your personality. You do not wish to have your carefully constructed good opinion of that personality disturbed. Such criticism shakes not only your belief in your ability as a speaker, but your faith in yourself as an effective individual. If you can find no way of nullifying the criticism, you may, as a last resort, turn on the critic with the irrelevant remark, "You're not so good yourself." Consequently you may never really have analyzed your skills and shortcomings as a speaker. You would much rather have your faith in yourself unshaken.

HOW TO LISTEN

However, there is a way to bring about such an analysis with a minimum of pain and disturbance. If you discover that one of your friends always increases his rate and raises his pitch when he feels that he is not getting attention from his listeners, you conclude that you are very observing, and may even start as an amateur analyst to discover the reasons for his behavior. Or you may note another speaker who commands attention by effective use of the pause. If you then set yourself the task of analyzing how more and more people behave in a variety of speaking situations, for better or for worse, you can build up skill in judgment through this listening and watching. The day will come when you think, with some impersonal curiosity and surprise, "Do I do what Jack does when I speak or read? He has interesting variety in his voice which makes people listen to him; can I acquire that trait?" Or you may think, "Jim's constant slurring of words makes him hard to understand, and people don't give the attention to his ideas they should. Do I have similar faults?"

You can be reasonably certain that you will not develop good listening habits unless you really want to do so. Listening, like any other skill, can be developed only by constant attention to it; haphazard listening, which takes place only during the hour when the speech class is in session, will do you little good. *Every minute of hearing others speak should be made a conscious part of your drill in listening.* You will hear many different types of speakers: the professors lecturing in your classes, preachers and other public speakers, radio announcers, bus drivers, paper boys, sand-lot baseball players, speakers you overhear on the bus, waitresses, salesgirls, actors. The number of different situations in which you can hear speech is unlimited, and each speaker and speaking situation presents a new challenge in listening. Some of the speakers you hear will have better voices and speech than your own; some will have poorer. You can learn from both.

But it is not enough simply to hear voices. You must have a method for analyzing them. If we were to give you a complete chart for analyzing voices at this time, it would be meaningless to you. This entire book is designed to help you regain your ability to hear your own voice, through critical listening to others and to yourself. In each chapter, you will find specific instructions for listening to others, analyzing their voices, and applying the results of this analysis to the study of your own vocal problems. Yet there are some things for which you can begin listening at once. The sooner you begin to attend to these things, the more rapid your progress will be.

WHAT TO LISTEN FOR

Levels of Usage

Speech situations vary in formality, in the intensity of the situation, in the size and complexity of the audience, and in the purpose the speaker has in mind. Each situation demands a different kind of speech. Listen carefully to speakers under each of the following sets of circumstances: a preacher reading from the Bible; a small boy describing how his team won a ball game on a home run in the last inning with two men out and the count three and two; a group of friends in your living room before an open fire; the executive committee of your fraternity discussing an important problem; a group of college students in a "bull session"; a well-known actor performing a Shakespearean role; your own speech during a conference with your English or speech teacher.

Try to analyze the differences between these speakers as you hear them. What differences were there in distinctness of utterance? Which speakers talked most rapidly? Which spoke most loudly? Which ones had the most pleasing tone quality? Which had the most interesting variety in their voices? What correlations can you see between the nature of the situation and the differences you observed?

If you have analyzed these speakers carefully, you probably have come to the conclusion that as the situation becomes more intense, the speaker's manner may become more animated; he may speak louder, and his rate may become faster. As the situation becomes more formal, the level of distinctness tends to improve. As the audience becomes larger, or the acoustics less satisfactory, the speaker may be required to talk louder and more distinctly, and he tends to increase the range over which he develops variety. In other words, speech which may be entirely adequate for simple situations, such as casual conversations with your friends, may fail completely as the situation becomes more formal, more intense, or more complex in terms of the size of the audience or the acoustics of the room.

Changes in the speaker's purpose may also vary the quality of his voice and his general style of delivery. The manner of the speaker who merely wants to inform his hearers is markedly different from that of the orator who tries to stimulate, the soldier who wishes to command, or the lover who seeks to charm. Vocal quality which serves one purpose well may be without effect in a different situation.

Listening, then, should first teach us to recognize levels of usage. We should try to determine what constitutes the good normal voice for pleasant and effective conversation. We then need to know how we can adapt the normal instrument to the needs of skilled speech in the more demanding situations which confront us. Finally, we must avoid the pitfalls of substandard voice and articulation in any situation. Careful listening, coupled with the reading of this book and the advice of your instructor, will teach you to develop adequate standards for each speaking occasion.

Specific Vocal Characteristics

In public performance, a speaker's personal worth, the intense interest of the audience in the subject, and the presence of strong emotions may compensate for the speaker's bad vocal habits. Lacking these conditions, however, few audiences will listen long or responsively to a speaker or actor whose projection or articulation makes him difficult to understand, whose voice is monotonous in melody or rate, or whose manner seems to indicate that he is indifferent to the audience or the subject. To put the emphasis on the speaker's vocal traits is not, of course, to minimize the importance of worthwhile materials for the speaker to present, but our primary concern here is with the voice.

At a formal reception you may mumble, "Happy to meet you," or, "Hope you drop dead," with equal lack of communication. Since no meaning is intended by either phrase, if the proper inflections and fixed smile are maintained, no one need be the wiser. But in most speaking situations, you are trying to make your voice a full instrument of communication—of your ideas, your attitudes, and your feelings. As a first step in training yourself to listen, you should ask yourself four questions dealing with this problem of communication. Apply them first to others. When you think you have developed some skill in analysis, turn the tables and apply them to yourself.

1. *Can you be heard by the listener?* This may seem simple enough at home in a quiet room with the listener seated a few feet from you, but it becomes a real problem as the physical situation changes. You may be as close to your friend as you were at home, but if you are now in a noisy restaurant or railroad station, the level of loudness which you used in the first situation may be far from sufficient to allow him to hear you. In large audience situations, mere physical distance reduces audibility, along with such factors as the acoustics of the room, the sounds made by the audience, and external noises which may filter in. In listening to others, if you have difficulty hearing, make note of the presence of any of these factors. In listening to yourself, if these factors are present, you should watch your hearers for signs of inattention or strained listening. Most college students underestimate the amount of sound necessary to be heard in an ordinary classroom. But if you will train yourself to observe your audience, you need not make this error. Chapters 3 through 6 should help you to understand this problem and deal with it. Meanwhile train yourself to listen for levels of loudness.

2. *Can you be understood by the listener?* Are you producing sounds with sufficient clarity to convey your meaning? If the listener merely hears vocal tones coming to his ear, and not the sounds of articulate speech, he cannot possibly get your idea. The problem involved here is closely related to loudness and is often confused with it. Many deaf people are annoyed by loud talking, saying that they hear perfectly, but that "people today don't talk as distinctly as they used to." Such individuals are the victims of high-

frequency deafness, which prevents them from hearing distinctly the slight differences between high-pitched consonant sounds of similar acoustic properties. But the same problems may arise for any hearer when the speaker does not articulate clearly, when outside noises interfere, or when echoes and dead spots in an auditorium confuse high-frequency sounds. You should therefore form the habit of listening to yourself, as well as to other speakers, to determine whether you make all of the sounds of speech clearly or whether you tend to slur them, run them together, or omit them. Self-analysis will be more rapid and accurate if you record your voice to assist you in hearing your articulation of sounds. If you discover that you have particular difficulties in this area, you will do well to work ahead of the class with Chapters 8, 9, and 10, which take up articulation problems in detail.

3. *Is your voice pleasant to listen to?* This is an intensely personal question, and the answer to it is intermeshed with fundamental problems of physical structure, personality, and emotional control. Some of these problems are discussed in Chapter 2. Some may require psychological advice. Other difficulties can be dealt with by understanding the mechanism which controls the voice and learning how to use it better. Chapters 5 and 6 will prove especially helpful in this analysis. But before any of the suggestions of these chapters can help you, you must hear your own voice and decide for yourself whether you would like to make it more pleasant than it now is. Detailed listening to others is particularly important here. You must formulate standards of judgment by listening to many types of voices; then apply these standards to discover the faults and virtues of your own voice. Here again, when you start to analyze yourself, the recording machine is indispensable. You must listen to your voice as if it were that of a stranger. Since few people hear themselves as others do, this is not so difficult as it might seem. It is perhaps more of a problem to persuade yourself that the voice you are hearing is really your own. But it is essential that you make that judgment if you wish to improve.

4. *Is your voice flexible enough to convey the shades of meaning and of feeling which you intend?* Is it an interesting voice? Is the rate continuously fast or slow, or does it change with the meaning? Is there variety in the melody of the voice, or does it stay on one level most of the time? Is the tone more resonant when strong feelings are present? The significance of these and other factors is developed in Chapter 7, but for the present you should resort again to extensive listening to others and to self-analysis through listening to recordings.

A PLAN FOR IMPROVEMENT

The material of this book will be of value to you only to the extent that you use it to plan a systematic program of improvement in the use of your voice. You cannot learn a new skill unless you have regular periods of practice and continually check your progress against both your starting point and your goal.

Develop Habits of Self-analysis

As we have noted in the preceding pages, the first step in your improvement should be the development of habits of self-analysis. But this is not a preliminary process, to be practiced at the beginning of the course and straightway forgotten. Self-examination, to be effective, must be continuous during the learning period. Throughout the book, as new problems are discussed, specific directions are given for self-analysis and listening. You must use these as they are presented, but you must also recheck yourself constantly on suggestions offered earlier. In this way you can fix the habit of listening to yourself and avoid dropping back into old habits when you have completed a semester of concentrated drill and study.

Distinguish Practice from Performance

It is difficult to establish new vocal skills in actual performance. To be effective, good vocal usage must be habitual, and in performance you must be free to direct your attention to communication rather than to the mechanical details of voice production. If you must constantly plan each step in vocalization, you cannot speak naturally, nor can you produce a voice which is free of strain and tension. The purpose of practice periods is to provide time when you can make mistakes and correct them without the social consequences of failure in performance. At the same time, we should note that appearances before the speech class are still within the practice framework. Public performances of plays or readings, public speeches, business interviews, and important social occasions should be classed as performances. Your aim should be to establish habits that will operate without effort in these situations.

Establish Automatic Control

Perhaps you can recall your first experiences in driving a car. All your attention was directed to the manipulation of the mechanical devices which kept the machine running. Probably you were tense, using more muscles and expending more nervous energy than were needed. After some experience, however, you began to relax unneeded muscles; your control over the car became a matter of automatic reflexes rather than of conscious thought, and you became a better driver in the process.

In the same way you should learn the new motor skills involved in improving your use of the vocal mechanism. You may improve your control over new habits by learning them so thoroughly that you do not need to think about them. Thus control becomes a matter of less attention to detail rather than more. Control need not involve tension; if good habits are thoroughly learned, you will find yourself using less physical activity than you did under your previous faulty habits of voice production.

Practice Continuously

While you are attempting to develop new vocal habits, you should, if possible, avoid public-performance situations, which often compel you to revert to your old habits. But in every other speaking situation, where social pressures permit, you should practice the new skills you are seeking to establish. For example, you may tell your friends and family what you are trying to accomplish, and ask them to listen to your voice in conversation, calling attention to your errors. With a little experimentation, you will find that you can practice vocal drills in time you now waste. You can practice breathing exercises while walking, phonation exercises in your shower, and articulation exercises while driving to school. So far as possible, once you have determined the nature of your new habit, you should avoid falling back into your old way of speaking in any situation whatsoever.

Concentrate on One Problem at a Time

If you have many vocal problems, do not try to remedy them all at once. Determine with the help of your instructor what is most important; then concentrate on that problem, moving on to others as you begin to make substantial progress. At the same time remember your ultimate goal—better communication in speech. Each skill you learn is a step toward that end.

SUMMARY

In the plan of this book, listening and self-analysis are constant tools for improvement. They are the means by which you may overcome your inertia and compel yourself to take positive steps to improve your voice. As you read the book, you should take advantage of the materials dealing with self-analysis and apply your findings to the development of new skills.

Exercises to Improve Listening and Self-analysis

1. Listen to a public speaker talking to an audience of 100 or more. Is his level of usage appropriate to the situation in which he is speaking? Can he be heard without effort on your part? Do his words and phrases reach you clearly so that you can understand them easily? Is his voice pleasant to listen to? Is his voice responsive to shades of meaning in his material? As far as you are able, at this point in your training as a listener, analyze the factors which influence the answers you have given to these questions.

2. Make the same type of analysis for as many of the following situations as you are able to observe: (*a*) the actors in a play you attend; (*b*) a friend or a member of your family conversing with you in a casual situation; (*c*) a person you overhear in casual conversation on a bus, at a party, or in a public place; (*d*) a group of children at play; (*e*) a professor lecturing in a classroom.

3. In the Columbia album, *I Can Hear It Now*, Volume I, listen to the voices of Will Rogers, Huey Long, Adolf Hitler, Joseph Stalin, radio announcer Herbert Morrison describing the burning of the Hindenburg, Fiorello La Guardia, Alfred E. Smith, Franklin D. Roosevelt, Winston Churchill, Harry Truman. As far as you are able to do so from the recordings, analyze these voices according to the standards set forth in Exercise 1. Some of these voices have marked faults. Are there compensating factors in the voices themselves, or would you have to know more about the speech situation and the personality of the speakers to discover why audiences were attracted to these men?

4. Make a record of your voice, preferably one side of a disk record which you can play on your own phonograph. Part of the record should consist of reading, and part of informal or extemporaneous speaking. Your instructor will help you to select suitable material. Listen to the record as if it were the voice of another person, and analyze it in the same way you did the voices in the previous exercises.

5. Keeping in mind the factors you noted in analyzing your voice recording, listen to your voice as you read aloud, as you converse with a friend, as you talk informally before the class. Can you hear the same problems?

2

Why You Speak as You Do

There is no index of character so sure as the voice.—TANCRED

In the preceding chapter, you were urged to listen to yourself and to answer the question, "What is my speech like?" To facilitate self-criticism and to give greater insight into your present habits, you now must answer the question, "Why do I speak as I do?" You need to discover what physical conditions have influenced you and how the environment in which you grew up has influenced your speech. You must also inquire whether your evaluation of yourself in relation to other people reveals itself in your voice.

It is easy to ask these questions. It may be harder for you to answer them. In this chapter, therefore, we shall introduce you to other people whose past and present physical condition, environment, or emotional adjustment has influenced their voices. When you can recognize these factors in others, look for them in yourself. If you can make a calm and objective analysis of your own background and personality, you will be aided materially in solving your voice problems resulting from these causes.

Let us begin by eavesdropping on a family argument. John had decided to "talk it out" with his father. The time had come when he had to follow his own ambitions instead of the career which his father had selected for him.

As they got up from the table, John began cautiously, "Mr. Stone was saying business was good. He has a nice place there." His tone was guardedly casual.

"How do you happen to be so interested?" his father asked sharply.

"Who said I was so interested?" John asked defensively, as if to protect himself.

"You've heard he's looking for a new man, haven't you?" the older man bristled.

"Well, what if he is? I've got a right to consider my *own* future, haven't I?" All the uncertainty of John's position was marked by the high pitch and the rush of his words.

The father's voice was ominously quiet. "All I want is an explanation."

So John explained, described, and grew enthusiastic about the position open to him, trying to make the older man see his point and share his feelings.

Since this is not a story, you will never know what happened. It is only an example of the many voice changes which take place quickly in a single, brief situation.

In this chapter we shall examine four factors in the speaker's background and experience which may influence his production of voice: (1) his physical structure and function, both past and present; (2) his environment, both past and present; (3) his personal adjustment to his environment; (4) the emotions present in the immediate speaking situation. These factors are interrelated and influence one another. In the story of John and his father you may readily recognize two of them. The personal relationship of the two men was quite evident, and the emotions present in the immediate situation could be judged by the tone of the voices alone, even without words. You might also have been able to tell some things about their physical and environmental backgrounds by careful observation of the men as they talked, but you probably would have needed more information than can be obtained from a single incident if you were to make a valid judgment on these influences.

You may discover how to analyze all of these causal relationships in yourself by examining typical speakers and speaking situations in which each of the four factors is at work.

THE INFLUENCE OF PHYSICAL STRUCTURE
AND FUNCTION UPON VOICE

Each of you in this class started out with a different physical equipment. The man next to you may have a powerful, deep voice. No forced lowering of your pitch is going to give you his low, resonant tone, because you may happen to have a smaller larynx and a different-sized throat and mouth. You can, however, with your particular structures, improve resonance and responsive quality at your normal pitch level, and you may develop a flexibility in usage that makes your voice more pleasant to listen to than his.

Note how the structures of the vocal mechanism alone can vary. Within your own class, notice differences in the size and shape of jaw, the arrangement of teeth, the development of mouth and lips, the size of larynx, and the construction of rib cage. You will not be able to see the tongue, the soft palate, and the vocal folds themselves, but after you have observed other differences, you can understand that these also may vary extensively from person to person.

These differences in relative size and shape of structures will affect the manner in which you produce sounds, but while you may be vocalizing or articulating in a way technically different from that of your neighbor, the audible results may be good. Even pronounced differences in structure need not cause speech defects. The moving parts of the speech mechanism can make a wide variety of adjustments.

However, structural deviations may sometimes be related to poor habits of voice production. One girl will lisp because her teeth protrude; another cannot be heard because her small mouth opening; a man may mumble because he has not learned to move his rather thick lips with agility. Sometimes the existence of former deviations in structure may have set up habits which continue even after the change in structure has been made. One girl in a speech class still held her upper lip down stiffly as if trying to hide an ugly protrusion of her teeth, although the teeth had been straightened years before.

If illness caused a prolonged state of lassitude when you were very young, you felt no inclination to use the voice in experimental vocal play and jargon which were the necessary preparation for speech, and thus you were delayed in speaking. A student reported that, because of illness, he had not learned to talk until he was three. Because of this delay, his articulation and voice were infantile for several years after he entered school. The concern of his parents, the criticism of his teachers, and the ridicule of the children had convinced him that his speech would be habitually poor. Even at twenty, he was still painfully self-conscious of his speech, with the result that his voice was uncertain, weak, and monotonous.

Hearing loss will also affect your acquisition of speech. If as a child you did not hear accurately the high-frequency sounds of s, f, and th, you could not imitate these readily. Similarly, if you did not hear pitch and loudness differences with ease, you may have acquired a monotony of melody and loudness in your speech.

You are aware, of course, that your present physical condition influences your voice. If you are fatigued or debilitated after a recent illness, the muscles of your body do not respond quickly. Speech production is a muscular process; when the body is run down, you cannot expect the high degree of responsiveness and fine muscular coordination necessary for good voice.

To understand the way you now use your voice, you need to consider both your past and your present physical condition. Your present vocal habits may be the result of early structural deviations or of the presence of illness when you were first learning to speak. Your voice will also be affected by existing structural differences and by the present state of your health.

THE INFLUENCE OF ENVIRONMENT UPON VOICE

Home Influences

As an infant you produced an amazing variety of vocal sounds. You gradually modified and combined these into speech by imitating those around you, by trial and error, by self-imitation, and by repetition of approved responses. Because of these processes of imitation and experimentation, members of a close family group often have the same habits of inflection, of rate, or of articulation and pronunciation. Young children unconsciously copy vocal patterns of parents, brothers, and sisters. Although there may be likenesses of structure among family members, these similarities in speech production are more likely to result from a common environment.

Sometimes imitation may set up habits which are not acceptable in college life. A young man, whose birth into a family of four girls had once probably caused a pleasant stir, discovered that his way of speaking was ridiculed. Although his voice was low pitched and his general behavior masculine, he had a preciseness of articulation and a reserved "niceness" of manner which suggested that all five women in his family had served as models for his unconscious habits.

Sometimes imitations may be deliberate, or if not consciously pursued, may indicate an individual's need for appreciation. A girl, tall and slow moving, had attempted to copy the animated voice of her small, excitable mother. Her present speech was hesitant, with hurried broken phrases and much stridency of tone. Similarly, a boy had forced his pitch down so low, in imitation of the powerful tones of his admired lawyer father, that he developed a chronic hoarseness. Both of these students had copied voices whose production was not suited to their particular physical structure and function.

The influence of the home upon your speech depends also upon the emotional environment provided for you as you grew up. If you competed strongly with brothers and sisters or even with your parents, in an attempt to assert yourself, the type of speech you now habitually use may reflect the outcome of that competition. Again, the family relationships may have involved strict discipline, or extremely protective attitudes on the part of your parents, or the insecurity of confusing and little-understood conflicts in the home. Negative-feeling states stirred up by interfamily relationships were reflected in physical tensions and behaviors which in turn caused you to speak in a certain way. Even though your living situation has now changed in adult life, some of your speaking habits may relate to those early emotions of aggression or submissiveness, of insecurity, of extreme dependence or independence, or of self-consciousness. Have you noticed that you now attempt to dominate a situation by the loudness, fast rate, and aggressive tone of your voice? Or do you find yourself talking in a cautious, overly restrained way, as if you expected criticism and strong opposition? Habits of using whining or strident qualities, of hurling the words out as fast as possible, or of abruptly starting a statement in a loud, high tone may once have served a purpose; they have outlasted the conditions which created them.

Poor speech models may have been introduced into the home environment. Someone may have been brought into the home to care for you, and you modeled your speech after hers. Your parents may have come from a foreign country; perhaps they lisped or stuttered or slurred their articulation. It was only when you went out from the family group that you noticed that the models you had for imitation when you learned to talk were different from those of other people whom you met. These factors are beyond your control. Fortunately, you can change your speaking habits and find models with more effective speech.

If you were that fortunate child who was brought up in a secure and happy family, who heard those close to you talking freely and effectively, you probably have great facility in speaking. You have profited by learning your good speaking habits in your home environment.

The Influence of Friends and Associates

Your relationships with friends and associates influence your speech. When you wish to be a part of a group, you tend to speak like that group. This applies not only to the use of the latest expressions, but to rate, inflection, voice quality, and pronunciations. Among small children, even good vocal habits learned at home may yield to the social pressures of the speech spoken by playmates in the local district.

Many servicemen during the war became acutely conscious of the differences between their local dialects and the speech of other men in their units.

The desire to conform was often great enough to make them change their Brooklyn, Ozark, or Pennsylvania Dutch dialects in the direction of more acceptable General American.

The child or adolescent may model his behavior on that of some hero of the moment. He may first copy the voice of the television cowboy or gangster; later, that of the movie star; and still later, the manner of an older boy in school or of some man whom he admires. You have probably imitated certain aspects of the speech of other people because you admired them. If these traits contribute to effective speech, the tendency is good. These self-selected patterns have influenced the speech of all of us. Only when they are extremely different from the speech of others, when they do not fit the appearance and general character of the speaker, do they become faults which attract attention to themselves. The chubby little girl with the breathily sensual voice of her favorite movie star had better move back again into the world of everyday existence and speak in a way which matches her personality.

The Influence of the School

The school is another major influence. Here you may have learned negative attitudes toward speech. If a nagging teacher insisted upon pedantic articulation and precise pronunciation, if good speech was unrealistically associated with formal presentation of dull book reports, uninspired debates, and routine oral reading, it is not surprising if you resent efforts by others to improve your speech.

If, on the other hand, you have gone through a school system where the emphasis was placed upon oral communication as a tool for learning, where talking was fun because it gave you individual satisfaction in group activity, you will probably be well ahead of your college speech classes in poise and fluency.

The Influence of the Locality

There are distinct differences in American speech from one area to another. Sometimes these differences are highly localized; sometimes they are characteristic of broad regions. In any case, it is possible that you and your family now live in an area where the dialect is different from that in which your speech habits were learned.

The culture and behavior patterns of a particular race or national group may also affect your speech. Within the city of Detroit, for instance, there is a section populated by Polish people. Here the customs and the language of their native land are kept alive. A student teacher, although neither she nor her parents had ever been to Poland, showed her foreign background in the articulation, inflection, and rhythm pattern of her speech. Many such sections exist within large cities. A man may not wish to change his speech while he still lives in such a locality. One student made his home in a section of a large Eastern city where the majority of the people were immigrants or children of immigrants. Like other residents, he said "dis" and "dat." When his teacher tried to show him how the tongue tip is held for the TH sound, he said, "Well, I *can* put my tongue between my teeth and say 'them,' but if I do, somebody in my neighborhood will clip me on the jaw and I'll bite my tongue off."

THE INFLUENCE OF PERSONAL ADJUSTMENT UPON SPEECH

All of you have met the man who talks too loudly with an exaggerated heartiness that deceives no one, or the effusive girl who praises everything with indiscriminate gushiness. Or you may know the aggressive student whose voice sounds as if he had to prove his simplest statement with continual argument. Again, you may recognize the inhibited person whose colorless speech is used as a barrier so that outsiders cannot intrude, by means of conversation, on his private world. Finally, you may encounter the defensive individual, endlessly explaining his actions in an apologetic tone. You will see all of these people in your classes. Their more exaggerated prototypes are common outside of the university where the battle to exist may have aggravated these habits of response.

Such people as these have unconsciously evaluated themselves in a particular way. One may have failed to adjust to a physical difference; perhaps he wanted to be handsome and admired and has not yet realized that a person with a big nose or a too thin body can nevertheless be appreciated and accepted. The problems of personal adjustment posed by such physical differences are so intense that at least two great playwrights have made them dominant themes in their dramas. Rostand and Shakespeare have made Cyrano's nose and Richard III's hump the central factors in plays of great emotional power. In productions of these plays, the voices of the chief characters reflect their bitterness toward their physical abnormalities.

A man's evaluation of himself in relation to his environment and to his appearance may stand in the way of easy communication with others. He sometimes becomes too anxious to please, or aggressively hostile, or easily defeated. He may be so hypercritical of his own behavior and so analytical of his successes and failures that he has little time left to be interested in others. Instead of responding to his companions' ideas, he is hounding himself with such questions as, "Do I look funny?" "Do they think I'm not as good as they are?" "Will they know I am uncertain of myself?"

What do these evaluations of his body, his environment, and his relations with others have to do with a man's voice? These factors shape his personality. Whatever affects personality affects speech, since language behavior and personal adjustment are closely allied and interact.

Listen for signs of exaggerated response, inhibition, hostility, and defensiveness in the voices of those around you. You hear these in the quality of the voice, the rate, the pitch changes, and the variations in loudness. Listen also for the highly acceptable vocal indications of friendliness and interest in others, of animation, assurance, and belief in oneself.

The increased observation of the relationship between a speaker's personal adjustment and his speech skills will lead you to examine yourself more closely. Do you perceive that the way you speak is related to aspects of your personality?

Courses in personal adjustment and mental hygiene will give you a more comprehensive knowledge of yourself, but for the time being, analyze your speech, relate it to the influences of physical structure, environment, and personal adjustment. If you come to a place in your thinking where you conclude that your voice is dull and unresponsive because poor personal adjustment is contributing to poor voice usage, you will have obtained some insight into both your speech habits and your social relationships, and will then be ready to move out of this type of habitual response into behavior which will be more satisfactory to you.

THE INFLUENCE OF EMOTION IN THE IMMEDIATE SITUATION

In any speaking situation, even the most casual, you have a purpose in using language. Closely tied up with this purpose are accompanying attitudes toward the situation, the idea discussed, your listener, and yourself as a speaker. Attitudes are emotional in nature and will be apparent to you in physical changes and feeling states. You enjoy a situation: that enjoyment is evident in muscle tonus, in the undisturbed activity of the life-maintaining processes, in what you may call the "aliveness" of the whole body. You resent a situation: the muscles of the extremities tighten, your breath and heart rates increase, you feel the tension within the body as if certain processes had been interrupted.

Speech is, of course, a muscular activity. As the physical responses of the emotion occur, the body changes affect the voice.

A moderate amount of emotional stress is an aid to a speaker. The best speakers and actors are never completely at ease when they go before an audience. Cicero recorded his opinion that "the better the orator, the more profoundly is he frightened by the difficulty of speaking." Similar views have been expressed by such modern speakers as William Jennings Bryan, George Arliss, and Booker T. Washington. In fact, it is a universal experience of speakers and actors that they are seldom at their best unless they are emotionally stimulated before they speak.

There is a simple physiological explanation for this. When you are confronted with circumstances which are unusual or which challenge your normal faculties of response, your body reacts with a safety mechanism to give you additional energy. Your success as a speaker, either on the platform or with a group of friends, depends upon how well you can channel this extra energy into useful activity. If you can turn it into meaningful gestures and strength and vitality of voice, you will be vastly more effective than if you had not been emotionally aroused. If you do not find an outlet for this extra energy, it will be expended upon purposeless and distracting activity. Your effectiveness will be lessened and you will feel uncomfortable before your listeners.

In examining your own speech habits, criticize yourself on your ability to channel emotional responses in such a way that they contribute to the effectiveness of your speaking.

These emotions of the moment which we have been discussing will of course be related to emotions of the past. Often the insight gained in analyzing personal adjustment will help you to understand and govern the sometimes unexplainable emotions aroused in the present situation.

SUMMARY

Good speech is accepted and valued by our society. Since you were very young, social pressures for continuous improvement have been exerted upon you in the home, in school, by movies, radio, and television, in business and professional life. You have been taught to associate speech skills with the successful, attractive man or woman.

With such pressures, why are not all of us near-perfect? The answer to that question lies in the fact that influences of physical structures, environment, and personal adjustment often prevent acquisition of skills.

The desire for social acceptance and approval is a basic motivation for all of us. With some, the connection between speech skill and advancement in a profession or business may constitute a very real drive. With others, ambition to use speech creatively in artistic expression for radio, television, and stage may be an incentive for improvement.

Ask yourself why you wish to improve. Develop habits of listening critically to others. Define your own skills and faults. Analyze the backgrounds of your speech habits. In this way, you will create a desire for an understanding of how the speech mechanism works and how the various processes involved in voice production may be made more efficient and more effective.

Exercises for Analysis

1. Write an analysis of the voice of a person whom you overhear or whom you do not know well. Attempt to describe personality traits which may be related to his voice habits.

2. Write an analysis of your own voice. Base this on three questions: (*a*) *What is my voice like?* Refer back to the suggestions made in Chapter 1. Seek comments from other people to contribute to the answer. Listen to the recording made of your voice. (*b*) *Why do I speak as I do?* You should present your answer freely, since this information will be confidential and read only by your instructor. You will benefit by setting the ideas down in full so that you can examine them objectively. (*c*) *How may I improve?* The material here may be sketchy, since you may not yet have a clear idea of the skills possible to you. You may add to this at a later date.

Take your time on this analysis. Return to the preliminary notes, check them, and add more. A hurried effort made the night before the assignment is due may fulfill requirements but will rarely contribute to your understanding of yourself.

3. Analyze the impression a stranger may have of your personality after listening to you on one of the following occasions: a dinner, a business interview, a conversation with an old friend, the presentation of a speech.

3

How Sound Is Produced in Speech

The sound must seem an echo to the sense.—POPE

There is no part of the body which is specifically designed by nature for speech. Even the most garrulous gossip must stop talking long enough to eat. The athlete finishing his race knows that his body's demands for oxygen take precedence over his wish to acknowledge the good wishes and congratulations of his teammates. The small boy soon learns that he cannot articulate clearly with his mouth full of bread and jam. The structures of the body are primarily designed for the biological needs they serve. The use of the same structures for producing speech sounds is secondary, and may be described as an *overlaid function*.

PHYSIOLOGICAL BASES OF SPEECH SOUNDS

There are many animals whose vocal mechanism is sufficiently complex to produce meaningful speech of a sort; yet no animal except man has learned to use his vocal organs to produce any other meaningful sounds than the fundamental cries of animal emotion. The difference lies in the greater complexity of the human nervous system. Man has learned to sort out, classify, and control the production of speech sounds, first by the random manipulation of the speech organs to produce sounds which cause others to respond to his wishes; then by habituating these responses so that control is automatic; then by deliberately developing new vocal patterns in agreement with other men, creating the infinitely complex structure of human language.

Voice Production as a Muscular Process

The entire process of producing speech sounds, from the inhalation of the breath to the articulation of consonants, consists in the contraction and

21

relaxation of muscles. This is why your voice is so responsive to your general physical condition. Fatigue and illness make it difficult for you to "lift a finger." They make it equally difficult to "lift a vocal fold." Your voice is likely to be dull and lifeless when you are tired or sick simply because your muscles will not respond properly under these conditions.

Your vocal muscles, like any other muscles in the body, are subject to local fatigue. After a long period of talking, they may not respond readily, and your voice may play tricks on you. Like other muscles, however, the muscles which control your voice can be trained to operate with greater efficiency, and the threshold of fatigue can be raised.

You will get a more accurate picture of the functioning of the vocal apparatus if you remember that muscles do not push. They can only pull. When a muscle contracts, it becomes shorter, and exerts a pulling force on the bone, tendon, or cartilage to which it is attached. If the bone, tendon, or cartilage is displaced by this force, it can return to its original position in one of three ways: by the force of gravity, by the natural resiliency of the substance or of other tissue pressing against it, or by the pulling force of other muscles acting in opposition to the first.

You can observe all three of these conditions by a simple experiment. Place your forearm on a table, with the palm up. With your other hand on the muscles of your forearm, slowly clench your fist as tightly as you can. You can feel the contraction of the muscles. Now relax these muscles, but make no effort to straighten your fingers. Note the natural resiliency of the tissue of your hand which causes it to open slightly. Now open the hand. Note that a different set of muscles is employed from those which clenched the fist. If you were to try the same experiment with your hand at your side, the fingers would be extended more as your muscles relax, because of the force of gravity.

Why Study the Vocal Mechanism

In Chapters 4, 5, and 6, you will be introduced to the mechanism which produces speech sounds and to its functioning. We shall not be concerned with the fine details of anatomical structure; that is material for more advanced study, and you will not even be given the names of many of the muscles, nerves, bones, cartilages, and connective tissues which enter into the production of voice. Some knowledge of anatomy is, of course, essential, but our primary concern will be with the functioning of the mechanism. We shall discover what parts of the body operate to produce voice; what their relationship is to each other; and how malformation or malfunction of any part may distort speech.

"But," you say, "why is it necessary to study physiology? Isn't it perfectly possible to have a good voice without knowing how it is produced? Haven't there been thousands of excellent actors and public speakers—even teachers of speech—who didn't understand the mechanism, or who may even have had incorrect ideas about it?"

The answer is obvious. It is possible to have a good voice, and even to develop a good voice, without the slightest knowledge of physiology. But as we acquire more and more knowledge about how the voice is produced, this haphazard approach to voice training makes less and less sense. Without some knowledge of vocal physiology, your chances of making improvement on your own initiative are severely limited; your understanding of the exercises suggested by your instructor is inadequate; your ability to hear your own defects and interpret them in terms of needed adjustments in the mechanism is circumscribed. The intelligent approach to voice training is to know how the mechanism operates and how to detect and change improper use.

PHYSICAL BASES OF SPEECH SOUNDS

Not only must we understand how the various structures in the body interact, but we also need to know something of the nature of sound itself. On any given day, most of us hear an infinite variety of sounds. The hum of automobile engines, the chirping of birds, the clatter of dishes in a restaurant, the blare of music from a juke box, the drone of a professor's voice in a dull lecture, the yelling of the crowd at a football game—these are only a few of the sounds that form a part of our everyday experience.

The sounds to which we give most frequent and careful attention are those of articulate speech. But all sounds have certain common characteristics: they are formed by the action of some force upon an object capable of vibration; they pass through some transmitting medium (usually, but not always, the air) in the form of waves; these waves set up similar vibrations in the receiving object, ordinarily the ear. When sounds have a clearly identifiable pitch, or a harmoniously blended series of tones, they are called musical sounds; when the pitch is confused or dissonant, sounds are termed noise.

Sound Sources

The most common sources of musical sounds are: strings, as in a piano or violin; rods, as in a tuning fork; plates, as in a gong; bells; membranes, as in a kettledrum; air columns, as in organ pipes; reeds, as in a clarinet; membranous reeds, as in the human larynx. While all of these sound sources produce musical tones, the simultaneous sounding of unrelated pitches by each of them would produce only noise. The noise of a passing automobile may be a combination of many of these sound sources plus others, in a sound wave of infinite complexity. Nonmusical sounds may be created by vibrating objects as diverse as the rustling of the wind through dry leaves, the striking of an ax against a tree, or the firing of artillery.

Sound Waves

In ordinary transmission of sound, the vibrations of the sound sources are communicated to the surrounding air and carried as *sound waves* to the ear of the listener. Sound waves are characterized by differences in *frequency*—the number of vibration cycles per second emanating from the sound source; and by differences in *wave length*—the distance between the vibration impulses as the wave moves away from the sound source. The frequency and the wave length are inversely proportional to one another, their product always equaling the speed of sound.

The speed of sound varies with the temperature of the air, the altitude, and other factors, but it is roughly 1,100 feet per second. Obviously sound could not be carried at such a speed by a continuous forward motion of the air, for that would imply winds many times faster than the most furious typhoon every time a sound was made. Sound waves are simply alternate periods of condensation and rarefaction (thinning out) of the air molecules. The initial energy derived from the sound source is transmitted from one particle to another, with only slight forward motion, and with each particle rebounding to its first position before the next condensation strikes it.

The movement of a single period of condensation in a sound wave may be illustrated by standing a number of dominoes on end at a distance from each other slightly less than the length of one domino. By touching the first piece, you may push over the whole row, as the initial energy is transmitted from one to another until all are down. If the dominoes could be made to return

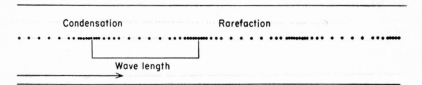

Fig. 1. Diagram showing condensation and rarefaction of air in sound waves

immediately to an upright position, another touch would start a second wave after the first. If this were done at regular intervals, the number of times it was repeated in a given period of time would be the *frequency*, and the distance between the impulses on the row of dominoes would be called the *wave length*. To put the figure back into terms of the sound wave, the distance between two condensations is the wave length, and the number of condensation-rarefaction cycles per second is the frequency.

Frequency and Pitch

The frequency of a sound wave is determined by the frequency of vibration of the object from which the sound comes. It is interpreted by the ear as the *pitch* of the sound, the same number of vibrations per second being heard as the same pitch, regardless of the source or loudness of the sound. A good point of reference in interpreting pitch is to locate middle C, a pitch made readily by both male and female voices. This pitch is approximately 256 to 260 vibration cycles per second, depending upon the musical standard adopted. The vibration rate doubles with each octave of the musical scale. Thus one octave below middle C is approximately 130 cycles, and one octave above is approximately 520 cycles. The human ear is able to detect frequencies as low as 12 and as high as 50,000, although there are wide variations in perception, particularly in the high frequencies. It is the exceptional ear which can hear frequencies higher than 20,000.

In vibrating objects like the human vocal folds, frequency is determined by four factors: (1) length—the pitch is lowered as the length increases; (2) thickness—the pitch is lowered as the thickness increases; (3) tension—the pitch is *raised* as the tension increases; (4) density—the pitch is lowered as the density increases. The force which sets the vibrating object into motion does not directly affect the frequency, although in the human voice, an increase in force is almost always accompanied by increased tension and a consequent rise in pitch. It is possible that there may be a causal relationship between these two conditions, but because the vocal folds are difficult to observe in a natural state, it is hard to determine how closely they are related.

All four factors are involved in the differences between any two voices. Thus the lower pitch of men's voices, as compared with those of women and children, is the result of longer and thicker vocal folds. In an individual voice, changes in length and thickness tend to cancel each other, and variations in pitch are largely the product of differences in the tension of the folds.

Amplitude and Loudness

When an object vibrates, the extent of its displacement from its normal condition is called the amplitude of its vibration. The greater the amount of force exerted upon the vibrating object, the greater the amplitude. The ear interprets amplitude as loudness. Since sound waves (unless prevented by reflection or absorption) move in all directions from the source of the vibration, this initial energy is dissipated rapidly. The amplitude of a wave decreases as the square of the distance from the sound source. If sound waves are to be used for communication, therefore, they must be controlled and directed to prevent the amplitude of the wave, and hence the loudness, from decreasing so rapidly that sounds cannot be heard by the listener.

In Chapters 4 and 5 you will learn how the interaction of the muscles which control the breathing mechanism and the movements of the vocal folds produces voices of varying pitch and loudness.

Overtones and Resonance

Few vibrating objects produce pure tones. They have one frequency which is dominant and determines the pitch you hear—the *fundamental* tone. But they also produce other frequencies, known as *overtones*, or partials, which are not heard as separate pitches but which determine the distinctive quality of the tone you hear. Thus the conductor can pick out of the orchestra the particular instrument which is off key, since he can recognize the overtones of the instrument. Similarly, no two voices, even in the same pitch range, have identical quality; you can easily recognize a familiar voice without seeing the speaker.

Usually the strongest overtones are those produced by segmental vibrations of the vibrating object. A violin string, for example, may vibrate not only over its full length, but also over one-half, one-third, or one-fifth its length, simultaneously with the stronger fundamental vibration. Segmental vibrations of this kind blend harmoniously with the fundamental and change its quality without the hearer's being particularly conscious of the existence of additional pitch levels. A complex vibrator like the human vocal folds, however, may produce some frequencies which do not blend with the fundamental; the number of different simultaneous vibrations produced by the vocal folds is much greater than is found in the simpler string.

Neither the fundamentals nor the overtones produced by musical instruments or the human voice are strong enough to carry any distance without some form of amplification. The overtones are so weak that without some way of increasing their intensity they may be lost altogether. Such a method of amplification is provided by the phenomenon called *resonance*.

Resonance is the result of three forces, usually acting together, although they may act independently. The first is the principle of *reflection of sound waves*. You enjoy singing in the bathtub because the hard walls of the tub and the room itself reflect the sound waves back to your ear and give the illusion of a much more resonant tone than you actually possess. If you try singing in a closet filled with clothes, the tone will seem stifled and dull, although the initial sound in the two cases may be exactly the same. The difference lies in the reflection of the waves, a phenomenon which does not occur in the closet because the waves are absorbed by the soft surfaces instead of being returned to you. In a band shell or a megaphone, sound waves are reflected and concentrated in one direction. The tone is loudest in front of the opening, and its carrying power is greater, because the initial energy has been increased by preventing its dissipation in other directions. It should be noted that hard surfaces, smooth contours, and open passages reflect a wider range of sounds more efficiently than their opposites.

In the human voice, reflective resonance is the primary means by which the fundamental tone is amplified. In Chapter 6, many of the exercises suggested for developing good resonance are based on the concept of an *open throat*. By developing an open throat, you will increase the efficiency of reflective resonance.

The second principle is that of *forced vibration* (sometimes called *sounding-board vibration*). When a tuning fork is struck and held in the air, its tone is barely audible at close range. When its base is held against a table top, however, the table is also set into vibration at the same frequency, and the tone may be heard at much greater distances. The vibrations of a piano string are communicated to the sounding board of the instrument, and those of the violin string to the wood of the violin. The differences in quality between clarinets made of wood, metal, and plastics are largely traceable to the different vibration traits of the respective substances, although they may be due in part to different reflective traits of the surfaces. Different overtones are given prominence, and the quality varies. In addition to such vibrations induced in solid objects, a body of air in a partially enclosed cavity may also be set into forced vibration if it is in close proximity to the sound source. There is much controversy about the role of forced resonance in the production of voice. There can be little doubt that the bones of the head and chest are set into forced vibration by the action of the vocal folds, but it seems quite dubious that much of this vibration is transformed into

audible sound through layers of soft flesh, membrane, and skin, to say nothing of clothing. Certainly this is the least important to voice production of
the three types of resonance.

The third principle is *sympathetic vibration.* If two sound sources are
tuned to the same frequency, and one of them is set into vibration, the other
object, if it is nearby, will also begin to vibrate. You may note this principle
by singing one or more notes while seated at the piano with the damper
pedal depressed. The strings corresponding to the tones you sing, and the
more prominent overtones, will vibrate in response to your voice.

More important to the production of voice, however, is the fact that not
only solid objects, but bodies of air in a cavity may be set into sympathetic
vibration by vibrating objects near them. The natural frequency of the air
in a cavity is determined by the volume of the cavity and the shape and size
of its openings. A cavity may be of a fixed size and shape or it may be capable
of great variations, as in the vocal mechanism; but in any given form, it will
respond sympathetically only to a narrow range of pitch.

If you take a number of large jars of the same size and shape and fill them
with water to different levels, you can observe this fact for yourself. Strike a
tuning fork and hold it over the mouth of each jar in turn. The vibrations
of the fork will be amplified only by those jars whose water level is such
that the natural frequency of the cavity is approximately equal to that of
the fork. In the same way, in the marimba, each tone is produced by the
vibration of a bar which is struck, reinforced by the sympathetic vibration
of a column of air, directly beneath it, tuned to the same frequency.

The fact that a cavity responds most efficiently to a narrow range of pitch
is important both to resonant vocal tone and to the complex series of reso-
nances that distinguish the various vowel and consonant sounds from one
another. The general shape and size of the resonance cavities of the nose,
throat, and mouth, and their interrelationship, determine the quality of
the voice. The great flexibility of the oral cavity makes possible the adjustments for the efficient resonation of the overtones that distinguish the quality of one speech sound from another. In Chapter 6 we shall point out the
specific ways in which the vocal mechanism makes use of the three kinds of
resonance in the production of speech sounds.

Unpleasant Resonance Traits

Resonators may also serve the function of suppressing some vibrations.
The presence of too many high-frequency overtones makes a tone sound
harsh and strident. A resonator having soft surfaces tends to damp out these

high overtones, at the loss of some carrying power, but with more pleasing quality.

Resonators having an entrance substantially larger than the exit, or having a common entrance and exit, create a cul-de-sac effect, similar to that produced by blowing into a bottle. This is the quality which characterizes the legitimate nasal sounds, M, N, and NG, and the vocal fault known as nasality.

The loudness of a sound is derived initially from the amplitude, or distance over which the vibrating object moves in producing the tone. Resonance chambers may increase the amplitude, but once a sound leaves the resonator, its loudness diminishes rapidly, since its energy is dissipated in all directions. As we have already noted, where there are few reflecting surfaces, the amplitude of a sound wave (loudness) diminishes as the square of the distance from its source. In a closed room the loss is much less, because the waves are reflected back from the walls. However, this in itself is a hazard to the speaker, because in some rooms, these reflected sounds may be delayed long enough to create echoes, interfering with new sounds being made, and creating only a noisy confusion. Thus a cathedral, with its many-angled hard surfaces, is well adapted to a solemn chant, but not to the rapid movement of a Bach fugue.

SUMMARY

Sound is the result of a force acting upon an object capable of vibration. The vibrations which are set up are transmitted to the surrounding air and carried as sound waves to the ear of the listener. Sound waves are characterized by frequency, the determinant of pitch, and by amplitude, the determinant of loudness.

The carrying power of sound waves is increased by the phenomenon of resonance, which concentrates and directs the initial energy of the wave. Sympathetic resonance makes possible the creation of different qualities from the same fundamental tone, including the infinitely complex resonance patterns of articulate speech.

Since the sounds of speech are created by the interaction of complex muscular structures, you will make more rapid progress if you understand how these structures work. The rest of this book is designed to give you that understanding and to help you to apply it to the improvement of your speech.

4

Breathing for Speech

*This being of mine, whatever it really is, consists of a little flesh, a
little breath, and the part which governs.*—MARCUS AURELIUS

As the swimmer climbs out of the pool after the race, he says to a friend, "I
could—have won—if Jack—Smith—hadn't been—in such good—shape."
You can see his ribs move in and out and his breastbone up and down as he
struggles to speak. His friend leans closer to hear him. The strenuous physical exercise has created a demand for increased oxygen and a need for faster
elimination of the waste products in the blood stream. The vigor of the
breathing activity distorts his speech.

When you speak, you need a steady control over the amount of air taken
in and exhaled, and over the rate and regularity of breathing. If physical
exertion or emotional excitement has changed your rate or disturbed your
rhythm, or if it has made you take in great quantities of air, you will find
yourself unable to control the steadiness of your voice, its loudness, and its
general rate and phrasing. Observe a man talking after exercise. His voice
production will be affected in these three ways.

Sometimes when an inexperienced speaker gets up on the platform, you
may notice signs of breathlessness, as if he had been running to class. An uncontrolled fear reaction prepares the body to meet an emergency. More air
is taken in with each breath; the rate speeds up. You will hear this speaker
gasp like the swimmer, as he struggles futilely for steady tone, adequate
loudness, and meaningful timing of what he wants to say. He, like the
athlete, must reestablish control over his breathing before he can talk
effectively.

STRUCTURE AND FUNCTION OF THE BREATHING MECHANISM

THE STRUCTURE

The bony structure of the thorax or chest, sometimes called the *rib cage*, is made up of the backbone; the sternum, or breastbone; and the twelve pairs of ribs. All the ribs are attached to the backbone. The six upper pairs are joined in front by cartilage to the sternum; each of the next four pairs is attached to the rib above by cartilage. Only the two lower pairs, called the *floating ribs*, have no direct frontal connection with the other ribs, and can therefore move more freely than those above. The type of attachment of the ribs to the backbone makes movement possible so that the rib cage is not a rigid structure. The sternum can be raised and the whole thorax lifted so that the depth of the chest is increased from front to back. The lower ribs can move outward and upward so that the size of the chest cavity increases from side to side. In forced, heavy breathing, both of these expansions permit a deep inhalation.

Within this thoracic cavity are the two large, conical-shaped lungs; the heart; blood vessels; the esophagus, or passageway to the stomach; and the trachea, bronchi, and bronchial tubes, which carry the air into and out of the lungs. The cavity is a completely walled chamber; muscles fill the spaces between the ribs, and the diaphragm forms the entire floor of the cavity, separating the chest from the abdominal region. The lungs and chest wall are normally always in contact. The apex of each lung rests just above the collarbone, while the base touches the diaphragm.

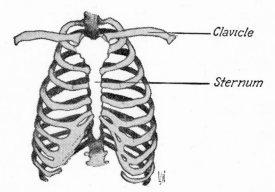

Fig. 2. The rib cage: diagram showing frontal view of the clavicles, sternum, and ribs

The air enters the respiratory mechanism through the mouth and nose, passes down the throat between the vocal folds and into the trachea, or windpipe. The trachea consists of a four- to five-inch tube held open by horseshoe-shaped, incomplete rings of cartilage; its back wall is of muscle. In the chest cavity, this tube divides into two bronchi, which in turn branch in the lungs into smaller and smaller tubes. The whole structure resembles an upside-down branching tree, with the trachea as the trunk.

Functioning of the Structure in Inspiration

The powerful diaphragmatic muscle is the chief muscle of inspiration. In its position of rest, the diaphragm is shaped like an inverted bowl. It consists of a central tendon, elliptical in shape, from which the muscles radiate outward to the inner wall of the thorax, and connect to the tip of the sternum, the six lower ribs, and the backbone. When these muscles contract, the diaphragm descends and becomes flatter, pressing against the abdominal viscera. Since the backbone and the pelvic structure restrict backward and downward movement of the viscera, the abdominal wall now bulges slightly under the pressure.

The action of the muscles between the ribs also increases the size of the chest cavity. If the upper part of the rib cage is fixed in position, the contraction of these muscles, the external intercostals, can elevate the ribs. Because of the bowed shape of the ribs, their movement is outward as well as upward as the muscles contract.

There are several other series of muscles which can elevate or depress the ribs. Some lie across the back of the thorax, some at the neck or upper chest. These need not be named in detail.

The action of the rib cage is sometimes compared to that of a bellows. As the handles of the bellows are pulled apart, the space within is increased

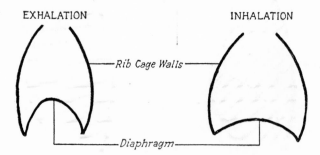

EXHALATION   INHALATION

———Rib Cage Walls———

———Diaphragm———

Fig. 3. Diagram showing the changes in size and shape of the thoracic cavity during breathing (front view)

and a partial vacuum created. To equalize the pressure between the outside and the inside, the air rushes into the small opening at the top and fills the bellows. In a similar way, as the bony structure of the rib cage moves out, the air, because of the atmospheric pressure outside the body, rushes into this enlarged cavity. The lungs are not active in any way in "drawing in" the air. They are merely reservoirs for air which are acted upon by the changes in size and shape of the thorax.

Let us now follow through the process of inhalation: the muscles of the diaphragm contract and the diaphragm descends, pressing against the viscera below; the upper chest is fixed and the ribs move slightly upward and outward; if the breath is deep, the breastbone moves forward and upward. As the thoracic cavity is increased in size vertically and horizontally, the air pressure within is lowered, and the air from outside pours in to equalize the pressure.

Functioning of the Structure in Expiration

If you are not speaking but are only breathing quietly, the relaxation of the muscles of inhalation is sufficient to force the air out. The abdominal viscera have been under pressure; in their elastic recoil, these organs press against the diaphragm, which relaxes and ascends quickly. Because of the weight of the rib cage, when the muscles relax, the ribs descend. In breathing for life, the inhalation is active, the exhalation passive.

Let us suppose that you are going to use the exhaled breath to set the vocal folds into vibration. You must now control the exhalation so that you can use it efficiently for long phrases, if necessary, with accompanying changes

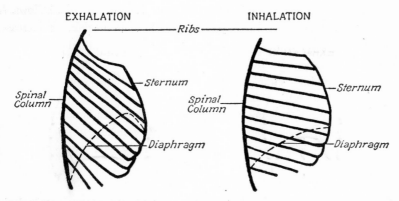

Fig. 4. Diagram showing the changes in size and shape of the thoracic cavity during breathing (from the right side)

in pitch, in loudness, and in resonance for the subtle expression of your desired meaning.

The muscles which actively control exhalation are situated in the abdominal region. Four powerful flat layers of muscles form the front wall of the abdomen; three of these are attached to the lower margin of the thorax. When they contract, they will pull the lower ribs down, in cooperation with muscles within the interior walls of the rib cage, and will press against the abdomen. This pressure forces the viscera up against the diaphragm. In life breathing, the diaphragm would now relax and the breath would pour out. In breathing for speech, however, a balance must be achieved between the controlled relaxation of the diaphragm and rib muscles and the firm pressure exerted by the abdominal muscles. The breath can move steadily upward under pressure, past the vocal folds, because the ribs press steadily inward against the lungs and because the diaphragm relaxes gradually under the pressure of the viscera below it.

BIOLOGICAL FUNCTION

The main function of breathing is the maintenance of life. Oxygen is supplied to the blood via the lungs on inhalation; the gaseous waste product of the blood, the carbon dioxide, is carried away on exhalation. The respiratory center in the medulla at the base of the brain automatically controls the inspiration-expiration cycle. If you are exercising, the oxygen or fuel for physical exertion is used rapidly and the waste products in the blood increase. The rate of breathing and the amount of air taken in are increased to meet the bodily needs. If you are in an emotional state, the body gets ready to meet the emergency, and since oxygen is needed in greater amount for the impending action, the breath is taken in more quickly.

Under quiet conditions, your breathing for life is rhythmical, with the inhalation and the exhalation approximately equal in duration. You use little of the total or "vital" capacity of the lungs because your breathing is shallow and frequent.

When you speak, this process is modified. The breath is now the source of energy which sets the tensed vocal folds into vibration to produce vocal sound. To make this vibration efficient and steady, you must control the breath stream being exhaled.

FUNCTION OF BREATHING IN SPEAKING

The Modification of Life Breathing for Voice Production

The production of voice modifies breathing for life in the following ways:

1. In breathing for life, the inspiration is active, the expiration passive; for speech, both are active processes. The exhalation is firm, steady, and controlled.

2. In breathing for life, the time cycles of inspiration-expiration tend to be equal. For speech, the inhalation is quick and the duration of the expiration is governed by the idea to be expressed.

3. Breathing for life, when you are quiet, is shallow. Breathing for speech is sometimes deeper, depending, of course, upon your immediate need for a long phrase or for increased general loudness. A word of caution should be given here. Deep breathing does not necessarily improve voice. The habitual taking of a deep breath before speaking can cause excessive tension, since it keeps the rib cage unnaturally distended over too long a period. If you mistakenly try to set up habits of deep breathing, you can spoil the rhythm of your whole speech and affect the quality of your voice.

Types of Breathing for Voice Production

There are several different types of breathing, any of which you may be using habitually. You may have developed certain breathing habits merely by chance, or you may have acquired them because of differences in your body structure or because some "authority" has advocated a method as beneficial. Of the various types of breathing, only the first one to be discussed below is consistently associated with poor vocal quality.

1. *Clavicular breathing.* The speaker elevates the shoulders and collarbones (clavicles) every time he inhales. This is a faulty action, because the contraction of muscles around the collarbone and in the neck will set the whole region of the larynx and the vocal folds into tension and cause a poor, strained quality of voice. Such a method also pulls the entire rib cage up, thereby tiring the speaker because of the extra, unnatural activity. Control of the exhalation should lie in the abdominal muscles, but with clavicular breathing, the speaker cannot control the flow of the breath adequately and is therefore likely to have a weak voice and the habit of gasping for air.

2. *Upper-thoracic breathing.* The speaker raises the sternum on inhalation and often pulls the lower ribs in. Occasionally, a man will learn this habit in physical training which requires the raising of the entire chest structure. If

the individual is muscular and large in build, this may not affect his control over breathing for speech. If he is small, he may have the same difficulties as the man with clavicular breathing.

3. *Medial breathing.* The speaker moves the lower ribs outward and slightly upward, increasing the dimensions of the whole lower part of the rib cage. There is, however, little movement in the abdominal region. If the movement of the ribs is steady and strong, he probably has good control over breathing.

4. *Diaphragmatic-abdominal breathing.* To the expansion of the lower rib cage on inhalation, the speaker adds the pronounced downward movement of the diaphragm, which causes the bulge of the abdominal wall in the center of the body just below the ribs. On exhalation, the pressure produced by the contraction of the abdominal muscles is balanced by the gradual relaxation of diaphragmatic and rib muscles. This process and its similarity to natural breathing for life have already been described. You can analyze the actions involved if you lie down, become relaxed, and perceive the gentle rise and fall of the mid-region of the body below the ribs. Speech which changes the normal life process as little as possible will show ease in production of voice. The parts of the chest which are not actually needed in voice production can remain relaxed. If the activity for breath control is centered in this mid-region, the speaker can also learn to relax the muscles of the neck and larynx and so improve the quality of his voice.

The type of breathing you use is also related to your habits of posture. If your posture is stooped, you are actually preventing the diaphragmatic-abdominal activity, since the position crowds that region. If you lean on the lectern as you speak, you pull the whole structure of the chest upward and forward and thus tend to use upper-thoracic breathing. A slumped, one-sided posture with the body thrown out of line will distort the position of your muscles and make abdominal control difficult.

ANALYSIS OF BREATHING HABITS

You may now use the information on the functioning of the breathing mechanism as a basis for the analysis of your own breathing habits. Perhaps you will find that your breathing is adequate and controlled for everyday speaking situations. You may not perceive a need for practicing breathing and vocal exercises until finer skills of control are required of you in public speaking, reading, or acting. On the other hand, you may discover that your faults of inaudibility, rapid rate, broken phrasing, or unsteadiness of tone

relate distinctly to poor breathing habits, and you will be motivated to practice exercises immediately. Analysis of present habits must, of course,
precede improvement.

The Importance of Control of the Breath Stream

The control of breathing, as it relates to effective voice, is vital for the following reasons:

1. It contributes to the steadiness of your vocalization. If the flow of air
coming up through the trachea and past the vocal folds is not steady, the
vibration it sets up in the vocal folds cannot be steady. If you allow the air
to come out rapidly on the first words, little breath will remain to sustain
vibration at the end of a phrase. The muscular activity centered in the abdominal and lower rib region can govern the steady flow of breath needed.

2. Control of breath flow is necessary for the increase in strength of tone
which enables you to be heard over some distance. If the flow is weak, the
vibration is correspondingly feeble. The control also permits the variations
in loudness which provide a means of conveying changes in your meaning.

3. Good breathing habits allow you to adjust the amount of air inhaled
to the length of phrase and the duration of the words which you emphasize
within the phrase. The manner of breathing will also relate to the general
rate of your speech and your ability to vary rate.

4. Control of breathing contributes to a feeling of ease of production. If,
as you speak, you experience no gasping for air or feeling of breathlessness,
and if you know that because of established control your voice can reach
all within the group and can change in loudness and rate to suit your meanings, then you have the confidence which results from the habitually efficient
use of the breathing mechanism. The lack of control, conversely, will disturb
your confidence. Poor breathing habits often influence detrimentally the pitch
changes and quality of tone. They induce muscular tension. Faults of phonation and resonation are frequently traceable to a basic breathing difficulty.

Observation and Self-analysis

1. First duplicate each of the four methods of breathing, exaggerating
the movements in order to feel the action of the muscles involved. Raise the
collarbone and shoulders as you inhale deeply. Next, place your open palm
against the breastbone. Raise the upper chest as you take a breath, allowing
the whole rib cage to be pulled up. Now, with the palms pressed against the
lower ribs, move the ribs out, first while taking in a breath, and again with
no breath being inhaled. Place one open hand over the triangular soft spot

where the lower ribs do not join in front, and the other hand against the ribs at the side. As you inhale, observe both the outward and upward movement of the ribs and the outward movement of the abdominal wall. Which of these types of activity seems easiest for you?

2. Repeat several short sentences as you reproduce each type of breathing. Can you analyze your own method?

3. During an animated conversation, for a brief time give attention to your manner of breathing. Are you raising the shoulders or gasping for air?

4. Observe in other speakers any tendency to raise the shoulders on inhalation for speech. Do they have good control over their voices?

BREATH CONTROL FOR STEADINESS OF VOCALIZATION

Self-analysis

1. Read aloud one of the more serious and slow practice selections in Appendix II, such as Number 4 or 23. Is your tone unsteady or weak?

2. As you read, do you tend to exhaust your breath supply quickly at the initiation of the phrase so that you run out of air and your tone becomes less firm at the end of the phrase?

3. In phrases which contain many of the friction sounds, like H, S, TH, and F, do you waste a great deal of breath? Mark these sounds in any passage and listen critically to yourself. This is in reality an articulatory fault, but it will be related to lack of steady tone on the vowel sounds.

Exercises for Improvement

Before you begin the exercises, make sure that your body is relatively free from tension. Standing on your toes, stretch upward as far as you can reach with your fingers, bringing your hips forward and your abdomen in, so that the entire body falls into line. Repeat several times.

Next, bend forward from the waist, allowing the trunk, arms, and neck to hang down limply. Begin to straighten slowly, inhaling as you come up; feel the pull of the muscles in the hip, thigh, and abdomen. Slowly assume the upright position, making sure that the large muscles of the shoulders and neck are relaxed.

Tighten the muscles at the back of the neck, pull the head back tensely, turn it from side to side, and then let it fall forward gently.

Examine your posture. The body should feel well balanced and at ease, with the weight on the balls of both feet. You should avoid the extremes of either the military or the slouched posture.

1. Place the open palms of your hands tightly against your lower front ribs. Inhale slowly and deeply through both mouth and nose, feeling the push of the lower rib wall against your hands. Hold the breath for about the count of five, noting that your ribs are held up and out. Now exhale slowly, pressing in with your hands but resisting this pressure by the slow lowering of the ribs. Turn your hands so that the fingers point toward the back; the open palms can now feel the rib movement of the side and back of the rib cage. Repeat the slow inhalation, the holding, and the steady exhalation until you are well aware of the desired movement.

2. Repeating this same steady breathing, place your finger tips on your shoulders. Inhale. Your fingers will tell you whether or not your shoulders are relaxed. Place one palm on the sternum. As you inhale, concentrate on the movement of the lower rib cage so that the hand on the upper chest moves only slightly. Repeat, until you can minimize the activity of shoulders and sternum.

3. To correct clavicular breathing, sit upright in an armless chair; grip the legs of the chair low enough so that your chest can remain erect and your shoulders cannot be raised; in this position, inhale and exhale, concentrating on the movement at the center of your body.

4. Repeat, this time counting aloud on the exhalation.

5. With your open palms again on the ribs, inhale quickly through your mouth, purse your lips, and blow a steady, forceful stream of air, as if you were trying to blow out a candle some distance from you. Continue blowing until most of your breath is exhausted; feel the inward movement of the abdominal wall and the gradual lowering of the ribs. Try this also with an actual candle, this time blowing evenly, with little force, so that the flame is merely made to bend steadily away from you but is not extinguished and does not waver.

6. Inhale to the instructor's count of "one," exhale to the count of "one, two"; inhale; exhale to the count of "one, two, three"; and so forth up to the count of ten, so that the ratio of inhalation-exhalation becomes 1:10. Be aware of steadiness of movement at the ribs.

7. Repeat, this time counting aloud on the exhalation.

8. As you inhale, hands on ribs, yawn gently. Maintain this relaxed openness of throat as you produce a breathy AH. On the second attempt, retain the relaxation in your throat, but consciously increase the clarity of the AH. Keep the ribs elevated without strain as long as possible, bringing the abdominal region in before the descent of the ribs begins. The tone does not have to be loud, but steadiness in flow should be sought. Close your eyes

as you vocalize; listen to see if breath is wasted at the initiation of the tone or if the tone becomes faint near the end of the production. If the tone wavers, concentrate on steadiness of movement at the lower ribs, rather than on any muscular adjustment in the throat. This ability to achieve a steady vowel tone without wasted breath or strain is your most important objective at this time.

9. Repeat the above exercise for each of the "long-vowel" sounds: A, E, I, O, OO, AW. Take the breath in quickly, but without exaggerating the amount or permitting audible intake; hold the vowel sound until most of the breath pours out. Do not strain; this is an exercise for steadiness of tone, not for duration.

10. Repeat all of the vowel sounds listed above on one exhalation, keeping the flow of breath steady as you change the position of the mouth.

11. Using long, sustained vowel sounds, chant the following phrases quietly and easily:

> How far away.
> How quiet it became.
> How slowly the waves roll in.

12. Inhale and count aloud from one to ten, from one to twenty, from one to thirty, using a firm, sustained tone. Listen to yourself to see if some of the breath is wasted on F's, TH's, and s's. How far can you count without a feeling of strain?

BREATH CONTROL FOR CHANGES IN LOUDNESS

AUDIBILITY

When a situation arises in which you must speak to a roomful of people or call to someone in the distance, the loudness of the conversational tone will not meet the needs of the situation. More energy is required in the vocalization to increase the carrying power.

However, the projection of speech to meet the requirements of distance demands more than loudness alone. Not only must the exhaled breath be under greater pressure, but the tone itself must be amplified more fully by changes in resonation, the rate must be slowed, the phrasing made shorter, the sounds longer, and the articulation more exact. The discussion of the projection of meaningful material will therefore be postponed until the other factors have been studied.

One of the main ways of increasing loudness is through the control of breath. To increase the amplitude of vibration of the vocal folds and the consequent amplitude of the sound wave required for the loud tone, the pressure of air beneath the vocal folds must be increased. To understand what is meant by this statement, find an opportunity to shout to someone. Notice that inhalation is quick, and if you are going to shout more than one word, somewhat deeper than usual. The muscles of exhalation now contract quickly and firmly, exerting pronounced pressure on the lungs, with a decrease in the size of the thoracic cavity. The breath coming up through the trachea to the vocal folds is thus under more pressure than usual. The sudden tone produced is loud.

A desired degree of loudness can be maintained if the pressure of the muscles of exhalation is firm and sustained during the phrase to be spoken. You should note several facts. First, under such pressure, air escapes from the lungs more rapidly than during quiet speaking. Thus each phrase spoken loudly must be relatively short, so that a new supply of air can be taken in to give support to the next phrase. Second, there must be enough air in the lungs to maintain pressure. For this reason, the inhalation, though quick, is often deeper than average. Third, the control which brings about the firm pressure lies in the diaphragmatic-abdominal region, not in the throat. You can, of course, increase the pressure of the breath stream, and loudness, by increasing tension at the vocal folds. Such tension, however, results in raising of pitch and may induce additional constrictions above the larynx, producing a strident quality.

Self-analysis

Examine yourself to discover the habits which affect your general audibility.

1. Can you make yourself heard in a large room?

2. When you are trying to make yourself heard, do you take a very deep breath and raise the shoulders and the upper chest?

3. Do you strain to increase loudness, and in so doing tense the muscles of the throat? Does your pitch rise? Does your quality of tone become harsh, strident, or squeaking?

4. Does a quantity of air pour out as you produce the first loud tone? Are you breathless, so that you immediately have to gasp for air?

5. Does the tone waver as it becomes louder? Does it diminish in volume, so that you start with a loud tone and then fade into an inaudible one?

6. Do you tire after the first four or five sentences? Does your voice break?

Exercises for Improvement

1. With the palms of your hands on the lower ribs, and your tongue tip behind the lower front teeth, yawn gently as you inhale; exhale slowly and steadily as you produce the long I sound. Inhale quickly and somewhat more deeply; exhale with more vigorous pressure at the central region of the body. Repeat a third time, being conscious of even greater muscular contraction. The last I will be energetic and short, and should easily reach across a large room without straining your throat muscles. Your mouth, of course, should be sufficiently open to permit the sound to escape without being muffled.

2. Repeat the above exercise, using the word "one" for vocalization. Hold the tongue in the position of the final sound until the breath stream has finished its objective of carrying the tone. Imagine on the first vocalization that you are speaking firmly to someone next to you and that this listener moves farther away for each of the succeeding four vocalizations. Be careful not to raise the pitch for each louder tone.

3. Run five "ones" together on one breath, steadily increasing the pressure of the muscles of exhalation so that the tone gradually and smoothly builds up in loudness.

4. Repeat Exercise 9 on page 40. Gently commence a yawn and produce a steadily controlled AH sound. Next, with the mouth wide open, yawn gently and produce a faint AH; gradually, through pressure at the central region, swell this tone in a crescendo without raising the pitch. As you gain skill in doing this smoothly and without straining the throat muscles, learn to start the faint tone, swell it gradually, and then allow it to diminish slowly. This may be practiced with all long-vowel sounds.

5. Contrast the fault of breath wastage with clarity of tone during loud production. Repeat the following sentences, pouring out excessive breath at the initiation of each phrase. Then, with the hands on the lower ribs, repeat the sentences in a clear, loud, sustained tone, getting full phonation from all exhaled breath on the voiced sounds.

> How do you expect me to go?
> He had to see the man today.
> We can't believe in this plan.
> I have told you again and again.
> Each of you must understand.

6. Repeat short phrases, such as "I know," "I will," using three degrees of loudness for each. Imagine you are talking to listeners at different distances. Keep the throat relaxed.

7. Read aloud a selection in Appendix II, such as Number 15 or Number 19: first, as if you were talking sincerely to one person; second, as if to a small group of people; third, as if to a large auditorium of listeners. In addition to the general increase in energy of production, you will notice that the larger and more extensive the speaking situation, the shorter the phrases become. Loudness uses up breath supply. The articulation must also be more exact, so that the sounds of speech can be recognized easily at a distance.

After practice at home, read other similar short selections to the class, first speaking to those in the first row, then increasing the distance your voice can be made to cover until the audience finally indicates that you are speaking too loudly.

CHANGES IN LOUDNESS FOR MEANING

Increase in general loudness is necessary to meet the requirements of audibility as the size of the audience or the room increases. To communicate specific meanings to the listeners, however, you need the additional skill of being able to change the loudness within the spoken passage to suit the meanings you wish to convey.

Your feeling states may be shown by your use of increased or decreased loudness. The angry man who shouts, "I don't care about it at all," discloses his emotion by his uncontrolled loudness. Continual loudness of tone is often associated by the listener with lack of emotional control and frequently should be saved for the most vital part of the idea, rather than dissipated over an entire passage. Increased loudness for obtaining attention is one of the more elementary skills which the child acquires early in life. The experienced speaker adds changes in timing, in melody, and in quality of tone in order to enrich the implications of his meaning.

Changes in loudness for contrast are effective. If a speaker has been explaining facts at a level of loudness suited to the situation and then drops his volume so that his listeners have to lean forward and attend carefully, he produces the effect of presenting valuable, exciting, and somewhat private data. The attention of the listener is caught immediately, if the device is not used too frequently. Again, an experienced speaker may, as he presents a series of ideas, build from a quiet level of loudness, increasing the intensity with each idea, until at the climax, the audience is carried toward emotional conviction by his vocal energy. Any change in loudness will attract the listener's ear momentarily; whether or not his attention is held will depend upon the speaker's ideas and his other skills of delivery.

Changes in loudness for emphasis contribute to the intelligent interpretation of an idea. The words which carry the greatest importance within the phrase are usually produced with the greatest energy. For example, read the following sentence, giving a different pattern of emphasis by means of increasing loudness on different words for each reading: "I saw you with him last night." Note how the meanings vary. The changes need not be pronounced or extreme.

The speaker who overuses loudness for emphasis will fall easily into a pattern of loudness changes. Any repeated way of emphasizing, such as making the first words the most prominent in the sentence, or hitting too many words in the phrase with a sudden increase in loudness, will become monotonous for the listener and thus will interfere with the speaker's communication. The use of mono-loudness is just as ineffective. If no word is louder than any other, meaning is obscured.

Self-analysis

The faults of extreme vocal energy and of lack of energy both call attention to themselves and away from meaning. Examine your speech critically to ascertain whether any of the following are true:

1. When you are earnest and emotional in proving a point, do you shout the whole idea, or do you confine the greatest display of energy to the most important part of the idea?

2. Do you hit words you want to emphasize with sudden changes in loudness? Have you heard another speaker do this?

3. Do you have a pattern of emphasis?

4. Do you speak all the words in a phrase with equal loudness so that, although the words may be said at different pitch levels, none is made with more energy than another?

5. Have you ever used gradually increased or decreased loudness for effect in building to a climax in a speech or argument? Have you ever been aware of this skill in the speech of others?

Exercises for Improvement

Continue the exercises for breathing and for control of increase in loudness.

1. Count from one to five, increasing the loudness steadily, as if the *five* were the climax of an idea. Keep the tone firm by steady pressure at the central region. Count steadily from one to ten, increasing loudness to a peak

at five, diminishing volume on the succeeding numbers, but keeping the tone unwavering.

2. Repeat the letters of the alphabet through F. State the letters as if they were: first, a casual idea; second, an increasingly vital concept; and third, in a loud, clear tone, as if they represented a main convincing argument.

3. Repeat the following groups of three sentences; increase the energy of production and loudness from the first to the third in each group.

   a. I believe in this man.
      What he says is true.
      I will follow his plan of action.
   b. I have come here today.
      I will come back tomorrow.
      I will stay until this is settled.
   c. There are five points to this plan.
      Not one can be discarded.
      Discount one, and you weaken the whole structure.

4. Try to reverse the process in Exercise 3, and produce a convincing effect by starting with average loudness and decreasing it on each of the three sentences in the group.

5. Read the following passage, exaggerating the increase in loudness on the important words. Repeat the reading, maintaining a tone of conviction but attempting to make the changes in loudness smooth and firm, rather than sudden and sharp.

The person who concludes that he is *exceedingly different* from his fellow men has several alternatives open to him. He can hide behind his difference, letting the *awareness* of his race, or his physical variations, or his family peculiarities become the *major part* of his personality. He then confides to himself that *no one* will ever *really* know him. Or he can *bluff* his way through existence, making so much *noise* and offering so many *varied distractions* that his fellow men—so he tells himself—will conclude that he *does not care.* Or he can sit down with himself and *examine* his difference, and come to the conclusion that he has *potential personality attributes* which can *outweigh any difference* that *birth* or *accident* or *circumstance* has imposed upon him. This *last* is the *man who becomes stronger* than *those who are never aware* of *possessing* a *difference. This* is the man whom *others* seek when they need *reassurance* and *security.*

6. Write out a statement of belief, working up to a climax, with the aim of convincing your listeners. The following may serve as suggestions:

   a. I believe that racial discrimination exists in this community . . .
   b. I believe that the present system of marking is unfair . . .
   c. I believe that this university should . . .

Ask for criticism from your listeners. Was the tone steady? Were you clearly audible? Did you use changes in loudness effectively to bring out differences in meaning? If you have had poor breathing habits, have you now been able to improve them in this real-life situation?

7. The following selections in Appendix II are recommended for practice on variation in loudness: Numbers 2, 12, and 22*b*.

TIMING AND BREATH CONTROL

Several factors contribute to the timing of your oral communication: the speed with which the phrase is presented, the interval of silence between vocalizations, and the duration of the individual sounds which make up the words. These three factors operating together determine the general rate or number of words spoken within a given time period.

All of these elements are affected by the control of the breath stream. If you run out of breath quickly or cannot sustain enough air in the lungs to support the tone adequately, you cannot achieve skill in the manipulation of timing and thus may not become effective in the expression of your meanings.

Counting the number of words which you speak within a minute gives you only a general notion of the effect which your time pattern produces upon your hearers. One speaker may utter 120 words a minute, hurry the phrases, give staccato production to all vowels, and yet allow long pauses between phrases. His timing may be interpreted by the ear as being too fast for intelligibility. Another man may repeat the same passage with slow phrases and long vowels but no appreciable pauses. Although the number of words produced per minute by both men is exactly the same, the interpretation of the meaning and the effect on the listener will be very different.

General Rate

The general rate for unemotional, spontaneous material presented in a situation with only a few listeners is between 120 and 140 words per minute. Reading rate is usually considerably faster, the average being about 160 words a minute. Rate, of course, is influenced by the nature of the idea and the emotions inherent in the situation.

Thus, as you describe an action scene, your fast rate indicates that you want your listeners to share your feeling of excitement and animation. If the topic is solemn or sad, the slow rate used can suggest the quietness or lethargy of the body in experiencing such a situation. Your feeling states are conveyed by this skill of changing general rate to suit your emotion. The listener responds quickly to such indications.

If you use a gradual increase in loudness to build to a climax, you will find that you often couple this with an increase in the rate of speaking. This means of displaying energy can arouse emotions and carry the listener forward to the climax of the idea.

Rate is influenced by the complexity of the thought you present. A simple report, well known to the listeners, can often be speeded up. A new problem, with aspects hitherto unanalyzed by the audience, will require time for comprehension.

It has already been mentioned that the size of the audience and of the room will affect timing. A dramatic scene upon the stage, while seeming to move swiftly, must still allow time for the lines to reach the audience. An angry question, such as, "What do you mean by that?" is said at great speed to the single listener. To a large audience, the intensity of the utterance must often supplant the natural inclination to hurl the words out quickly.

You may now argue that another factor influences general rate profoundly: the characteristics of your own personality. "I am excitable," you may say. "My rate is always fast." Or, "I am naturally slow moving." The type of person that you are will modify your general rate, but the assumption that your personality characteristics are static and cannot be varied when the need arises will interfere with the growth of your skill. Your purposes for using your speech fluctuate from hour to hour. The adaptation of your speaking habits to those purposes is your goal.

In practicing speech, you need to analyze your immediate purpose or intent in reading, speaking, or acting, and to think how changes in timing may be suited to the emotional content, the complexity of the idea, and the audience situation, so that the listeners can receive the full implication of your communication.

Analyze yourself to see if poor breathing habits are affecting your rate. If you have the habit of taking a breath and then speaking as long as seems physically possible before you gasp for air, you will tend to speak rapidly, particularly if you do not have control over the breath stream. The result is an uncertain and breathless production. Often, practice in improving breathing habits will overcome the excessive rate. The breathy, unsteady tone associated with clavicular breathing may cause the speaker to feel unsure of his voice, and self-consciousness will induce him to use a fast rate to get through the speaking situation as soon as possible.

Phrasing and Pauses

The phrase is the thought unit of speech. Phrasing refers to the process of grouping words together so that the relationship between the words will convey your immediate meaning. No criticism of "correct" or "incorrect" can be placed upon oral phrasing, provided that the grouping of the words fulfills your purpose and is meaningful to the listener.

Pauses, which serve to separate phrases from one another, are oral punctuation marks. Originally, written punctuation was a set of symbols designed to represent the oral grouping of the words. In recent writing, however, punctuation has become formalized, and the marks are not always accurate representations of the oral thought groupings. In reading aloud, therefore, you should not rely on punctuation alone to determine where to pause, although punctuation marks are usually helpful.

The oral phrasing of the first sentence below quite logically follows the written form:

1. John,/ unaware that they had gone,/ continued to talk.

The second sentence, with a more personal or emotional connotation, will need your own way of phrasing:

2. "We are now far into the fifth year/since a policy was initiated/with the avowed object and confident promise/of putting an end to slavery agitation."—LINCOLN

The way in which a passage is phrased, then, depends upon the meaning intended by the reader, actor, or speaker. Good phrasing contributes both to intelligibility and to emotional expression. Poor phrasing tears down the meaning and produces a feeling of confusion in the listener. As a matter of fact, poor phrasing is used deliberately in a dramatic production to indicate the uncertainty or emotional tension of the character.

While you must remember that length of phrase and use of pause are governed by meaning, you must also recognize that there are physical limitations to the use of these devices. You cannot prolong a phrase without adequate breath. Pauses must occur frequently enough for you to renew your breath supply. For skill in speaking, you must learn to combine the interpretations of meaning with efficient use of the breathing mechanism.

Phrases can be fast, slow, or average in speed. The timing of a particular phrase will depend on the specific emotion to be conveyed, the complexity of the idea, or the relative importance of the phrase in relation to those surrounding it. Vary the rate of the following phrases until the most meaningful combination is achieved. Make sure that breathing is controlled.

1. He was shouting wildly, and even though I could not hear the words, I knew what I had to do.
2. Language grows out of the social context.
3. Because of this, I understood his plan.

Notice that if you wish to subordinate a phrase, you hurry over it.

4. As I mentioned before, there are five points to remember.
5. You should repeat, whenever possible, the main points of your argument.

This ability to vary the timing of phrases makes your meaning clear, through the use of contrast, and also continually attracts the listener's ear by the variety of expression.

Pauses may be used for emphasis and dramatic effect. If, with the intent to be forceful, you declare, "These—are mine," you make the first word stand out with great significance. You may build toward an effect, directing your listeners, by your manner of presentation, to take particular notice of the final words in a sentence. "What you may be experiencing is a will—to fail." Pauses before, after, or around single words or short phrases will attract attention to the specific idea.

The length of the pause is dictated by the effect you seek. If your idea has been profound or new, for example, you may wish to pause for some time so that your listeners can consider the thought and continue to "think with you" as you go on. The size of the room will also affect the pause. If the sound does not carry well, it will be necessary for you to have frequent and long pauses so that the sounds of speech may be understood.

The average speaker is unwilling to pause for even a short time. He feels that, in this competitive society, the conversation will be taken away from him if he permits a break to occur. In the speaking or reading situation, he believes that attention will lag. An actor often places a more accurate interpretation on the pause; he knows from experience that its use will contribute to suspense—provided, of course, that he has the attention of the listeners in the first place. Probably the use of AH or ER to fill what would otherwise be a natural pause comes from the unfortunate feeling that some noise must be made continually to indicate that the speaker has not yet finished.

A pattern of pauses is often just as detrimental to meaning as the use of too infrequent or too short pauses. The speaker who says a phrase, pauses, says another, and so forth, and the speaker who gives the same-length pause and the same-length phrase over and over are both monotonous.

Two common breathing faults are frequently associated with poor timing. If your supply of breath is inadequate, you may break the phrase by gasping for air in the middle of a logical grouping of words. On the other hand, too deep an inhalation may induce you to use an interminable phrase while your listener waits anxiously for you to run out of breath.

In practicing phrasing and use of pauses, you need to be highly aware of the effect you wish to produce on the listener. A responsiveness to the implications of your idea and your purposes in speaking will frequently give you skilled variations in timing without any analysis of techniques. The techniques stand you in good stead when the responsiveness is temporarily disturbed by some factor in the immediate speaking situation.

Probably a recording of your reading and of your spontaneous speech is the best way for you to study your habits of phrasing and pausing and their relationship to breathing.

Duration of Sounds

The sounds of the language vary normally in length or duration of production. An isolated AH, as in *father*, is longer than the I in *sit*. An L has greater duration than a T. The length of sounds, particularly of vowels, will change with the accenting of the syllable. The material on articulation of sounds will present some of these factors later in the text.

The duration of the sounds of speech often relates to the speaker's general rate. If a person speaks rapidly, he may have the habit of clipping, or shortening, all of his sounds, thus producing a staccato effect. If he is a slow speaker, he may drag out, or drawl, all of his vowels regardless of the meaning of his communication.

The basic meaning of the sentence will suggest the general duration of all the sounds in a passage. For instance, you would get a very strange effect if you produced the sounds of the following line in a staccato manner:

Roll on, thou deep and dark blue Ocean—roll!

Nor can you suggest excitement and action if you lengthen all the sounds in the sentence: "As he raised his arm to strike, the other man suddenly darted away."

The vowel sounds of speech can be classified, in rather a loose way, as *long* and *short*. Poets are well aware of this fact and use it to achieve certain emotional effects in their poems. Notice the use of long vowels in the poem by Tennyson:

And sl*o*wly answered *A*rthur from the b*a*rge,
"The *o*ld *o*rder ch*a*ngeth, y*ie*lding pl*a*ce to n*ew*. . . ."

An opposite staccato effect is sought by Browning:

K*e*ntish S*i*r B*y*ng, st*oo*d for his k*i*ng,
B*i*dding the cr*o*p-h*e*aded Parliament sw*i*ng . . .

The variation of the duration of sounds is one of the main ways of emphasizing ideas. Read the following sentence with conviction and then decide which of the vowels are the longest: "I know that this story is true."

In everyday conversation, we continually give longer duration to the words or the accented syllables of the words within the phrase which carry the most meaning. The natural rhythm of spoken language evolves from this variety of emphasis. Sometimes a speaker can make his communication more effective by reviewing his habits of the use of duration to see if he lengthens sounds in too rhythmic a pattern or if he gives most of his sounds equal duration.

For your own practice, mark a reading selection to indicate phrasing, pauses for emphasis, and increased duration of key words within phrases. A well-written advertisement, conversational and interesting in context, will serve your purpose. Reread it after marking. Do these visual indications remind you to make the vocal changes?

One reader may mark a passage in a different way from another. The particular meaning intended at the moment is the criterion. Here is an example of such marking. Does it differ from your interpretation?

I *now* become *aware* of *something* interposed between the *page* and the *light*—// the page was *overshadowed*:// I looked up,/ and I *saw* what I shall find it *difficult*,/ perhaps *impossible*, to *describe*.// It was a *darkness shaping* itself *forth* from the *air* in very *undefined outline*.// I can not say it was of a *human* form,// and yet it had *more resemblance* to a *human* form,/ or rather *shadow*,/ than to *anything else*.// As it *stood* . . . its *dimensions* seemed *gigantic*.—BULWER-LYTTON

Self-analysis of Timing

Examine your speech objectively as you consider the following questions:

1. Is your speech to the single listener, before the small group, or in front of the large audience, too fast for comprehension? Is it too slow to maintain interest? Do you always hurry or drag out your words no matter what the topic?

2. Do you take a deep breath and continue to speak until the breath is exhausted, then break the phrases in the middle to gasp for air? Do you consistently break phrases to search for a word? Are all your phrases long or all short?

3. Does your rate vary from phrase to phrase so that a listener can tell that some are more meaningful than others?

4. Are you willing to pause long enough between phrases to look at the listeners and to judge their reactions to your ideas, or do you hurry on? Do you fill the natural times for pauses with a vocalized AH or ER? Do you permit time for comprehension of complex or new ideas?

5. Is your speech staccato in effect? Do you have a pattern of timing? Does your speaking sound so even and rhythmical in timing that the effect is monotonous?

6. Listen to recordings of your speech made when you were reading and when you were talking spontaneously. How many words did you speak a minute? Does the general rate permit intelligibility and is it suited to the idea expressed? Are your phrasing and use of pauses effective?

Exercises for Improvement

1. By timing yourself as you read the following passage aloud, ascertain your general rate on simple material. The average reader will not complete the 185 words within the minute, but will reach the dash in the last sentence (160 words per minute). If you finish sometime before the minute limit, you are probably going too fast for the audience's comprehension. If you do not finish the first sentence of the third paragraph, you are going too slowly for interest.

Your rate, when you read factual material, is faster than your rate for factual, spontaneous speech. The words are provided for you on the page, and even though you take time to react to the ideas and to make sure that the listeners respond, the words will still flow out faster than they would if you were creating your own phrases.

If the reading material is simple, your speed may even approach 180

160 wpm.

or 190 words per minute. At these faster rates, articulation must be particularly clear to permit understanding.

The moment the spoken material suggests an emotion, changes in rate occur. If you describe a quiet scene, you allow time for your listeners to react to your appreciation of the details. Introduce a horseman galloping across this scene, and your rate must change. Philosophize about the desolation of the picture, add a humorous detail, follow the horseman on to a climax in action—for each aspect of the idea you present, you will use a rate suitable to the feeling states you wish to evoke in your listeners.

If you are told that your rate is rapid, practice the selection until the time limit catches you in the middle of the last paragraph. The insertion of longer pauses alone will not change the listener's criticism. The phrases themselves must be slower and the words within the phrases longer in duration, to decrease the effect of hurrying.

2. Go back over the same selection and mark the phrases. Indicate where you would take a breath. Reread the selection, observing the breath marks.

3. Several selections will now be presented, each quite different in complexity of idea and in emotional connotation. Analyze each selection according to the following plan:

a. Should the general rate be fast, slow, or intermediate? Should there be progressive changes in rate within the passage? Why?

b. Mark the phrasing given in several of the selections, rereading the material as marked, until the grouping of the words seems logical and the length of the phrase is adjusted to your breathing habits.

c. Where might pauses longer than usual enhance the effectiveness of the reading?

d. In Selection 5, underline the phrases which, because of their importance, should be spoken more slowly than surrounding phrases. Reread the selection until you can hear your use of contrast between fast and slow rate on phrases.

SELECTION I

The changes wrought by death are in themselves so sharp and final, and so terrible and melancholy in their consequences, that the thing stands alone in man's experience, and has no parallel on earth. It outdoes all other accidents because it is the last of them. Sometimes it leaps suddenly upon its victims like a Thug; sometimes it lays a regular siege and creeps upon their citadel during a score of years.—STEVENSON

Slow Rate

SELECTION 2

Then there is the beefsteak. They have it in Europe, but they don't know how to cook it. Neither will they cut it right. It comes on the table in a small, round, pewter platter. It lies in the center of this platter, in a bordering bed of grease-soaked potatoes; it is the size, shape, and thickness of a man's hand with the thumb and fingers cut off. It is a little overdone, is rather dry, it tastes pretty insipidly, it rouses no enthusiasm.

Imagine a poor exile contemplating that inert thing; and imagine an angel suddenly sweeping down out of a better land and setting before him a mighty porter-house steak an inch and a half thick, hot and sputtering from the griddle; dusted with fragrant pepper; enriched with little melting bits of butter of the most unimpeachable freshness and genuineness; the precious juices of the meat trickling out and joining the gravy . . . and imagine that the angel also adds a great cup of American home-made coffee, with the cream afroth on top, some real butter, firm and yellow and fresh, some smoking hot biscuits . . . —could words describe the gratitude of this exile?—MARK TWAIN

SELECTION 3

On, then all Frenchmen, that have hearts in your bodies. Roar with all your throats, of cartilage and metal, ye Sons of Liberty; stir spasmodically whatsoever of utmost faculty is in you, soul, body, or spirit, for it is the hour. Smite, thou Louis Tournay . . . smite at that Outer Drawbridge chain, though fiery hail whistles 'round thee. Never . . . did thy axe strike such a stroke. Down with it, man, down with it. . . . Let the whole accursed Edifice sink thither, and Tyranny be swallowed up forever.—
CARLYLE

SELECTION 4

The President stood before us as a man of the people. He was thoroughly American, had never crossed the sea, had never been spoiled by English insularity or French dissipation; a quite native aboriginal man, as an acorn from an oak; no aping of foreigners, no frivolous accomplishments, Kentuckian born, working on a farm, a flatboatman, a captain in the Black Hawk war, a country lawyer, a representative in the rural legislature in Illinois;—on such modest foundations the broad structure of his fame was laid. How slowly, and yet by happily prepared steps, he came to his place.—EMERSON

SELECTION 5

The only way to write a popular history, as we have already remarked, would be to write it backwards. It would be to take common objects of our own street and tell of how each of them came to be in the street at all. And for my immediate purpose it is really convenient to take two objects we have known all our lives, as features of fashion or respectability. One, which has grown rarer recently, is what we call a top-hat; and the other, which is still a customary formality, is a pair of trousers. The history of these humorous objects really does give a clue to what has happened in England for the last hundred years.—CHESTERTON

4. To gain a better appreciation of the duration of sounds, read the following selection. Lengthen all of the vowels, with the exception of those in unimportant words. Do not drawl, but sustain the tone steadily for each long vowel sound. Be aware also of control over your breathing.

Life is a narrow vale between the cold and barren peaks of two eternities. We strive in vain to look beyond the heights. We cry aloud, and the only answer is the echo of our wailing cry. From the voiceless lips of the unreplying dead, there comes no word; but in the night of death, hope sees a star, and listening love can hear the rustle of a wing.

He who sleeps here, when dying, mistaking the approach of death for the return of health, whispered with his latest breath: "I am better now." Let us believe, in spite of doubts and dogmas, of fears and tears, these dear words are true of all the countless dead.—INGERSOLL

5. Read an excerpt from a modern story to the class. Choose a selection which will show your skills in suiting rate to type of material and in varying timing for effect.

6. Describe an action scene for the class, building to a climax through increase of rate and loudness.

These selections in Appendix II are suggested for practice on timing: Numbers 2, 8, 11*b*, 20, 23, and 25.

SUMMARY

In the production of your voice, the exhaled breath passes between your vocal folds. Control over steadiness, loudness, and timing of the volcalization will then depend, in great part, on control of the breath stream which sets the folds into vibration.

The structure of the breathing mechanism includes the rib cage, which is comprised of backbone, sternum, and twelve pairs of ribs; the diaphragm and tendons which provide a dome-shaped floor for the thoracic cavity; the two large conical-shaped lungs; the bronchial tubes; and the trachea which leads up to the larynx.

When you inhale, the large diaphragmatic muscle contracts and descends; by means of muscle contraction, the ribs are raised and lifted slightly, and the sternum rises a little. This process increases the size of the thoracic cavity in three directions: up and down, side to side, and back to front. Air rushes in to fill the lungs. On exhalation in life breathing, the diaphragm and muscles between the ribs relax, the raised structures descend, and with this increased pressure upon the lungs, the breath pours out. In breathing for speech, however, the breath stream must be expelled more slowly. The abdominal muscles assist in control. As they contract, they exert steady pressure on the viscera within, which are thus forced back up against the diaphragm. The diaphragm and rib muscles relax slowly, so that there is a nice balance achieved between the relaxation of the inhalation muscles and the firm pressure of the abdominal muscles. The breath now moves steadily upward under this controlled pressure.

There are four general types of breathing for voice production: clavicular, upper thoracic, medial, and diaphragmatic-abdominal. Clavicular breathing, which involves elevation of the shoulders and collarbones, is to be avoided because it usually results in tension, fatigue, and poor control over the exhalation. The medial and diaphragmatic-abdominal are the most similar to the natural breathing-for-life process.

The control of breathing is important because (1) it contributes to steadiness of vocalization; (2) it permits the use of increased loudness when the speaking situation and the meaning necessitate this; (3) it allows you to vary the timing of your material, permitting changes in the length of phrases and pauses and in duration of words which you emphasize; and (4) it brings with it a feeling of ease and a growing assurance that you can develop skill of varying loudness and rate to suit your particular meanings.

In practice, drills for improvement of phonation and of breathing complement each other. Consequently, as you read in this book the material on phonation and resonation, you will find it helpful to go back over the exercises on breathing. Respiration, phonation, and resonation are not three independent processes. Much of your skill in the other phases of vocalization will depend upon control of breathing.

5

Tone Production – *Phonation*

The tones of human voices are mightier than strings or brass to move the soul.—KLOPSTOCK

When the noisy welcome of a recent national political convention had died away, the governor of a prominent state stepped up to the rostrum to make the most important nominating speech of the convention. He began with energy and enthusiasm, but in a high-pitched voice. As he proceeded, his voice became higher and higher until it went above its normal pitch level to at least three tones above middle C. Finally he was able to speak only in a shrill and hoarse whisper, stopping at the end of every sentence in an attempt to relieve the evident distress of his strained vocal folds. He was barely able to finish his ten-minute speech because of the unnatural strain which he had placed upon his vocal folds and the muscles of his larynx.

A good sportscaster, on the other hand, can speak with enthusiasm, vigor, and excitement for two and a half or three hours, reporting a football game, at a pitch level which is easy for him and pleasant to the ears of his listeners. He will still have plenty of voice left when the game is over and will feel little strain on his vocal folds or the muscles of his larynx. He has achieved the fine balance of tensions and relaxations necessary for the production of excellent tone. The governor, however, upset that balance with extreme tension.

Faulty muscular control of the vocal folds as they vibrate to produce sound, through too much tension, too little tension, or improper adjustment, makes for poor tone production. This chapter is designed to help you achieve tones which may be "mightier than strings or brass to move the soul."

57

STRUCTURE AND FUNCTION OF THE LARYNX

STRUCTURE

We have shown how the controlled exhalation of breath provides the motive power for vocalization. As this stream passes through the larynx and past the vocal folds within this structure, the sound starts. You can locate your larynx in the region of the Adam's apple. Placing your fingers there, hum vigorously; you can feel the vibration of the folds immediately behind the cartilage.

When the breath leaves the lungs, it goes up through the many small bronchial tubes, to the two large bronchi, passes through the trachea, and

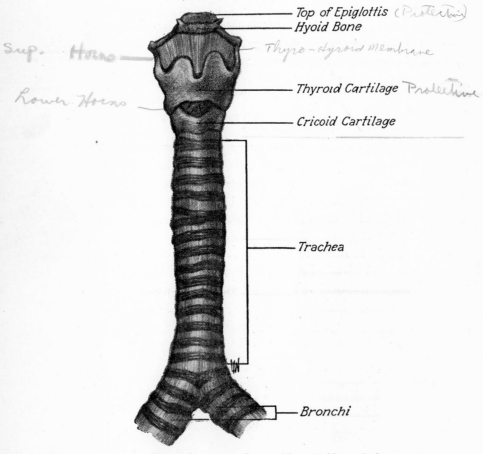

Fig. 5. Larynx, trachea, and bronchi (front view)

into the larynx. The larynx is composed of cartilage, connected with ligaments, membrane, and muscles. You will find the whole structure far from rigid if you place your hand on your throat as you swallow, or as you move your head back and forth and up and down.

Immediately above the top of the trachea and joined to it by ligaments is a large, heavy ring, called the *cricoid*. Whereas the cartilages of the trachea are not complete circles, since they are completed at the back of the tube by connective tissue, the cricoid is an actual ring. It derives its name from its shape, that of a signet ring, with the wide signet at the back of the larynx and the narrow band in front. The cricoid is the lower part of the larynx.

Resting on the cricoid is the largest cartilage of the structure, the *thyroid*. It is roughly shield shaped, or shaped like a cupped hand, and is made up of two plates of cartilage which meet in front in a **V** and diverge behind. Place thumb and forefinger on the Adam's apple and move them back and out; you will feel the sides of this shield.

The Adam's apple is the most prominent projection of the thyroid cartilage. Directly above this you can feel the notch of the thyroid at its top edge. On the other side of the cartilage from where your fingers rest, the vocal folds have their anterior attachment.

The sides of the thyroid cartilage extend outward at an angle. On the rear end of each side there are upward and outward extending projections,

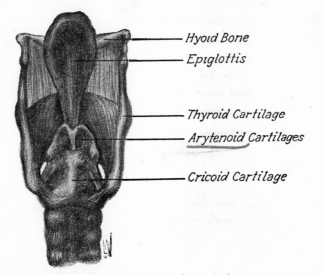

— Hyoid Bone
— Epiglottis

— Thyroid Cartilage
— Arytenoid Cartilages

— Cricoid Cartilage

Fig. 6. The larynx (back view)

vocal bands are attached to the Arytenoid Cartilage

in front to the thyroid notch

Glottis = space between the vocal bands
Ventricle = space above the larynx

known as *horns.* Above the larynx, curving in the bend between the neck and the turn of the throat, the horseshoe-shaped *hyoid* bone lies embedded at the root of the tongue. The superior horns of the thyroid cartilage connect with the posterior ends of the horseshoe-shaped bone by means of ligaments and small additional cartilages.

The lower pair of horns of the thyroid articulate with the cricoid cartilage below. The joint is not fixed; the thyroid cartilage can tilt back and forth in this small joint and can also slide a small distance.

The signet part of the cricoid cartilage is raised like a small platform in the space behind the spreading sides of the thyroid. Resting on the upper edge of this platform are a pair of very small cartilages, called the *arytenoids.* These are shaped like irregular three-sided pyramids and articulate with the cricoid on their fourth side or base. The arytenoids, by means of their muscular attachments, can rotate toward and away from each other and slip back a short distance over the edge of the cricoid cartilage. These small cartilages are important to speech because they form the posterior attachments of the vocal folds, and by their actions manipulate the folds.

The vocal folds and their accompanying muscles extend from the front prominence of the thyroid cartilage, just below the notch, to the two arytenoid cartilages at the back of the larynx. These structures, which

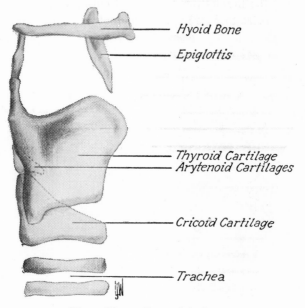

Hyoid Bone

Epiglottis

Thyroid Cartilage
Arytenoid Cartilages

Cricoid Cartilage

Trachea

Fig. 7. The cartilages of the larynx

vibrate for the production of tone, are two flaps, or lips, of muscle, triangular in cross section, whose inner edges are comparatively thin and outer ones thick. They are covered with the mucous membrane which forms a continuous lining for the larynx, pharynx, and mouth. The inner edges of the folds are of fibrous tissue, pearly white in color. The opening between the folds, which is triangular in shape during quiet breathing, is called the *glottis*. The sides of the folds extend out to the inner part of the cricoid cartilage. Thus, when the glottis is closed and the folds brought together, the passageway is completely cut off; air can go neither in nor out. A thin elastic diaphragm is formed across the larynx by this closure, with the closed slit down its center. The folds do not lie on the horizontal, but each slopes upward from the outer attachment at the cricoid to the central free edge. Directly above the true vocal folds lie the false vocal folds; they are thicker than the true folds and do not have the fibrous edge.

Also attached to the thyroid cartilage is the *epiglottis*, a leaf-shaped cartilage. It is connected by its stemlike part to the inside of the thyroid directly above the anterior attachment of the vocal folds and extends at an upward angle toward the back of the pharynx. The horseshoe-shaped

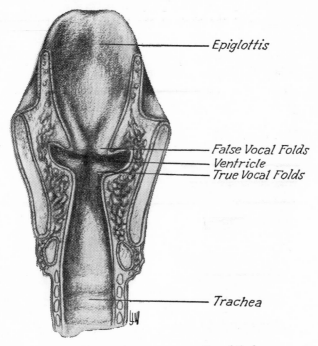

Fig. 8. The anterior transverse section of the larynx

hyoid bone partially encircles it. The hyoid bone, as we have mentioned, is buried at the base of the tongue. It forms the point of attachment for the principal muscles of the tongue; also from it a curtain of muscle and membrane extends to the top of the thyroid cartilage. Thus the entire larynx can be said to be suspended from the hyoid bone.

Directly behind the larynx is the *esophagus,* or food passage. This is a tube of muscle and connective tissue which leads from the level of the top of the larynx to the stomach.

The entire larynx and associated structures are interlaced with muscle and connective tissue. As we have no conscious control over individual muscles of the larynx, there is no need to name them individually. There are both paired and single *intrinsic* muscles within the larynx itself, which act upon the arytenoids and thus control the action of the vocal folds. *Extrinsic* muscles join the parts of the larynx on its exterior and extend to other parts of the mechanism, such as the hyoid bone or the sternum. These change the general position of the whole larynx.

BIOLOGICAL FUNCTION

The basic function of the larynx is to act as a valve at the entrance to the trachea. When you swallow, the tongue rides back, the larynx is raised, the epiglottis is tilted back to assist in diverting food or liquid away from the entrance into the larynx, and the vocal folds are brought together, closing the glottis. If, in spite of this protective action, food or other foreign matter enters the larynx, an instantaneous reflex is set up to expel it. The

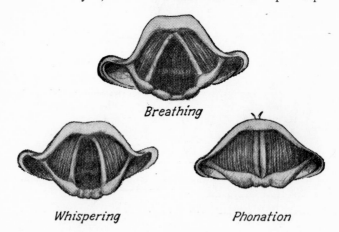

Fig. 9. The glottis during breathing, whispering, and phonation

vocal folds are closed tightly, air pressure is built up by the contraction of the abdominal muscles, the vocal folds are forced apart, and a blast of air is released under pressure, forcing out the foreign matter. This is what you label a *cough*. Similarly, by closing the glottis and contracting the abdominal muscles, pressure can be maintained in the chest to give a firm base for lifting or for other heavy strain.

These biological functions of the larynx take precedence over the functioning of the larynx for speech, making phonation an overlaid process. When it is necessary to use the larynx for any of them, speech functions of the larynx are disrupted.

FUNCTION IN PHONATION

The whole adjustment and movement of muscles and cartilages in phonation will be oversimplified in the following discussion so that you can understand the most important activities and those over which you have some conscious control.

During breathing, the glottis is open and is triangular in shape, with the apex of the triangle at the front. The arytenoids are separated and rotated slightly outward to maintain this opening. To produce tone, the intrinsic muscles of the larynx act upon the arytenoids to slide them together and rotate them inward, thus closing the glottis. When the edges of the folds are brought together, air pressure is built up beneath the glottis by the action of the muscles controlling exhalation. Because they are taut, the folds resist this pressure and are forced apart by it and set into vibration. This vibration is the action which produces tone. It occurs simultaneously in both folds and moves outward from the glottis in a wavelike motion of the entire fold. The vibrations are transmitted to the air column as a sound wave. In the rapid vibrations of phonation, the edges of the folds may touch hundreds of times a second as the glottis is opened and closed. An antagonistic set of muscles returns the arytenoids to the open position when phonation is finished.

The tone produced by the folds in vibration is determined principally by the action of the various *intrinsic muscles* of the larynx altering the position of the laryngeal cartilages. Muscles which stretch and elongate the vocal folds are called *tensors;* those which relax and shorten the folds are called *relaxors;* those which bring the folds together are known as *adductors;* those which swing the folds apart are termed *abductors.* These muscles produce the fundamental movements necessary for the production

Tongue – Most important single articulator

of tone. As we cannot consciously control the action of these individual muscle groups, it is not necessary to name them or to discuss their individual functioning. However, their activity determines the condition of the folds at any given instant, and, therefore, the pitch level of the tone produced.

The extrinsic muscles of the larynx serve chiefly to raise and lower the larynx from its normal position in relaxed breathing. Their main activity is related to such life processes as swallowing. Place your fingers on the thyroid cartilage and swallow; you will notice that the whole larynx rides up with the pull of the extrinsic muscles. Any marked raising or lowering of the larynx in phonation will, undoubtedly, affect the tensions in the larynx and, hence, the pitch. Some upward and downward movement of the larynx is necessary to good phonation, as you can feel if you place your fingers on the thyroid cartilage and speak a sentence or two. However, extreme movements, especially if the larynx is held at the top or bottom of its range of action, are to be avoided.

As a number of different forces are at work at the same time influencing the conditions of the folds, it is difficult to decide which influence determines a specific pitch level. The relationship of the various factors determining pitch has never been fully determined by research. While length and thickness help to determine the tone, they tend to cancel each other in influence; the final pitch is probably determined largely by tension. In whispering, the glottis is only partially closed, and friction noises, instead of tone, make up the vocalization.

For phonation, the glottis must be closed; air pressure must be built up beneath the folds, forcing them apart and setting them into vibration. The action of the intrinsic and extrinsic muscles of the larynx sets up conditions of length, tension, thickness, and density in the folds which determine the pitch produced.

ANALYSIS OF PHONATION HABITS

Since you have limited conscious control over specific muscle movements in phonation, you must learn to feel the presence or absence of muscle tensions in the mechanism of phonation as you speak. You must learn to associate particular kinds of muscular activity with the characteristic sounds which these activities produce. In this way you will develop a feeling sense for the muscular contractions necessary for good tone production, for the unnatural tensions which distort tone, and for the variations in tension responsible for pitch changes.

The Importance of the Control of Phonation

Learning to control phonation is important to the speaker for the following reasons:

1. Improper phonation may influence your breath control. If too much air escapes between the vocal folds as you phonate, no matter how good your breathing habits, you will run short of breath, lack control for changes of loudness, and interrupt your control for proper timing.

2. If there is muscle strain in either the intrinsic or the extrinsic muscles of the larynx, you cannot have easy vocalization. This tension may upset you and make you lose confidence in your own abilities. It will make phonation an effort instead of an easy, pleasant process.

3. Faulty phonation resulting in hoarseness, harshness, or raspiness will have an unpleasant effect on the ear of the listener and may be a distinct barrier to social acceptance and even to efficient communication.

4. Inefficient phonation often results in the inability to control and vary pitch for connected speech. When this occurs, the melody changes which suggest the variations in meaning are absent; communication is thus interfered with.

Self-analysis and Listening

Intelligent analysis of tone production through ear training is of major importance. Until you can hear critically the skills and faults of phonation in the voices of your classmates and in your own voice, you can do little toward self-improvement.

1. You should begin with an analysis of the muscle tensions present in your own phonation.

a. With your finger tips on the thyroid cartilage, produce an easy, pleasant, sustained AH sound loud enough to be heard easily by a person six feet from you. Notice the position of the larynx; are the extrinsic muscles above and below it tense or relaxed?

b. Without moving your fingers, sustain AH on as high a pitch level as you comfortably can. Notice how the larynx moves up. Is there tension in any of the extrinsic muscles?

c. Keep the fingers in position and sustain AH on your lowest comfortable pitch level. Notice how the larynx moves; note the tensions in the extrinsic muscles below it.

d. On one breath go from the low to the high AH sound without interrupting the tone. Do you feel muscle movements and changes in tension within the larynx as the pitch changes? On which pitch level do you feel the greatest tension? On which the least?

2. Listen to your phonation while sustaining AH at a conversational level of loudness, while reading aloud at conversational level, while reciting or performing in class, and while you are conversing with your friends. Does the phonation sound easy and pleasant? Do you sound hoarse or harsh to yourself by comparison with a voice which you judge as excellent? Do you feel any marked tensions in the extrinsic muscles? Within the larynx?

3. Do you hear in your own voice the same factors in tone production which your instructor and classmates report?

4. Listen to the recording of your voice which you made at the beginning of the semester. Do you hear any faults in your phonation? What are they?

5. Listen carefully to the normal phonation of your friends and that which takes place in the exercise assignments in class. Can you recognize clear, pure, unstrained production? Does your ear distinguish better phonation in the speech of one person than in that of another? When you hear phonation which is not pleasant and which sounds strained, try to imitate in your own mechanism the muscle tensions which the other person has in his; duplicate the tensions and phonate. Does your tone ordinarily sound like his?

PROBLEMS OF PHONATION

You should be acquainted with several specific and common voice problems which arise from improper phonation. We are not concerned with problems caused by organic defects of the larynx and the associated mechanism, such as paralysis of the folds, vocal nodes (corns on the inner edges of the folds which prevent their approximation), or malformation of the laryngeal structure. These are problems for the physician or the speech pathologist. We are interested here in the malfunctioning of the "normal" structure which can be corrected through training. While there is a wide variety of such difficulties, we shall classify them into a few general categories for analysis and retraining.

BREATHINESS

Breathiness is a condition caused by an incomplete closure of the glottis in phonation. The vocal folds are not brought together completely before air pressure is built up beneath them. As a result, there is air escaping which is not being used. This may happen on all phonation, or, as is common, only on the initiation of a vowel. The person with a breathy tone seems to be whispering everything he says; there is a fuzzy or feathery edge to all of his vocalization. The tone is not necessarily unpleasing, but it lacks carrying power, gives the impression that the speaker is airing his secrets in public, and frequently leads to monotony. The speaker who uses it puts forth a tremendous amount of effort in attempting to project with sufficient volume to an audience of any size.

GLOTTAL SHOCK

Glottal shock is a condition which is almost the direct opposite of breathiness. It is a staccato click, or tight, coughlike explosion of the vocal folds, frequently observed on the initiation of vowel sounds. Its presence is an indication that tone is begun with the throat in a strained condition.

This phonatory fault is caused by a tense, complete closure of the glottis under breath pressure. The vocal folds are then blasted apart, as in a light cough, when tone is initiated. In normal vocalization, the vocal folds touch each other lightly without the need of any pressure from the external throat muscles. Any voluntary cramping of the throat muscles interferes with this normal functioning, and a harsh, unpleasant initiation of tone results. The same tensions which produce glottal shock frequently lead to high pitch and to a flat tone which is deficient in resonance and tone color.

HARSHNESS

Harshness is related both to tone production and to resonation. It is the result of excessive muscle constriction throughout the vocal mechanism from top to bottom, and not in the larynx alone. The tension is particularly noticeable in the extrinsic muscles of the larynx; ordinarily, the larynx is held at the top or bottom of its range of movement. These tensions do not allow free and easy vibration of the vocal folds, and extraneous friction noises may be introduced in the passages immediately above the folds. The woman who talks at the top of her range with a shrill, high quality, or the man who forces his voice to the bottom of his range, so that it sounds gravelly and harsh, are both examples of this type of phonation.

Hoarseness

Hoarseness is generally associated with some abnormal physiological condition of the vocal folds, which may be either temporary or chronic. A temporary condition in the folds may cause them to swell, and the muscles may become less responsive to stimulation than normally. When you have a severe cold which "goes down your throat," the folds swell; they will not approximate easily or vibrate freely. When you yell continuously at a football game, you strain the muscles of the larynx and irritate the vocal folds by rubbing their edges together, so that hoarseness or complete loss of voice results. In the same way, if you give a speech with unnecessary tension in the larynx and strain the folds, you will become hoarse before you are through and may find it difficult to speak at all. A common cause of prolonged hoarseness is postnasal drip from hay fever, sinusitis, or other infection which causes constant inflammation of the folds.

These more or less temporary conditions, which have brought on the irritation in the larynx, may disappear and the irritation go away; yet you may continue to be hoarse. In this instance, either you have set up a pattern of muscle response which maintains the temporary tensions or you are still trying to adjust to an irritation which no longer exists. When a prolonged irritation of the folds leaves, you may still be trying to protect the folds as you did when they were sore, and so the hoarseness continues even though there is no longer a physical cause for it. The voice sounds raspy and strained.

Self-analysis and Listening

1. Read aloud a selection of vigorous, direct, communicative speech. "A House Divided," Number 18 in Appendix II, is that type of material. Record the selection and play the recording for analysis.

a. Are you breathy? Do you sound as if you were whispering?

b. Notice the vowel sounds at the beginning of words, particularly when a vowel begins a sentence. Is it initiated easily and smoothly? Do you hear a "click" or "shock" as you start it? Do you feel any unusual tension in the larynx as you start the vowel sounds?

c. Do you hear strain in your voice? Does the tone sound clear and pleasant? How does your tone sound by comparison with the best voices in the class?

d. Try to remember how the tone of your voice sounded when you had a bad cold, hay fever, or after you had done a lot of cheering at a ball game.

Was it unpleasant? Was there a feeling of strain or tension in the muscles of the larynx?

2. Do you hear any of the four problems of phonation in the voices of your friends or classmates? How do you react to the faults when you hear them? Do the faults seem to interfere with efficient communication?

3. Do you hear in your own voice any of the problems of phonation which your classmates and instructor report?

Exercises for Improvement

Exercises for both general improvement and correction of specific defects are presented here. They should prove helpful to all of you, regardless of your individual problems. The exercises should be regarded not only as remedial measures, but as tests of your ability in phonation. Plan and carry out a regular program of practice.

Breathing exercises should be continued as part of the work on phonation. It will be difficult for you to produce a pure and relaxed tone unless there is proper breath support. The most helpful exercises are those listed under *Breath Control for Steadiness of Vocalization* in the preceding chapter.

RELAXATION

Relaxation is basic to good phonation. It is necessary that the mechanism use only those muscles which are needed in each act and use them with the minimum of strain. Hence, the first exercises in this section are designed to relax the mechanism of phonation. Use these exercises each time before you do those for specific phonation faults.

1. Hold the head upright. Relax the muscles holding it and let it fall forward with the chin touching the chest. Be sure that it is falling forward of its own weight and that you are not pulling it forward. Repeat this several times.

2. Let the head fall forward as in Exercise 1, and then rotate it slowly and with as little muscular effort as possible up to the right shoulder. Now let the head fall backward and then rotate it forward over the left shoulder, letting it fall forward again. See that the jaw drops open of its own weight as the head falls back. As you rotate the head backward, inhale. Exhale as the head moves forward. Repeat this slowly; reverse the direction and do it several times more.

3. Relax the jaw by letting it fall open of its own weight as the head is held upright. Be certain that you are not pulling the jaw down, but letting

it fall. Close the mouth and repeat the exercise several times, getting the feeling of relaxation in the jaw muscles as the mouth falls open.

4. Repeat the syllable SUH, keeping the tongue relaxed and letting the relaxed jaw fall open after the consonant sound. Repeat this several times.

5. Take a deep breath; by relaxing as completely as possible, let out a deep sigh. Try to let the muscles of the throat and mouth go as you release the air. Feel that those muscles are relaxed. Repeat several times and then vocalize an easy, soft AH sound as you sigh. Try for pure tone without increased tension. Repeat, using the vowel tones OH, AW, OO, and EE.

BREATHINESS

Breathiness may be corrected through the systematic use of the following exercises.

1. Start a whispered AH; gradually add phonation on the sustained whisper until you have a clear and nonbreathy tone. Repeat this several times, being sure each time that the final tone has no breathiness in it.

2. Practice the sounds AH, OH, OO, and EE, starting each one with a firm glottal closure; sustain each for at least a count of three. Be sure that there is neither leakage of breath on the initiation of the sound nor breathiness as you hold the tone. Repeat several times with each of the sounds.

3. Starting with the lowest tone which you can produce with ease as *do* and sounding each note as a sustained AH, sing up the scale. Make each tone as long and loud as possible without strain, and be sure that it is not breathy. When you reach the top of the octave, reverse the scale and go back down to your original note. Breathe between tones. Repeat the exercise several times.

4. In reading the following paired words, pay no attention to breathiness on the vowel in the first word, but be sure that there is none on the vowel in the second word of the pair. Read through the list again and reverse the words in each pair. This time, eliminate the breathiness on all vowels. Do this a number of times.

hair	air	hat	at	hate	ate
hold	old	helm	elm	harm	arm
hit	it	high	eye	heel	eel
had	add	heat	eat	hall	all

5. Read the following words, guarding against all breathiness: *who, home, hunt, him, hem, whole, hand, wreck, wave, this, them, thick, several, finish,*

and *stool*. Repeat a number of times, lengthening the vowels on some of the trials.

6. Read the following paragraph as loudly as possible and without breathiness; then reread it, gradually reducing the loudness until you reach a conversational tone. Reread it as many times as is necessary to reduce the volume to the desired level. Be sure that there is no breathiness at any time. Making a record of this will assist you.

If you have breathy tone quality, you must make every effort to correct the fault. Hearing the defect is the first step toward this rehabilitation. A thorough course of exercises, practiced every day, will help to establish the new habit. Have your classmates check on the progress which you think you are making.

GLOTTAL SHOCK

If glottal shock is one of your problems, then you should work with the following exercises to help eliminate it.

1. Whisper the AH sound and gradually begin to phonate the tone at your habitual pitch level and with conversational volume. Be sure that the sound is easily initiated and that there is no click as the folds approximate on the initiation of the tone. Hold the sound steadily for a count of three. Repeat on the sounds OH, AW, OO, and EE.

2. Practice starting the vowel AH a number of times. Be sure that you get a smooth, easy initiation of tone without noise. Hold the sound, as in Exercise 1. Repeat on OH, AW, OO, and EE.

3. Use the paired words in Exercise 4 under *Breathiness* as the basis for this exercise. Read the first word of the pair, breathing the H sound and sliding easily without shock into the vowel; now read the second word of the pair without the breathed H, but with the same easy initiation of the vowel sound.

4. In the following sentences, the sounds on which you are apt to have glottal shock have been italicized. Read the sentences aloud, paying particular attention to the marked sounds, trying to get an easy initiation of sound on them. In each phrase, be sure that you blend the words so that the sounds flow smoothly without any break between them.

   a. *I*mmediately *a*fter the *e*nthusiastic *e*ncore, the *a*rtist *a*nswered his *a*pplause.

   b. Our *a*unt *e*mphasized the *i*dea that *a*n *a*ttitude of *a*ttentiveness *i*s obligatory.

    c. Each orator ought to outline an alternate argument.

    d. His inaccurate estimate of expenses was not only exaggerated but annoying.

    e. I invited Irene and Emma to accompany us all along the avenue.

    f. Honest effort is its own reward, asserted the old Oriental.

    g. Is Alex an expert at acrobatics?

    h. Insist upon inclusive information in appraising any insurance.

    i. Ella agreed to assist all eligible amateurs.

    j. Every alley entering the avenue is open to everyone.

HARSHNESS

Harshness can be materially helped through the use of the following exercises. You will find that the exercises for relaxation and for glottal shock are also helpful.

    1. Place the tip of the tongue behind the lower front teeth; open the mouth and throat as if to yawn. Maintaining this relaxed position, phonate an easy AH sound and sustain it for the count of three. If you feel any tenseness or rigidity in the muscles at the back of the throat, as you do in a completed yawn, relax and begin again. Practice the same exercise with OH, AW, OO, and EE.

    2. Following the same directions as for Exercise 1, start with the OH and gradually blend it into the AH sound. Start with OO and EE and blend in the same way. Keep the tone free and relaxed.

    3. Keep a relaxed throat and repeat the following sentences slowly, sustaining all of the vowel sounds, being sure that they are not harsh.

    a. Where are you?

    b. Green grow the lilacs.

    c. The moon is mellow tonight.

    d. Few were ready to go.

    e. Aim high if you are in earnest.

    f. Roll on, thou deep and dark blue Ocean—roll!

    g. Thou art merciful unto him.

    h. Blow a low, low tone.

    i. Hear how the sea moans today.

    j. Hold high the hero.

    4. The following selections provide good practice for eliminating harshness. Practice them, sustaining the vowels and listening for any sign of harshness.

a. Sweet and low, sweet and low,
    Wind of the western sea,
  Low, low, breathe and blow,
    Wind of the western sea!
  Over the rolling waters go,
    Come from the dying moon, and blow,
  Blow him again to me;
    While my little one, while my pretty one, sleeps.
                  —TENNYSON

b. Blessed is the man that walketh not in the counsel of the ungodly, nor
    standeth in the way of sinners, nor sitteth in the seat of the
    scornful.
  But his delight is in the law of the Lord; and in his law doth he medi-
    tate day and night.
  And he shall be like a tree planted by the rivers of water, that bringeth
    forth his fruit in his season; his leaf also shall not wither; and
    whatsoever he doeth shall prosper.
  The ungodly are not so: but are like the chaff which the wind driveth
    away.
  Therefore the ungodly shall not stand in the judgment, nor sinners in
    the congregation of the righteous.
  For the Lord knoweth the way of the righteous: but the way of the
    ungodly shall perish.
                  —PSALMS I

c. Teach me your mood, O patient stars!
    Who climb each night the ancient sky,
  Leaving on space no shade, no scars,
    No trace of age, nor fear to die.
                  —EMERSON

d. Selection 21 in Appendix II.
e. Selection 12 in Appendix II, CLXXIX.

HOARSENESS

If your hoarseness is pathological, caused by chronic infection or irritation, you have more need for medical care than you do for voice exercises.
If it is not pathological, then you should use the relaxation exercises and

those for glottal shock and harshness. It is not necessary to set up new exercises for this condition. The following exercises are particularly useful.

1. *Glottal Shock:* Exercise 1.
2. *Glottal Shock:* Exercise 3.
3. *Harshness:* Exercise 1.
4. *Harshness:* Exercise 2.
5. *Harshness:* Exercise 3.

PITCH

Habitual Pitch

In your vocalization you will have a habitual pitch level, the level of pitch at which most of your vocalization is done and to which you return after any excursion up or down the scale. This habitual pitch level is determined by the action of the muscles in the larynx controlling the vocal folds. These are conditions largely determined by habit and training, making this the level at which you usually speak. General health, specific conditions associated with the larynx, general emotional states, and the present emotional condition all go toward determining this pitch level. Experiments with a group of men and women with trained voices have shown that for the men in the group the median pitch was 141 cycles and for the women 233 cycles. Your habitual pitch may change from day to day, or even from hour to hour, as you become tired, ill, emotionally upset, or depressed; or conversely, elated or excited.

Finding the habitual pitch level. It is difficult to discover your habitual pitch level without aid from the instructor or a member of the class. A piano or a pitch pipe is almost a necessity for accuracy. Three methods are suggested below for you to try.

1. Read a selection of prose in an easy, conversational voice. As you go along, try to hear the level of pitch which you use most often and to which you return after any variation up or down the scale. Pick a word or syllable which seems to be on that note, and prolong the sound. Locate the pitch on the musical scale. Try the experiment several times, and average the results to get an approximation of your habitual pitch level.

2. Read a selection as suggested above while sitting at a piano. As you read, try various tones on the piano around middle C (or C below middle C for a man's voice) until you find the one which comes closest to your habitual level. Repeat the experiment several times to be sure you have the right tone.

3. If you do not have a piano available, but do have a pitch pipe, try Exercise 2, using the pitch pipe instead of the piano. It is possible to do this by yourself, but much easier if someone else uses the pitch pipe to help you locate the pitch level.

4. Read a selection and have someone else at the piano lightly sound the notes around middle C. The person at the piano should be able to locate your habitual pitch level. Repeat several times. Naturally, this experiment will be the most successful if the person helping you is trained in voice, particularly in listening.

Optimum Pitch

There is an optimum pitch level for every individual, the pitch level for the most efficient and effective phonation with the minimum of muscular action. For it there is selective contraction of muscles, and no unnecessary tension. Only those muscles are tensed which must be used for the production of the tone; all of the others are at rest. It is the pitch level at which the purest, richest, and fullest tone is produced. Its production involves not only the larynx and the vocal-folds, but also the whole speech mechanism, particularly the resonators. Optimum pitch is, in reality, dependent upon the action both of the vocal folds and of the resonators. For maximum efficiency of operation and the most pleasant phonation, the optimum pitch should be your habitual pitch. Generally, the optimum pitch level is about one-third of the way up from the bottom to the top of your range. If you will experiment you will find that your tone is more easily produced, fuller, and richer at one pitch level than at any other; that is your optimum pitch.

Finding the optimum pitch. The optimum pitch level is relative. It is the level at which the tone seems to sound the purest and the fullest. At best, any method available to you for finding it is crude and only approximate. Three possible methods are suggested.

1. Sing down to the lowest note you can comfortably produce. Let this be *do*. Sing up the musical scale to *sol*. Your optimum pitch should be at or near this tone. Using this pitch, say, "I am going home," on a monopitch. Try the same exercise one tone higher, and then one tone lower. Listen to your voice and have some other person listen, to determine which pitch produces the purest and fullest tone with the least effort. The tone which meets these requirements should be your optimum pitch.

2. Stop up your ears with your fingers and hum M up and down the scale until you find the pitch level at which the sound seems to ring the loudest in your head. This will be approximately your optimum pitch.

Test your ability to use this pitch by repeating the procedure suggested in Exercise 1.

3. Using a piano, go down to the lowest note which you can comfortably produce; follow along on the piano note by note. Now sing back up the scale, as suggested in the first exercise, sounding each tone on the piano as you do so. When you reach the *sol* in this experiment, try sounding it with the piano, and then sounding tones just above and below that level. Listen to hear which one sounds the richest and fullest; that is your optimum pitch. It is best to have someone with a good ear to assist you in this exercise.

If your habitual pitch level and your optimum pitch level are the same, then you need not be concerned about your voice in this regard. However, if there is any wide discrepancy between the two then you must work to reconcile the difference and bring your habitual pitch closer to the optimum pitch for the most efficient, effective, and pleasant phonation.

Pitch Range

Besides establishing your best possible pitch level, it is necessary that you make full use of the pitch range of your voice. This range is determined by the limits from the lowest to the highest pitch which you use in speaking. Persons whom you would judge as having good voices have a pitch range of an octave or more, while a highly trained voice will often have a range of at least two octaves. President Roosevelt's normal speaking range was from 96 to 256 cycles, a range of about one and a half octaves, with the top tone at about middle C. On the other hand, many persons with poor voices have a pitch range which is limited to not more than two full tones each way from the habitual pitch level. The mechanism of the larynx is capable, if it is in good physical condition, of operation which will give a range of at least an octave. Research has shown that there is little if any difference in the muscular development of the larynx in the person with a wide pitch range and one with a narrow range. It is up to you to discover whether your pitch range is adequate for good vocalization, and, if it is not, to make every effort to increase it.

Determining the speaking range. At best, the two exercises below are not entirely satisfactory methods of determining your range. However, without the aid of instruments such as those in a voice laboratory, they are the best methods available to you.

1. Read a prose selection which, by its very nature, seems to call for variation in pitch level. Try to locate the highest tone which your voice

reaches while reading, and sustain that tone; that is the top of your reading range. Do the same for the lowest note which you reach in reading. Repeat the experiment several times and with different materials.

2. Using a piano, repeat the reading which you used in the first exercise. When you sound the tone which you think is the highest, sustain it and locate it on the piano. Do the same with the lowest tone. This will give you your range. Try the experiment with several different selections and with conversational speech; note the differences in range and try to strike an average.

There is a distinct relationship between habitual pitch, optimum pitch, and range. If the habitual pitch is either so low or so high that it is near the bottom or the top of the range, then no matter how wide the range may be, it will be difficult for you to achieve real variety; all of the change of pitch will be either up from the bottom or down from the top. However, if you are using your optimum pitch level as your habitual one, then, even though the range is limited, there will be an opportunity for variety both up and down the scale within the range of your voice. Naturally, the wider your range, the greater chance there will be for effective variety. Hence, it is important for you to explore your habitual and optimum levels and your range and, if necessary, work to change or broaden them.

Self-analysis and Listening

1. Listen to yourself in three typical speaking situations: reading aloud, performing in class, and conversing with friends. Does your habitual pitch sound right to you? Is it too high or too low? You will be able to analyze yourself more effectively by recording your voice.

2. Can you find a level where the tone is easier, richer, fuller, and more pleasant than any other? What happens when you try to use that level as your habitual level? How does your fullness of tone then compare with that of your friends and classmates?

3. Is the pitch monotonous as you read aloud? Is there change from the highest to the lowest tone you produce? Do you have as great a range as others in the class with good voices?

4. Do you hear in your voice the faults in habitual pitch level or pitch range which your instructor reports?

Exercises for Improvement

1. Beginning at your lowest comfortable pitch, intone the sound OH. Glide up to your highest comfortable pitch; take a breath and glide down

again. Listen to yourself to see if there are any breaks in pitch level. Repeat several times, trying to extend the range in both directions, but do not strain.

2. Starting at a comfortably high pitch, count down the scale, using speaking rather than singing tones. Repeat, extending the scale at both ends, as far as you can without strain.

3. Starting at about the same pitch level used in Exercise 2, count to three on a descending scale. Continue to count to ten, using the same pitch level on which you produced the count of three. Repeat, descending to four, five, six, and so on, until you have completed the scale to the count of ten.

4. Repeat the above exercise, using an ascending scale.

5. Read each line of the following selection on a descending scale. Try to extend the range in both directions on each succeeding line.

> I wandered lonely as a cloud,
>> That floats on high o'er vales and hills,
> When all at once I saw a crowd,
>> A host, of golden daffodils;
> Beside the lake, beneath the trees,
> Fluttering and dancing in the breeze.
>> —WORDSWORTH

6. Using a low pitch level, read the following passage (*a*) in a monotone; (*b*) with a limited pitch range; (*c*) with the widest possible range.

The speaker who has a very narrow pitch range will have difficulty giving full expression to his ideas. If your mechanism is in good physical condition, you can extend your range through careful exercise. While it may be difficult to do this without the aid of the piano, still you can train your ear to help you. A few minutes each day is all that you need to use on this type of exercise.

7. Repeat the three different types of reading of the above passage, using a high level of pitch. Repeat again on an intermediate level.

8. Repeat the passage in Exercise 6, starting on a monotone near your optimum pitch, and gradually widening the range to your broadest one before you reach the end.

MELODY (*Inflection*)

Besides assuring yourself that you are using your optimum pitch and that you are making full use of an adequate range, you must have melody—the changes in pitch which express your emotional and intellectual meanings. Melody is the variation of pitch up and down the scale in the multitude of combinations used in connected speech. Each spoken dialect has its own basic melody pattern, even within the same language. When we refer to an Irish lilt, we are speaking of a melody pattern. However, we are concerned here, not with the characteristic patterns of dialects, but with the individual melody variations which help you to express your ideas in speaking, reading, or acting.

Melody and Meaning

The ability to achieve variety of melody is of basic importance to the communication of meaning. Probably such variety does more than any other single vocal element to give the listener the meaning which the speaker intends. In the sentence, "You are going to school," if the pitch falls on the end of the word "school," the listener receives a positive impression—that the person addressed *is* going to school. If there is a rise in pitch on the end of the final word in the sentence, the listener realizes that the speaker is asking a question. Other combinations of pitch changes will give other variations in meaning. For example, a combination of rising and then falling on the word "going" will indicate that the speaker thinks that the person addressed is foolish if he goes to school. The variety of meanings which can be expressed by these pitch changes is almost infinite. Naturally, these variations in pitch must be coupled with changes in time and loudness for complete expression.

The speaker who has a restricted pitch range, or keeps his pitch on one level without any variation, certainly cannot have the advantage of the many subtle cues to meaning which only melody changes can convey. Similarly, the speaker who repeats a pattern of melody is limiting himself in the possible expression of meaning. You have heard the speaker who starts every phrase on a high pitch and then lowers it on the last word of the phrase, repeating the pattern over and over again. Such a pattern may exist in any combination of melody changes. No meaningful variety is possible when this condition persists. The monotony of either approach, the mono-melody or the melody pattern, soon will become apparent in the loss of audience interest.

In the public-platform situation, the variety which you may have on the conversational level must be extended over a broader range in order to be effective for the larger group and greater distance. It is important, too, that you have easy use of your range. If the range is wide, but you can use only the narrow center of it without self-conscious effort, you might as well have only the limited range. Of course, you will not wish to use the broad, sweeping changes in pitch characteristic of old-time oratory, but when the audience increases in size, you must make suitable adjustments in your variation in pitch.

If your habitual pitch level is not near your optimum pitch, it will be difficult, if not impossible, for you to use melody efficiently. When you talk at the lower level of your range, so that your voice always seems to be scraping bottom, the only variety you can achieve is through a rise in pitch. On the other hand, some persons seem to talk constantly at the top of their ranges, and all of their variety comes from falling pitch. Neither of these two habitual pitch levels allows the individual speaker subtle variety. With your optimum pitch and your habitual pitch established at the same level, you can have adequate melody changes in either direction, and can achieve the variations necessary to express your meaning.

In preparing to speak before any group, you should not, of course, predetermine the melody which you are going to use and impose it upon the words you speak. No matter how much variety you achieved in a wide range of pitch by such a method, the effect would be ridiculous and artificial. This practice of imposing melody pattern upon the material helped to bring elocution into disrepute. All that the speaker, reader, or actor can do is to use the optimum pitch and the broadest possible range in the practice of exercises. In the actual speaking situation, the meaning which you wish to convey must determine the melody you use. The conscious practice of vocal exercises will help to develop a mechanism sufficiently flexible to respond quickly and automatically in communication.

Speech Melody and Song Melody

You must distinguish between the term "melody," as we have been using it to describe speech, and the familiar concept of melody in song. Song melody, of course, has great variety, but it is not suited to speech. Its pitch range is very wide, and the pattern is set by the composer and must be followed by the singer without individual variation. Moreover, there are wider jumps from pitch level to pitch level than are normally used in speech. In speech melody, the range is more restricted, and the performer improvises the melody pattern as the material, the feeling tone, and the inspiration of the moment dictate. Pitch changes in speech melody are often glides from one level to another, whereas pitch changes in song are definite and follow a formal scale. In addition, the singer prolongs tones in a way that would be disturbing in speech. Speech melody has more subtle changes than song melody and is a great deal more complex than the comparatively simple pattern of song.

Careful listening to the speech which you hear about you, especially to some of that from the pulpit, will give you examples of the intrusion of song melody upon speech, and the accompanying deterioriation in communication. The characteristic features of this intrusion, often called "ministerial cadence," is the sustaining of pitch and prolonging of tone, usually arranged in a rather definite and repeated pattern. The minister who says,

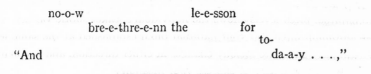

```
             no-o-w                le-e-sson
                 bre-e-thre-e-nn the        for
                                            to-
     "And                           da-a-y . . . ,"
```

(with the melody pattern and prolonged tones suggested) not only fails to communicate meaning, but also distracts the audience by the pattern itself. It should not be difficult for you to see the pitfalls of song melody when it is applied to speech. There are times, especially in reading certain types of poetry, when you may use modified song melody; generally, however, you should avoid it scrupulously if you wish to be genuinely communicative.

Key in speaking does not have the same meaning as it does in singing. In speaking it is closely associated with habitual pitch level; they are considered to be the same thing by some authors. However, here we are referring to key as the average pitch level at any given instant, depending upon the physical condition and mood of the individual and the ideas with which he is dealing. Hence, the person who is in good physical health and in a light and happy mood will generally speak in a higher average key than will the person who is not well or is in a dark or depressed mood. More important to us is the speaker's key in relation to the emotional mood of the material which he is speaking. His average pitch level will change with the changing emotions of the idea. In light, buoyant material the key will be higher than in material where the mood is depressed and sad. Listen to those about you and observe these differences in key.

The Inflection

The inflection is one of the methods through which you achieve variety of melody. An inflection is an upward or downward glide—a change in pitch within a single phonation. It is a change accomplished by sliding through the intervening pitch levels in moving from one pitch to another, without any cessation of tone. The rising inflection is an upward glide. Such an inflection usually denotes doubt, uncertainty, indecision, questioning, suspense, or unfinished thought. The falling inflection, ending on a lower pitch level, denotes certainty, positiveness, finality, or finished thought. The rising inflection is frequently used to end a question, while the falling inflection generally ends a positive statement of fact. You will impair the effectiveness with which you can use inflections, however, if you fail to note that there are many exceptions to these generalizations.

The circumflex inflection is a subtle inflection used to express fine shades of meaning. It may be a rising inflection followed by a falling one; it may be a falling inflection followed by a rising one; or it may be any one of a number of combinations of the two. A circumflex inflection may give an idea a double meaning, or one which is not inherent in the words but which the speaker wishes to imply. A classic example is the line from Shakespeare's *Julius Caesar*, when Antony is addressing the crowd saying, "For Brutus is an honorable man." The use of rising and falling inflections, particularly on the word "honorable," gives the listener the subtle meaning exactly opposed to what the words say, but which Antony wishes to convey.

Inflections help to convey the logical meaning and mood of the speaker to his listeners. They suggest the attitude of the speaker toward his ideas. By means of inflections, the speaker can give different meanings to the same words. Try saying "no" or "yeah," first with a falling, then a rising, and finally a rising and falling circumflex inflection. Note the differences in meaning achieved by the inflectional changes alone. It is important for you to be able to produce these various types of inflections so that your vocal instrument will be responsive to the changes in thought and feeling as they occur in your materials.

The general changes in pitch within a group of phonations are called an *intonation*. You must be careful not to repeat the same intonation pattern in each phrase or sentence you speak. If you are responsive to the fine shades of meaning and allow individual inflections to express them, you will avoid this pitfall.

The Step

In the inflection, the change in pitch is gradual, but in the *step* there is an abrupt change without a noticeable glide. In the transitions between words or syllables, and even more frequently between phrases, a skilled speaker will change his pitch because of a shift in thought or feeling. Between the major tonal elements of adjacent syllables there is a clear and discrete pitch change. In the following examples, the position of the words indicates the places where steps might be used in speaking.

```
                    red,
                        white,
    The colors are             and
                                   blue.

    This is the
                    place!

            so excited!
    I am

                here.
    I have it

            far,
                far
    It was          away.
```

The speaker may use the step to give emphasis to a word or group of words by placing them on a higher or lower pitch level than the remainder of the phrase. Also, it may help the speaker to convey emotional mood and atmosphere, and at the same time, to fix spatial relationships for the listener. The step is more direct, positive, and assertive than the inflection. As it is one of the methods for achieving variety, you should test your ability to use and hear the step. Further examples of the use of the step will be found in Exercise 5, page 86. In many of these sentences you will be able to note the significance of the step when it is used between phrases.

Personality and Melody

Your own emotional responsiveness will in large part act as a determining influence for variations in speech melody. If you are emotionally unresponsive, you will not have much melody change; and what you have will be in a narrow range. If you are excessively responsive, you are likely to have changes which are too abrupt and too wide and sweeping. Your habitual tensions will be reflected in your basic pitch and the pattern and variety of your melody. This is something which you must listen for in your own speech and ask others to criticize. If such patterns are present as the result of your personality, you must analyze yourself to find the root cause, and then make conscious efforts to break the old habits.

Subtle cues to the personality of the speaker are given by his use of melody. Consider the speaker who has many positive, falling inflections; generally, other things being equal, he will give the impression that he is a positive, even a didactic, person. Mr. Milquetoast will use many rising inflections, indicating his doubt and uncertainty about everything. When a man overuses a subtle pattern of combinations of circumflex and rising inflections, a certain femininity in character will be suggested. A constant series of rising inflections and a song pattern on the high pitch level associated with the gushy hostess denote the insincerity inherent in such an individual. These patterns limit the effectiveness of the speaker, because they all tend to impose themselves upon speech regardless of the meaning required by the words spoken. The effective speaker, therefore, must work not only to modify the pattern itself, but to change the personality traits from which it is derived.

Your emotional state in the speaking, reading, or acting situation may influence the melody, too. If you feel no unnatural tensions in the situation and have a responsive mechanism, you will probably make the changes necessary for meaning. However, if you feel unnatural inhibitions, engendered by the immediate situation, your mechanism may not respond freely; the variation in melody will be restricted to a narrow range, be almost entirely absent, or fall into a distorted pattern.

Self-analysis and Listening

1. Read aloud a selection from Appendix II, such as "Hamlet's Advice to the Players," Number 16. Listen to the melody as you read. Is there variety of melody, or does all of the vocalization center around one or two tones? Do you start most of your phrases on a relatively high pitch and then work your way down in pitch to the end of the phrase? Or do you have other melody patterns?

2. Listen to the recording you made at the beginning of the semester. Try to plot a curve on paper representing your changes in melody as it moves up and down the pitch scale within your range. Is there easily recognizable variation? Does the variation follow any set pattern from phrase to phrase? Do you use both steps and inflections?

3. In your conversational speech, can you recognize inflections? Steps? Do they occur frequently or rarely? Do these pitch changes help you to express your meaning?

4. Listen to your friends and classmates. Do you hear Mr. Milquetoast, the didactic informer, or the gushy hostess? What melody factors contribute to making the impression? Are any of those factors present in your own voice?

5. Can you hear in your own voice the things about melody which the instructor and your classmates report to you?

Exercises for Improvement

You should consider the phonation exercises dealing with *range*, on pages 76–78, part of the exercises on melody; review them before you undertake the exercises listed here.

1. Analyze the speech melody of the recording which you made at the beginning of the term. Answer the following questions about it:

a. Does the analysis you made in Exercise 2 of the self-analysis section suggest a pleasing voice? An interesting one? An effective one for the communication of all the meanings in the selection?

b. What changes might you make in the melody to make your voice more pleasing, interesting, and effective?

c. Read the selection again, trying to change the melody as your analysis suggests. Record the new reading on a wire or tape recorder and compare it with the first reading. Experiment until you are satisfied that you have made substantial improvement.

2. The following drills are useful in testing your ability to achieve variety in melody. Be sure that each tone is easily initiated, full, and clear. Do not strain or go beyond the easy limits of your speaking range.

a. Chant the vowel sound AH in steps through the middle octave of your speaking range, from the lowest to the highest tone, taking a fresh breath on each pitch. Hold each tone for a duration of three seconds. Repeat with OH, OO, EE, and AW.

b. Inflect each of these vowel sounds through the same octave to the top note and continue down to the lowest one. Repeat from top to bottom and back to the top.

c. Try Exercises *a* and *b*, exploring the full limits of your speaking range.

3. Read each of the following words and phrases with a final falling inflection, a final rising inflection, a circumflex inflection, and on a monopitch without inflection. Try each of the phrases with a rising step and then

with a descending step to the final word. Notice the various shades of meaning which you give to the material with the melody changes.

a. Please	*i.* Friend	*q.* You would
b. Yes	*j.* Go	*r.* Keep quiet
c. Where	*k.* Mother	*s.* Not at all
d. See	*l.* Robber	*t.* Oh, look
e. Maybe	*m.* Look out	*u.* Children play
f. Fire	*n.* Don't go	*v.* We stand
g. No	*o.* See here	*w.* Follow me
h. Help	*p.* Who's there	*x.* Page thirty

4. Read each of the following sentences in the upper, middle, and lower keys of your speaking voice. Introduce all of the melody changes which are essential to meaning. Strive for variety and freedom from pattern. Decide in which key you are most expressive.

a. It was a foggy, gray day, and I felt especially low as I realized that I had flunked two of my midsemesters.

b. First you could hear the low roll of the muffled drums, and then the funeral procession came slowly around the corner with the flags draped in crepe and the hero's body on the flag-covered caisson.

c. He jumped into his convertible and raced to the beach where he knew he would find his gang waiting for him.

d. In this class tomorrow we will have a discussion and demonstration of the uses of melody in connected speech.

e. What a party! Everything seemed to go wrong! No one had the right address, half of the food was missing, and everyone was fighting with everyone else.

f. Another verse of the hymn arose, a slow and mournful strain, such as the pious love, but joined to the words which expressed all that our nature can conceive of sin, and darkly hinted at far more.—HAWTHORNE

g. A ship captain is a good man to marry if it is a marriage of love, for absences are a good influence in love and keep it bright and delicate.—STEVENSON

h. If one is to improve his speaking voice, he must constantly strive to establish new vocal habits in place of old ones.

5. In the following sentences, be sure that you are getting variety through the full use of the inflection and the step. Analyze each sentence, marking the places where you might use an inflection or a step for meaning; indicate

the type of inflection or step which you would use. Practice the sentences, following your markings and revising them as necessary.

   a. Before him lay the river; beyond it the yellowing fields of the farm; and in the distance the blue hills which he had never explored.

   b. She posed before the mirror, admiring the fluffy yellow folds of her first real evening dress, showing off the gold slippers, adjusting her brown hair just so, and trying on the little white fur jacket.

   c. When the brilliant orange, red, and yellow of the sun had faded from the sky, the clouds were tinged with purple and gray which added to the somberness of the fog sweeping in from the ocean.

   d. The garden was laid out in a formal pattern with the low flowers in prim beds in the foreground, backed by rows of tidy, clipped shrubs, and the whole topped by regularly spaced oaks and elms.

   e. Far, far in the distance she could hear the low moan of the train whistle, reminding her that she could never go home again.

   f. In a riot of red, yellow, and blue the gypsies whirled in the dance, going faster and faster to the ever increasing tempo of the music.

   g. He was only three, so he had never gone alone beyond the garden fence to the distant henhouse, nor the even more distant barn, which lay before him like a foreign land.

6. Strive in the following selections to achieve variety of melody for meaning; avoid mono-melody or pattern.

   a. Private theatricals, as I have figured in them in country lyceum-halls, are one thing,—and private theatricals, as they may be seen in certain gilded and frescoed saloons of our metropolis, are another. Yes, it is pleasant to see real gentlemen and ladies, who do not think it necessary to mouth, and rant, and stride, like most of our stage heroes and heroines, in the characters which show off their graces and talents; most of all to see a fresh, unrouged, unspoiled, highbred young maiden, with a lithe figure and a pleasant voice, acting in those love-dramas which make us young again to look upon, when real youth and beauty will play them for us.—HOLMES

   b. First a shiver, and then a thrill,
     Then something decidedly like a spill,—
     And the parson was sitting upon a rock,
     At half-past nine by the meet'n house clock,—
     Just the hour of the Earthquake shock!

—What do you think the parson found,
When he got up and stared around?
The poor old chaise in a heap or mound,
As if it had been to the mill and ground!
You see, of course, if you're not a dunce,
How it went to pieces all at once,—
All at once and nothing first,—
Just as bubbles do when they burst.

End of the wonderful one-hoss shay,
Logic is logic. That's all I say.

—HOLMES

c. With malice toward none; with charity for all; with firmness in the
right, as God gives us to see the right, let us strive on to finish the
work we are in; to bind up the nation's wounds; to care for him who
shall have borne the battle, and for his widow, and his orphan—to do
all which may achieve and cherish a just and lasting peace among
ourselves, and with all nations.—LINCOLN

d. Gather ye rosebuds while ye may,
    Old Time is still a-flying;
And this same flower that smiles today
    Tomorrow will be dying.

. . . .

Then be not coy, but use your time,
    And while ye may, go marry!
For, having lost but once your prime,
    Ye may forever tarry.

—HERRICK

e. The Lord is my shepherd; I shall not want.
    He maketh me to lie down in green pastures: he leadeth me beside
        the still waters.
    He restoreth my soul: he leadeth me in the paths of righteousness for
        his name's sake.
    Yea, though I walk through the valley of the shadow of death, I will
        fear no evil: for thou art with me; thy rod and thy staff they
        comfort me.

Thou preparest a table before me in the presence of mine enemies:
thou anointest my head with oil; my cup runneth over.

Surely goodness and mercy shall follow me all the days of my life:
and I will dwell in the house of the Lord for ever.

—PSALM 23

f.   Come, my tan-face children,
Follow well in order, get your weapons ready;
Have you your pistols? Have you your sharp-edged axes?
Pioneers! O Pioneers!

For we cannot tarry here,
We must march, my darlings, we must bear the brunt of danger,
We, the youthful sinewy races, all the rest on us depend,
Pioneers! O Pioneers!

O you youths, Western youths,
So impatient, full of action, full of manly pride and friendship,
Plain I see you, Western youths, see you tramping with the foremost,
Pioneers! O Pioneers!

—WHITMAN

7. The following selections in Appendix II are particularly good for work on melody: Numbers 5, 9, 10, 17, 22.

8. Write a 100-word description of a landscape; keep it subdued and without action, but phrase it in colorful language. Read it aloud, trying to picture the scene for your listener. Listen to your tone production. Is there variety of melody? Do you make use of inflections and steps? Are there any regular, monotonous melody patterns? Do individual color words have melody changes on them?

9. Prepare a two-minute extempore speech based on a personal experience. If possible, try to work in a description of some action. When you give it in class, keep the delivery alive and animated. What do your instructor and classmates say about the melody variety in your voice? Record the speech and do your own analysis of your use of melody.

PHONATION AND LOUDNESS, TIME, AND QUALITY

Changes in loudness are the result of changes in amplitude of vibration of the vocal folds. Increased amplitude is brought about by greater breath pressure at the glottis. For the best phonation, as we have already noted, control of this pressure should be achieved by control of breathing. It is perfectly possible to increase the pressure, however, by narrowing the opening of the glottis through increased tension of the vocal muscles. This tension, of course, inevitably produces higher pitch, and if it is the only method of increasing pressure, the tones will be harsh and unpleasant. We do not mean to suggest that a controlled rise in pitch should not be used simultaneously with an increase in loudness, as a means of interpreting meaning. These changes will be both effective and pleasant, however, only when they are attained without excessive tension in the laryngeal muscles.

The problem of duration involves both time and phonation. You must be able to maintain a steady, pure tone for a sound of any length. If the sound is short, you must be able to initiate it easily and smoothly. The sound of long duration requires not only easy initiation, but also the ability on your part to maintain the tone steadily and evenly. Exercises under both phonation and melody deal with this problem.

Phonation and quality are closely connected. In the discussion of optimum pitch, it was suggested that optimum pitch was the product of both phonation and resonation. What the ear hears as tone is the result of both the action of the vocal folds and the influence of the resonation cavities on that sound. It is necessary that the proper relationship be maintained between the tensions in the folds determining the basic pitch and the adjustments of the resonating cavities. If you were able to find your optimum pitch, you noted that one tone was fuller and richer than all of the others when you reached the ideal relationship between the vibration of the folds and the action of the resonating cavities. The discussion of quality in the next chapter will make this problem clearer to you.

SUMMARY

The larynx is the housing for the vocal folds; it is composed of four major cartilages: the thyroid, the cricoid, and the paired arytenoids. The vocal folds are flaps of muscle attached in front to the inner edge of the thyroid, in the rear to the arytenoids, and at the sides to the inner edges of the cricoid. The entire larynx and associated structures are interlaced with muscles and connective tissue, and the interior surfaces are covered with mucous membrane. The basic biological function of the larynx is to act as a valve at the entrance to the trachea.

For phonation, the glottis must be closed; air pressure must be built up beneath the folds, forcing them apart and setting them in vibration.

Conditions of length, tension, thickness, and density in the folds will determine the pitch produced. When the vocal folds do not function properly, such problems of phonation as breathiness, glottal shock, harshness, or hoarseness may arise.

In your vocalization, you have a habitual pitch level and an optimum one; as nearly as possible these should be identical. Your melody is based upon your pitch range, and you must try to develop melody by the use of the inflection and the step so that you will communicate meaning effectively.

As you do not hear the tone directly as it comes from the vocal folds, but only after it has been resonated, an understanding of resonation is necessary for the complete analysis of tone production. If you find that you have a phonation problem, read ahead in Chapter 6 to see how poor resonation may be contributing to it.

6

The Resonating Process

The art of delivery deals with the voice: how we ought to manage it to express each several emotion.—ARISTOTLE

How often have you listened to the radio and formed a mental picture of the speaker whose voice you heard? Try it. The effusive voice of Gabriel Heatter or the strident quality of Walter Winchell's voice will produce in your mind a voice picture suggestive of the person; at the same time, it may arouse varied emotional responses in you. As you hear Winchell, Heatter, Louella Parsons, or Ronald Colman, you may experience feelings of alertness, skepticism, anger, or pleasure. It is difficult to explain or justify these reactions, but they occur. People's voices affect us; they soothe or disturb, please or irritate us.

This personal quality of voices depends to a considerable extent upon a process of reinforcement and amplification of the sound originally produced by the vocal folds. This process is known as *resonation*. It is the means whereby the weak, colorless laryngeal note is amplified and enriched as it passes through the cavities of the human resonating system.

STRUCTURE AND FUNCTION OF THE RESONATORS

We pointed out in Chapter 3 that resonance is the product of three physical phenomena: the reflection and concentration of sound in a single direction through open passages; the forced vibration of solid objects in contact with a vibrating body; and the sympathetic vibration of solid bodies or partially enclosed cavities filled with air, in response to a vibrating object tuned to the same natural frequency. In the human voice, as sound waves

92

pass through the cavities of the pharynx (throat), oral cavity (mouth), and nasal cavity (nose), all of these factors operate to amplify and modify the tone produced at the larynx.

STRUCTURE

We shall now examine the structure of each of the resonance cavities, and indicate what modifications in their size and shape are possible. We shall also discover what effects such modifications produce in the fullness and quality of the tones heard by the listener.

The Oral Cavity (m outh)

If you take a mirror and hold it before your open mouth, you will observe that the outer boundary consists of the mobile lips, behind which are the fixed gums and teeth. Move the tip of your tongue back from the inner side of the upper front teeth. At this point you will notice a definite gum ridge, which is called the *alveolar ridge*. Then, continuing back for a little more than an inch, is the bony, rigid, concave roof of the mouth known as the *hard palate*. Behind the hard palate, and continuing in what appears to be a part of it, is the sheet of muscle fibers covered, like the hard palate, with mucous membrane; this is known as the soft palate or *velum*. This can be further identified by its terminal pendent tip, called the *uvula*. Unlike the

THE MOUTH

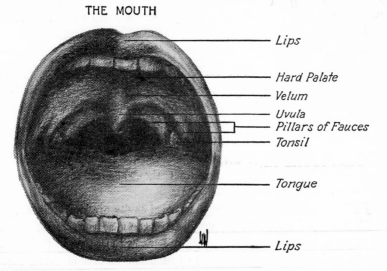

- Lips
- Hard Palate
- Velum
- Uvula
- Pillars of Fauces
- Tonsil
- Tongue
- Lips

Fig. 10. The mouth

immovable, rigid, hard palate, the velum is flexible and may be raised or lowered to open or close the entrance into the nasal passageway directly behind and above it. Extending downward from the velum are two muscular arches, known as the anterior and posterior *pillars of the fauces*. Your tonsils are located on either side between these arches. The fauces, acting in co-operation with the muscles of the velum and the tongue, aid in opening or constricting the entrance into the pharynx. By changing the area of this entrance, called the *isthmus of fauces*, you change the resonating qualities of the entire system.

The tongue consists of a large mass of muscular fibers tapered at the front tip and widening and thickening at the back. It goes much farther down into your throat than you realize, and its root connects with the lower jaw and the hyoid bone. It possesses extreme agility. It is able to stretch forward, draw back, thin or thicken, broaden or groove, and raise or lower itself. Because of its extensive ability to alter its shape and position, the tongue serves greatly to change the size and shape of the oral cavity.

The interaction of all these structures of the mouth enables the oral cavity to undergo considerable variation in size, shape, surfaces, and openings, as well as to perform selective coupling with the pharyngeal and nasal cavities. Because of these numerous and complex adjustments, and because the oral cavity is the largest cavity resonator, it may be said to serve as a balancer for the other resonators. It may improve or distort the quality of the resonated tone. Furthermore, not only is it extremely important in resonating the various partials composing the complex laryngeal note, but it also functions in shaping and resonating the different vowel sounds.

The Pharyngeal Cavity

Most efficient resonator

The pharynx, or throat, is a passageway approximately five inches long. It extends from the area just above the false vocal folds and the esophagus up to the posterior opening of the nasal passage. The pharynx communicates with the larynx, the esophagus, the mouth, the nose, and the Eustachian tubes leading to the ears. Three sheets of paired, overlapping muscle fibers, called the *constrictor* muscles, contract the walls of the pharynx in swallowing.

The three main divisions of the pharyngeal cavity are known as: (1) the *laryngopharynx*, which is immediately above the false vocal folds; (2) the *oropharynx*, which is behind the mouth in back of the pillars of the fauces, reaching from above the epiglottis to just below the velum; and (3) the *nasopharynx*, which is just above the velum, continuing on into the nasal passage.

The size, shape, and adjustability of the pharynx enables it to function admirably as a resonator. The pharynx may be shortened by raising the larynx on high-pitched sounds, thus contributing to the brilliance of the resonated tone. It may be lengthened by lowering the larynx on low-pitched sounds, thus influencing the mellowness of the resonated tones. A reduction in the length of the pharynx may also be effected by raising the velum against the back wall of the pharynx, thus blocking off the nasopharynx and eliminating the top section of the pharyngeal tube. Because of the adjustability of the velum, the pharynx can employ the mouth and the nose, either separately or together, as its opening. This action will obviously affect the quality of the resonated tone. In addition to these changes in size, shape, and openings, the pharynx has the muscular ability to vary its diameter, surface tension, and texture, further affecting resonation. Relaxed pharyngeal musculature promotes a rich, mellow tone by damping out the high frequencies and strengthening the fundamental and lower overtones. Tense, constricted pharyngeal musculature, on the other hand, has a tendency to produce a hard, harsh quality by reflecting the higher overtones as well.

It may be seen, then, that the great adjustability of the pharyngeal cavity enables it to function as our most efficient and important resonator.

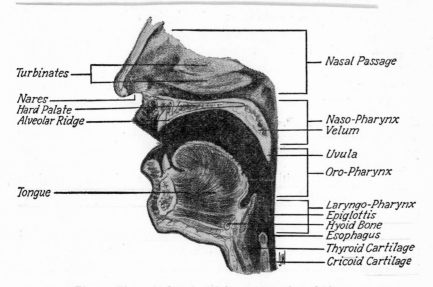

Fig. 11. The sagittal section of the nose, mouth, and pharynx

The Nasal Cavity

The nasal cavity continues the tube of the nasopharynx on out through the anterior *nares*, or nostrils. The nasal cavity might more accurately be referred to as two cavities, since it is divided into two sections by a thin bone, called the *medial septum*. Each of these sections contains three shell-like bones, called *turbinates*, which project horizontally from the septum. Although, on most drawings showing the various cavities of the head, the nasal cavity appears to be much larger than either the oral or the pharyngeal cavity, actually it is considerably smaller because of the presence of the septum and turbinate bones. Its size is further decreased by the fact that, like the other cavities, its entire surface is covered with thick mucous membrane.

In addition to its limitation in size, the nasal cavity is further restricted as a resonator. Except for movements of the velum which change its posterior opening, and muscular constrictions at the region of the nostrils which slightly change its anterior opening, it is unable to vary its shape. The nasal cavity, therefore, is our least adjustable and least versatile resonator. Of all English speech sounds, only three, the nasal continuants M, N, and NG, are primarily, if not completely, the product of nasal resonation.

Considerable difference of opinion exists as to the extent to which the nasal cavity functions in general resonation. Views vary all the way from regarding it as inadequate to serve as a selective resonator, to assuming that it serves as a supplemental, multiple resonator for a wide range of frequencies. Because of the relatively small size of the nasal cavity and the presence of the small pockets formed by the projecting turbinate bones, there seems to be sufficient evidence to accept the opinion that the nasal cavity does function at least as a supplemental sympathetic resonator for high-frequency overtones.

The Sinuses

Since all the sinus cavities communicate with the nasal chamber, and because the statement is sometimes encountered that the sinuses "act as resonators," we need to consider them briefly. Although the sphenoidal, ethmoidal, maxillary, and frontal sinuses are of appreciable size, the last two being an inch or more in height, depth, and breadth, the ducts connecting them with the nasal cavity are probably too small and too long to accommodate the sound waves. Their main function appears to be that of lightening the bone weight of the head; in this respect they may influence the de-

There is also a sounding board type of resonator. (Bones of chest)

gree of forced vibration of sounds. But it is extremely doubtful whether the sinus cavities themselves function as resonators.

BIOLOGICAL FUNCTION OF THE CAVITIES AND STRUCTURES

Resonation, like all other aspects of voice, is an overlaid function of the vocal mechanism. The cavities, structures, and muscles involved in resonation are biologically intended to serve the primary purposes of breathing and eating. Furthermore, these biological activities frequently are in conflict with the muscle movements necessary to produce good, resonant tone. . The muscles we use for tone production and resonation are the same muscles which are used for gagging, coughing, sucking, chewing, and swallowing. Some individuals who otherwise are well adjusted have never mastered the small muscular coordinations needed for a good voice. Some of the muscular activities of coughing, chewing, and swallowing have not been eliminated; they intrude upon the speech process. The coughing and gagging muscles constrict the opening from the larynx to the laryngopharynx and also unduly tense the vocal folds, the chewing muscles tighten the jaw and constrict the mouth opening, and the swallowing muscles raise the larynx and crowd it against the base of the tongue. Each of these actions tends to narrow the space available for resonation and to constrict the passageway for the breath stream so that friction noises may occur, or otherwise to interfere with and distort the normal resonance channels.

FUNCTION IN RESONATION

In order to secure normal resonation of the human voice, your throat, mouth, and nose must not be constricted or distorted by any interference from the biological functioning just described. The structure of these cavities is such that the tones of speech are reflected, and are concentrated before being released through your mouth and nose, thus providing the primary resonance of the fundamental tone. If these passages are constricted or narrowed, the desired reflection and amplification of tone will not take place.

You must realize that your pharyngeal and oral cavities are capable of wide variations in size and shape, and thus can respond sympathetically to many different overtones. Moreover, the breadth of range to which they respond is further increased by the fact that your pharynx may be coupled to either your oral or your nasal cavity, and that the openings connecting your cavities are capable of considerable variation in size and shape. Your mouth opening, too, is capable of great variation. The relative size and shape of this opening and of your oral cavity serves to differentiate one vowel sound from another. This flexibility of adjustment, when not interfered with by biological muscular tensions, enables your cavities to function admirably as "tuned" resonators.

We have noted earlier that the extent to which forced resonation contributes to the fullness and quality of the voice is a matter of considerable dispute. Certainly the bones of the head and chest, the teeth, and the walls of the pharyngeal and oral cavities are set into forced vibration by the laryngeal impulse. Some authorities contend that the entire body acts as a sounding board for the resonation of tone. There is much doubt, however, whether these vibrations are transmitted to the outer air and actually contribute to the sound we hear.

In the absence of conclusive evidence as to the function of forced resonation in contributing to the production of voice, we must assume that probably the principal factor in resonating the fundamental tone in most voices is the reflection and concentration of sound in the open tube structure of the pharyngeal and oral cavities. On the other hand, research has shown that the distinctive quality of a voice is primarily the product of sympathetic vibrations set up in the cavities in response to overtones ranging between 400 and 2,400 vibrations per second. Different qualities in the same voice and the special characteristics which distinguish one speech sound from another are the result of modifications in size and shape of the resonance cavities, which cause them to respond sympathetically to a different set of overtones.

Selective Activity of Muscles

The statement has been made that relaxation is necessary for good resonation. Obviously, however, since every aspect of voice production involves muscular activity, speech itself would be impossible if all the muscles were relaxed. The sense in which relaxation for speech is advised is that you should activate *only* those muscles which are necessary to the production of the effect you desire.

This selective activity is the process of learning, which is used in acquiring any motor skill. A newborn baby, for instance, responds to every stimulus with his entire body. When he is uncomfortable, he cries, but his crying involves every muscle of his face, contortions of his body, and even the wriggling of his toes. An older child will repeat this identical over-all activity when he is in a temper tantrum; an unstable adult in hysteria will also react with every muscle of his body. A skilled athlete, on the other hand, improves in proportion as he eliminates unnecessary motions and muscle tensions. He learns to bring into play only those muscles which contribute to the goal for which he is striving. The same holds true for the skilled speaker or actor. A common term for any one of these performers who is off form is that he is "tied up." He is using too many muscles.

Your aim in voice production, therefore, should be to relax all the muscles of the throat which are not actually used in the formation and resonation of tone. This particularly refers to the heavy throat muscles used in chewing and swallowing, as well as to the muscles which raise the shoulders or tighten and draw down the chin. Relaxation of the general throat region is necessary so that the tone passage may be free from any interference by the biological functions; it is also necessary so that the highly delicate adjustments of the larynx and the resonating cavities may occur. In emotional states, temporary or chronic, these adjustments break down, and the more fundamental biological reactions tend to reassert themselves. Thus, people with poor physical coordination and people who are emotionally unstable tend to have unpleasant voices.

If you are successful in effecting this type of selective relaxation, you will produce the best tone of which your individual vocal mechanism is capable. And if your vocal mechanism is not impaired by the presence of some organic abnormality, this will usually be a pleasing tone.

Optimum Pitch and Resonation

Selective relaxation also enables you to provide the desirable conditions required for your voice to function at its optimum pitch level. This optimum pitch level, together with an optimum melodic range responsive to your thinking and feeling, will not only allow you to amplify and strengthen your tones with the least expenditure of effort, but will also provide maximum resonation. Furthermore, since optimum pitch is intimately connected with the development of desirable vocal quality, it is important that you discover and employ those pitch levels at which your voice achieves its fullest and richest resonation. Therefore, because of the inextricable relationship between phonation, resonation, and vocal quality, you should now refer back to Chapter 5 and review the exercises pertaining to the establishment of optimum pitch.

ANALYSIS OF RESONATION HABITS

Importance of Control in Resonation

It is important for you to recognize that your breathing and phonation habits will materially influence resonation. Tensions occurring in the performance of either one of these activities affect the areas acting in resonation. What we have previously written about control in breathing and phonation has a direct application in this matter of resonation. So it would be well for you to review those earlier sections and apply their teachings to your efforts to attain effective resonation.

If desirable breathing and phonation habits have been established, your vocal instrument will be more responsive in resonation. In addition to control of the acts of breathing and phonation, awareness and control of the actions of your tongue and soft palate and of your swallowing, chewing, and gagging muscles are extremely important. The muscles of the structures involved in resonation must be alert and responsive. Sluggish muscular action will have a tendency to dull and deaden your vocal quality; tense muscular action will have a tendency to sharpen and harden your vocal quality.

Central in this whole matter of control in resonation will be your ability to apply the principle of selective relaxation. If you do not exercise this control, faulty resonation and poor tone quality will result. You must learn to develop controlled relaxation of those chewing, swallowing, and gagging muscles which are not directly needed in tone production. If you succeed in accomplishing this, your resonating system will have a better chance to function normally.

Observation

Examine your own speech habits critically and try to determine to what degree these are in accord with the principles of good resonation presented in this chapter. Investigate whether you are able to exercise the kind and degree of selective relaxation and control of muscular activity required.

1. Take a small mirror and observe the changing shape of your lips and mouth when you pronounce various speech sounds.

2. Perform these same sounds with tightened cheek and throat muscles and clenched jaw. Observe the characteristic tensions of the chewing muscles involved. Next, repeat these sounds, employing selective relaxation and responsive jaw action. Notice and compare the patterns of muscle action involved in these two demonstrations.

3. Assume the position for the open AH sound, with the tip of your tongue against the lower front teeth. Observe the size and shape of the megaphone-like opening of your mouth.

4. Phonate the AH sound. See whether your jaw and throat muscles are bunched and tense or relatively relaxed.

5. Check the action of your soft palate and tongue and the degree of opening into your throat during vocalization.

a. Pull your tongue back into your pharynx and talk with it bunched in this position. You will find that you sound like Donald Duck.

b. Swallow, and hold the muscle tensions created by this action. Place your hand at the junction of your chin and neck and feel the constriction of these muscles. Maintaining this condition, try speaking. You may notice a pronounced nasal twang combined with gutturality. This indicates what happens to your voice when you fail to modify the action of your swallowing muscles.

6. Assume the basic AH position again. Inhale through your mouth as though commencing to yawn. Feel the current of air passing through the isthmus of fauces and into your pharynx. Watch yourself in your mirror, and observe how the back of your tongue lowers, your soft palate rises, and your isthmus of fauces widens and opens the entrance into your pharyngeal cavity. Repeat this action until you establish the sensation of a rising soft palate and an open throat.

Listening

1. Listen to class members and friends when they speak. Do their voices seem muffled and blocked or open and free?

2. Listen critically to various speakers and actors; try to evaluate the resonance characteristics of their voices. Compare their voices with your own. What resonance traits are present that you would like to emulate? What faults are present that you would like to avoid?

3. Listen to your own voice. To the best of your ability, try to determine where it is "placed," that is, what muscular adjustments seem to affect its quality. Does it seem to issue from the back of your throat? Does it seem to come from your nose? Does it seem to be blocked by your tongue somewhere in the middle or back of your mouth? Or does it seem to flow out freely and brightly from the front part of your oral megaphone?

4. Ask your friends to describe your voice in terms of its resonance characteristics. Is it strident and hard? Flat and dull? Nasal or whining? Thin and weak? Muffled or booming? Do these comments agree with your own

analysis? Listen again to your voice, and check those factors in which you and your friends disagree.

RESONATION AND VOCAL QUALITY

Resonation is simply the reinforcement and amplification of the fundamental and its overtones. It may vary in degree according to the amount of amplification employed. In this sense, a speaker's voice may be said to possess less or greater resonance than that of another. But resonation itself is not the identifying characteristic of a good voice. A voice may be unpleasant and still be resonant.

Efficient resonation implies the smooth and unrestricted functioning of the structures and cavities involved. It is absolutely necessary for the development of a pleasing voice.

Vocal Quality Defined

Vocal quality, on the other hand, is the identifying characteristic of an individual's voice. It is the listener's interpretation of resonation. It is what he hears and what he responds to. You have frequently observed that the vocal qualities of any two people are never precisely alike. In fact, if you consider for a moment the speech of people of your acquaintance or of actors you have observed, you will notice that the voice of each of these individuals possesses a distinct personality which differentiates it from that of any other. You may describe their personal vocal quality as shrill, metallic, hard, strident, whining; muffled; or smooth, mellow, and rich. These possible classifications are almost endless, but they are subjective rather than scientifically definitive.

Physically speaking, however, vocal quality is the complex result of the selective combination of the fundamental and its overtones. It must be remembered that your resonators can amplify only those overtones present in the original phonation. Therefore, the condition and action of the vocal folds themselves contribute to quality. As we have already indicated, tension changes in the muscles governing your resonating cavities cause alterations in their size, shape, and surface texture, resulting in the selective amplification of different overtones for each change of condition. In addition, vocal quality involves not only these delicate adjustments of your vocal mechanism, but action of the gross muscles of your entire body. All these actions and modifications selectively affect the relative intensities of the various overtones and the fundamental. The tonal result of this selection is what we hear as vocal quality.

Factors Involved

Vocal quality may thus be seen to be the result of the interaction of a number of factors. These may be classified under the following heads:

1. *The way your vocal mechanism is constructed.* There may be just as many physical differences between any two vocal mechanisms as you might find between two pianos or two cellos.

2. *The general health of your vocal mechanism.* For example, muscular or surface irritation and inflammation of the throat area will seriously affect vocal quality. Most of you are familiar with the change in voice quality that accompanies a severe cold.

3. *Your habitual manner of vocalization.* Your posture may be poor, your chest slumped, your breathing shallow. You may have acquired poor habits of phonation, and these may exercise a direct influence upon your vocal quality.

4. *Your emotional state and your responsiveness.* You all have heard an angry voice, a joyous voice, a bitter voice. Not only strong emotions, but moods and attitudes may affect vocal quality. The person who is lazy and dull will have a vocal quality which reflects those characteristics, no matter what he is saying. The same holds true for the individual who is in a constant state of excitement and tension. Both of these persons, at emotional extremes, tend, after a while, to become monotonous and will fail to express emotional meanings appropriate to the ideas being presented.

Aspects of Vocal Quality

In judging the vocal quality of other speakers, we have a tendency to apply subjective terms such as "good" or "poor" to the qualities we hear. By good vocal quality, we mean a tone that is free from impurities and pleasant to the ear. If your vocal mechanism is operating efficiently, without any physical interference or strain, the quality will be good. The agreeability of an individual's voice may determine not only the kind and degree of attention which you give to his remarks, but, rightly or wrongly, it may influence your judgment regarding his character, background, training, and culture. It seems wise, therefore, to strive for that quality of voice which is not only pleasing to the ears of listeners, but which also reveals the thoughtful responsiveness to ideas and feelings indicative of a well-integrated human being.

By poor vocal quality, we mean a tone that is unpleasant to hear because of some structural abnormality or functional distortion in the resonation of the tone. For example, if adenoids are present or if unnecessary tensions interfere with the resonation of the tone, then denasality, throatiness, stridency, or some other defect in quality will occur.

In addition to these general concepts of good and poor quality, you also respond to the speaker's *changes* in quality as he attempts to convey meaning and feeling to you. As you read in Chapter 2, your personal adjustments and your immediate emotional attitudes in relation to what you are saying produce modulations in the tone. These changes in vocal quality are frequently referred to as "tone color."

Open Throat

It has been indicated that characteristic adjustments of your resonators accompany each particular sound. It is your good fortune that, if no organic or functional impediments are present, these adjustments will take place automatically. However, you can assist this process by providing the physical conditions necessary for all good tone production. Specifically, this means sufficient selective relaxation of your facial, jaw, and throat muscles so that the automatic adjustments may function without interference.

Among these adjustments, one of the basic conditions required for effective resonation is an open throat. This has already been described under *Observation*, and it will pay you to refer now to Exercise 6 on page 101. Open throat is a condition of wideness and openness in the oral and laryngeal divisions of your pharynx. This area should be free from any constricting tension. Any bunching of the back muscles of your tongue or constriction of the pillars of fauces will narrow the opening into your throat. In addition, there may be contraction of the swallowing muscles in your pharyngeal walls which will decrease the size of the throat itself. These actions will muffle and block the tone. If you relax and lower the back of your tongue, raise your soft palate, and relax your swallowing muscles, you will increase the size of the entrance into your throat as well as the dimensions of the pharynx itself. This will help you to produce a free, full flow of tone.

"Tone Placement"

Tone placement is a term commonly encountered in reading about resonation. Singers and speakers are frequently told to "place" their voices in the front of their mouths rather than in the back of their throats. However, it is generally agreed that this term has no basis in physiology. It is physically impossible to place tone anywhere but where nature has already put it—in your larynx.

Although tone placement is merely a figurative term, it and its companion term of "frontal placement" serve a useful purpose. They are convenient concepts, providing distractive techniques which help us make small and beneficial adjustments in the size and shape of our oral and pharyngeal cavities through influencing muscles not under our voluntary control. Therefore, if you think of "aiming" your tones against your upper gum ridge or against your upper front teeth, you will, in all probability, open your throat and achieve a brighter, clearer quality of tone.

Supported Tone

With your throat in the desired condition of openness, tone must be adequately supported by breath in order to achieve the steadiness of vocalization so necessary for effective resonation. Therefore, we recommend that you review these sections in Chapter 4: *The Importance of the Control of the Breath Stream* and *Breath Control for Steadiness of Vocalization.*

Exercises for Improvement

ESTABLISHING OPEN THROAT

1. Place the tip of your tongue against your lower front teeth. Gently inhale through your mouth; then easily roll your head toward the right, allowing it to fall toward your chest; exhale through your mouth as your head falls. Repeat, moving toward the left. Continue in this fashion until you experience a feeling of ease and relaxation in the region of your throat.

2. Assume the basic AH position with the tip of your tongue against your lower front teeth. Inhale through your mouth as though commencing to yawn. Feel the current of air passing through the isthmus of fauces and into your pharynx; this sensation indicates one of the desired conditions for openness of throat. Repeat this action until you establish the feeling of a rising soft palate and an open throat.

3. Repeat the conditions described in Exercise 2. Keeping your throat passage as open as possible, chant an easy, sustained AH sound. Prolong it for the approximate count of five. Repeat, changing to an AW sound. Next, practice gliding from AH to AW and retain the feeling of an open, relaxed throat.

4. With the tip of your tongue against your lower front teeth and your jaw as relaxed as possible, practice the following sounds, employing a fresh oral inhalation for each sound: HAH, PAH, BAH, FAH, VAH, YAH. Repeat several times.

5. Keep your jaw as open, relaxed, and motionless as possible. In this position, repeat the following sounds with gross movements of your tongue but keep the tongue tip against your lower front teeth: HAH-HAH-HAH-HAH, YAH-YAH-YAH-YAH, YAW-YAW-YAW-YAW, YOH-YOH-YOH-YOH, YAH-YEA-YEE-YEA-YAH-YAW-YOO-YAW.

TONE PLACEMENT

1. Test the operation of what is called "tone placement" by phonating the vowel AH in such a manner that it appears to be produced far back in your throat. To facilitate this, pronounce AH and try to imagine that you are making the sound AW. You will notice that the sound acquires a throaty, muffled quality. Follow this by phonating the same AH sound as though you were producing it at the upper front gum, and imagine that you were making the vowel sound EE. In this instance, you will notice that the same AH sound now acquires a firm, brilliant quality.

2. With the tip of your tongue against your lower front teeth, pronounce the word *we* several times. Carefully produce the vowel sound of this word so that it seems to achieve great fullness of tone toward the front of your mouth.

3. With the tip of your tongue against your lower front teeth and the sounds as though aimed at your upper front gum, repeat the following: WAH, WAY, WE, WAY, WAH, WAW, WOO, WAW. Chant these singly and as a continuous phrase.

4. Chant the vowel sounds AH and OO alternately on different pitch levels. Try to concentrate the tones in the front of your mouth by aiming at your upper front gum. Carefully keep these tones full and open and keep your throat muscles relaxed.

5. Repeat Exercise 4, using the vowels EE and AH. Also practice these sounds as a single chant, carefully gliding from EE to AH.

6. Keeping your throat open and relaxed, and concentrating on frontal placement, practice the following sentences and selections.

 a. Hello.
 b. How are you?
 c. Away we go.
 d. The water level fell lower and lower.
 e. The ball rolled away.
 f. Over the valleys and over the plains.
 g. High on a hill.
 h. He will soon be here.

i. The university team easily won the contest.

j. They held onto the table with all their might.

k. Cool, blue evening shadows slowly moved across the green lawn.

l. A little learning is a dangerous thing.

m. In a drear-nighted December
Too happy, happy Tree
Thy branches ne'er remember
Their green felicity;
The north cannot undo them
With a sleety whistle through them,
Nor frozen thawings glue them
From budding at the prime.

—KEATS

n. The splendour falls on castle walls
And snowy summits old in story;
The long light shakes across the lakes,
And the wild cataract leaps in glory.
Blow, bugle, blow, set the wild echoes flying,
Blow, bugle; answer, echoes, dying, dying, dying.

—TENNYSON

o. She walks in beauty, like the night
Of cloudless climes and starry skies,
And all that's best of dark and bright
Meet in her aspect and her eyes;
Thus mellowed to that tender light
Which heaven to gaudy day denies.

—BYRON

p. Willows whiten, aspens quiver,
Little breezes dusk and shiver
Thro' the wave that runs forever
By the island in the river
Flowing down to Camelot.
Four gray walls, and four gray towers,
Overlook a space of flowers,
And the silent isle embowers
The Lady of Shalott.

—TENNYSON

q. The weary wanderer went slowly up the hill. Far in the distance, the shadowy woods blurred into the twilight. Not a sound was heard. Then, while time itself seemed to stand still, night came down and covered the countryside.

7. Selections 3, 12*b*, and 23 in Appendix II are also recommended for practice. Keep your throat as open and relaxed as possible and try to "place" the tones toward the front of your mouth.

PROBLEMS OF VOCAL QUALITY

STRIDENCY AND THROATINESS

Stridency is a fault of resonance. The prominence of the higher overtones produces a harsh, sharp quality. It is usually caused by excessive tension in the pharynx and in the muscles of the soft palate. The firm surfaces of these areas contribute to very "efficient" resonation, so that, instead of many of the higher overtones being damped out by the relaxed, soft surfaces of the oral and pharyngeal cavities, all of the overtones are reflected. The throat may be held open, but the whole area is tense. You may have heard strident voices in political speeches, particularly among speakers accustomed to speaking to large audiences, who have not yet tempered their method of voice production to the requirements of public-address systems.

In some individuals, the strident tone is high; if it is accompanied by a drawing out of the vowel sounds, it can be called whining. In others, the tensing of the pharyngeal muscles may so constrict the opening that a friction sound accompanies phonation. The tone then becomes grating as well as sharp, made more unpleasant by the additional noise components.

Stridency frequently occurs with rapid rate, since both may be due to habits of nervousness and excitability.

The *throaty tone* is produced when the lower part of the pharynx is constricted and when the posterior part of the tongue crowds back into the throat. The tone is often low in pitch, with a guttural quality produced by constriction of the pharyngeal passageway and with the same grating and friction sounds which may accompany stridency. The riding back of the tongue will also muffle the tone.

Throatiness is sometimes the response to the effort to lower the general pitch. The external muscles of the larynx may contract and pull down on the entire larynx, holding it in this lowered position while voice is produced. This, coupled with the inner pharyngeal constriction, will interfere with good resonation.

Either stridency or throatiness may result when the speaker tries to project the tone but lacks the necessary control over the breath stream. He attempts to create subvocal pressure, not by diaphragmatic control over breathing, but by constricting the passageway directly above the larynx. Breathing examination and exercises should precede attempts to correct these faults of resonance. If the breath cannot be controlled either for steadiness of tone or for increased loudness, the speaker almost always responds with tenseness of the throat area.

The presence of physical differences may cause the initial use of the generally harsh tone. If the throat is inflamed and sore, the speaker may try to protect it by preventing movement in the area. If there is a great deal of mucus on the vocal folds or the pharyngeal wall, the person may clear his throat frequently, an activity which tends to keep the muscles of the velum and pharynx in a state of tension.

Listening and Self-analysis

1. In the Columbia album, *I Can Hear It Now*, Volume I, listen to the voices of Adolf Hitler, Wendell Willkie, and Fiorello La Guardia, watching for elements of stridency and throatiness.

2. Listen to the voices of your classmates and see if you can hear faults of stridency or throatiness. Observe any unusual muscular actions accompanying these qualities.

3. Listen to the record you made at the beginning of the semester. Do you have either of these faults?

Exercises for Improvement

1. Review all of the exercises in Chapter 4 dealing with steadiness and loudness of tone.

2. Review the exercises in Chapter 5 dealing with glottal shock, hoarseness, harshness, and optimum pitch.

3. Practice the exercises for open throat and tone placement given earlier in this chapter. Both stridency and throatiness are the antithesis of open throat.

Nasality and Denasality

As we noted in Chapter 3, the quality known as nasality results from the entrapment of the vibrating breath stream in a cavity in which the entrance is substantially larger than the exit, or in which there is a narrow common entrance and exit. This blind-alley, or cul-de-sac, type of resonance is produced most frequently in the nasal resonator, from which the term "nasality" is derived. When the velum is relaxed, leaving a wide opening from the oro-pharynx to the nasopharynx, the narrow exit through the nares completes the factors characterizing nasality. The three normal nasal sounds in English speech, M, N, and NG, are all resonated in the nasal cavity, with a supple-mental cul-de-sac provided by the oral cavity. The differences in quality among these three nasal sounds are created by the changes in size and shape of the oral cul-de-sac. The whole cavity is used for M, a smaller part for N, and a narrow pocket at the back for NG.

The basic characteristic of nasality is a foghorn quality. If this quality appears on sounds other than the three nasal continuants, it is generally regarded as a fault in English-speaking voices. Normally, nasality is the re-sult of excessive relaxation of the velum, but speech clinicians have also recognized nasality in cases where the subject clearly made an adequate closure of the soft palate. In such instances, the cul-de-sac must be sought elsewhere. One obvious answer in many cases is an inadequate mouth open-ing. A small mouth opening clearly duplicates the conditions for nasality produced in the nasal resonator by providing a wide entrance into and a narrow exit from the oral cavity.

A special problem in nasality is the so-called *nasal twang*, which is usually accompanied by high pitch and stridency. Although this problem is not fully understood, it is probable that the same tensions which produce the other faults also operate to create pockets along the sides of the resonance passages in which cul-de-sac resonance occurs. At any rate, it is certain that in such cases relaxation of the throat muscles will usually remedy the condition.

It is important to distinguish between the fault of nasality and the use of the nasal resonators as a normal supplement in the resonation of primarily oral sounds. So long as the posterior opening of the nasal cavity is smaller than the opening of the nares, nasal resonance is a positive contributing factor to fullness of tone, and the foghorn quality of nasality is not heard. Careful listening to the tones you produce will help you to distinguish be-tween supplemental nasal resonance and the fault of nasality.

Denasality is the lack of nasal resonance—cold-in-the-head speech. Any blockage of the nasal passage, caused by a cold, hay fever, deviated septum, broken nose, or enlarged adenoids blocking the nasopharynx, may produce this quality. If any of these factors persist for some time, inactivity of the velum may become so habituated that removal of the obstruction may be followed by marked nasality until new habits can be formed.

It should be noted that both nasality and denasality, under certain condi-tions, may be present in the same voice. If the temporary or permanent blocking of the nasal passageway is in the anterior portion of the nares and the soft palate is inactive, the vocalized breath for vowel tones may be entrapped in the posterior portion of the passageway. Such a condition causes vowel sounds to become nasal and at the same time blocks and distorts the normal nasal resonance character of the M, N, and NG sounds.

Listening and Self-analysis

1. Listen to a recording of your voice. Do the M, N, and NG sounds have a clear nasal quality? Are your vowel sounds free from nasality?

2. Observe the movement of your lips and lower jaw as you speak in front of a mirror. How wide is your mouth opening? Does it seem to be as wide as the posterior opening into your oral cavity?

3. Looking into a mirror, open your mouth wide. Hold your tongue down and forward. If you have trouble doing this, use a tongue depressor or spoon handle to keep your tongue down. Now inhale sharply through your mouth, and exhale through your nose, keeping your mouth wide open. Notice the movement of your velum as it rises on inhalation and moves down in contact with your tongue on exhalation. Observe the same phenomenon as you phonate NG-AH-NG-AH. If you can get vigorous action of your velum, you should have no difficulty controlling nasal resonance.

Exercises for Improvement

1. Practice the exercises for open throat given earlier in this chapter, under *Establishing Open Throat*.

2. Sound AH at your optimum pitch. Without stopping the tone, close your mouth to get M. Move back and forth from one sound to the other several times, without allowing nasality to creep into the vowel sound.

3. Repeat the procedure of Exercise 2, using the vowels AW, OH, EE, E (as in *bet*), and A (as in *bat*). Repeat the same procedure for each vowel, using N and NG.

4. Pronounce each of the following words slowly, and then repeat more quickly, giving full value to the M, N, and NG sounds, but eliminating nasality from the vowels: *am, time, gone, sang, fine, dance, seem, soon, song, moon, mat, gnat, neat, singing, finger, can, ram, ran, rang, ten, met, fame, rain, length, land, friend, spend, lame, mean.*

5. The following sentences contain no nasal sounds. Speak them without nasality.

   a. He was awake at five o'clock.

   b. He walked to the store and asked for cigarettes.

   c. They hurriedly left for the gold fields.

   d. Be sure to go to bed early.

   e. This is the house that Jack built.

   f. Today is the last day to go to the Catskills.

OTHER PROBLEMS

Some teachers of voice use additional terms to refer to vocal faults, such as *flatness* of voice, *thinness*, and so forth. The faults covered by these terms usually involve the functioning of the entire vocal mechanism. If you can learn to develop an adequate breath stream, to initiate tones without shock, and to sustain full tones through open resonance passages, you should have little difficulty in overcoming these problems.

We cannot emphasize too strongly that defects in vocal quality, except those caused by physical differences, are often deeply rooted in early habits based on environmental influences, in fundamental personality problems, or in emotional disturbances. If you have serious problems in vocal quality, therefore, you should reread Chapter 2, examine your whole background of habit and emotional response, and try to make adjustments which may remove tensions contributing to poor vocal quality.

CHANGES IN VOCAL QUALITY TO EXPRESS MEANING AND FEELING

The many variations in vocal quality needed to represent the shades of meaning and feeling of emotionally charged material are not within the primary scope of this book. As we have indicated, most of these are dependent upon the emotional responsiveness of the individual speaker, reader, or actor. No amount of emotional responsiveness will suffice, however, unless the speaker responds sensitively to meaning and emotion by modifications of resonation which reflect his feelings.

Muscular Tensions and Emotional Response

One of the effective ways in which your vocal instrument may be made more responsive in this respect is to consider vocal quality in relation to muscular tensions and emotion. For the successful use of vocal quality in speaking, reading, and acting, you must covertly, if not overtly, engage in general body tensions and relaxations corresponding to the tensions and relaxations of the emotional states involved. These physical responses cannot be considered as tensions and relaxations of the resonators alone, or even of the whole vocal mechanism, but must be of the entire body. In the discussion of the other elements of voice, you have seen how the functioning of the whole body operates in determining the vocal result. The effect of the gross muscles—those of the arms, legs, and torso—on the fine muscles of the vocal mechanism, especially on the resonators, is of tremendous importance for vocal quality.

If you are extremely angry, you are angry with your whole body, not with only a part of it. The muscles of your extremities are set to fight, and the effect of these tensions makes itself felt on the vocal mechanism. You cannot say, "I am so angry I could knock his head off," and give full significance to the words, unless you respond with body tensions of anger. If you try to say this sentence with your body as relaxed as possible, you will fail to express the full meaning of the phrase. However, if you actually engage in the muscle tensions of the emotion, attempting to "suit the action to the word, the word to the action," your words will increase in meaning. The states of anger, anxiety, and fear, are generally expressed as the result of strong, positive muscular tensions affecting your vocal mechanism, while depressing states of grief, sorrow, or boredom generally receive their appropriate tone color as the result of the relaxation of muscular tensions.

You cannot approach vocal quality from a mechanical point of view. If you should say to yourself, "Since this passage calls for the expression of fear, I will use such-and-such a tone quality," you will succeed only in being patently artificial and false. You must remember that vocal quality is the expression of what you are—your health, your habitual emotional states and patterns of responses, how you think and feel, and your emotional condition at the particular moment of utterance. These responses cannot be supplanted by the application of a studied, prescribed vocal quality.

Something must happen within you. Therefore, if you possess at least a modicum of emotional responsiveness, you must attempt to re-create within yourself the broad muscular tensions implicit in the particular emotional state. You should encourage these energies to sweep through you and influence vocal quality. Try to apply this principle, and you will discover that a responsive body will help you to develop a responsive and colorful voice. The following exercises should help you to develop your skills for the communication of meaningful material.

Exercises for Improvement

1. The following sentences express a series of moods: (*a*) simple statements of fact; (*b*) irritation; (*c*) positiveness; (*d*) deep conviction; (*e*) excited en-

thusiasm. Try to analyze the changes in muscular tensions that accompany these feelings. Then speak these sentiments as if they were your own. Take notice that variations in pitch, force, and time accompany the vocal quality changes produced.

a. We went to the show.
   The lock on the front door is broken.
   The house was built in record time.
   The auditorium was crowded.
   The sun was so hot that the sand along the shore burned our feet.

b. You should have known better.
   I hardly suppose that anything I can say will make any difference.
   I can't stand him, no matter what you say to the contrary.
   Do you have to make that noise?
   How many times do you expect me to tell you?

c. This particular product is the best of its kind in the entire world.
   That kind of literature is beneath me.
   Modern architecture provides the perfect solution to the needs of contemporary living.
   People who don't like modern jazz simply don't appreciate good music.
   Extracurricular activities are just as important as an academic education.

d. Something went wrong from the very beginning.
   This problem is one which confronts us all.
   Literature itself is a form of living.
   Beginning as a slave, the machine, in many respects, has now become our master.
   There is no fate more regrettable than to work without joy.

e. We had a wonderful time last night.
   I never knew that sailing could be such fun.
   There's no food so fine as fresh lobsters broiled right on the beach.
   If you get the chance, by all means go to see that show.
   What a marvelous idea!

2. Formulate sentences of your own, involving definite moods and attitudes, and practice them in the manner described in Exercise 1.

3. The following sentences and selections should be practiced for the purpose of applying the general principles of good resonation. Observe all breath pauses and keep your tones well supported. Prolong the vowel sounds. Keep your throat muscles selectively relaxed and your pharyngeal

passage open and free from interfering constrictions. Arouse yourself to respond both intellectually and emotionally to the ideas, moods, and prevailing spirit of these exercises.

a. He took the long road home.

b. The cabin was half buried under huge drifts of billowing, white snow.

c. There is no music quite so soothing as the sound of a bubbling stream hidden in deep woods.

d. Illustrations have been employed as aids to the definitions.

e. The far-streaming smoke of the freighter drifted slowly over the calm sea.

f. The curfew tolls the knell of parting day,
The lowing herd winds slowly o'er the lea,
The ploughman homeward plods his weary way,
And leaves the world to darkness and to me.

Now fades the glimmering landscape on the sight,
And all the air a solemn stillness holds,
Save where the beetle wheels his droning flight,
And drowsy tinklings lull the distant folds:

Save that from yonder ivy-mantled tower
The moping owl does to the moon complain
Of such as, wandering near her secret bower,
Molest her ancient solitary reign.

—GRAY

g. Our revels now are ended. These our actors,
As I foretold you, were all spirits and
Are melted into air, into thin air:
And, like the baseless fabric of this vision,
The cloud-capped towers, the gorgeous palaces,
The solemn temples, the great globe itself,
Yea, all which it inherit, shall dissolve
And, like this insubstantial pageant faded,
Leave not a rack behind. We are such stuff
As dreams are made on, and our little life
Is rounded with a sleep.

—SHAKESPEARE

4. The following selections lend themselves to the development of vocal strength, projection, and full resonance of tone. You will discover that these exercises require more vigorous breathing and greater management of the outgoing breath stream. No increased muscular effort in the region of your throat is required. Keep your throat passage open and relaxed.

a. Boot, saddle, to horse, and away!
   Rescue my castle before the hot day
   Brightens to blue from its silvery gray.

   CHORUS—

   Boot, saddle, to horse, and away!

Ride past the suburbs, asleep as you'd say;
Many's the friend there, will listen and pray,
"God's luck to the gallants that strike up the lay—

   CHORUS—

   Boot, saddle, to horse, and away!"

Forty miles off, like a roebuck at bay,
Flouts Castle Brancepeth the Roundheads' array;
Who laughs, "Good fellows ere this, by my fay,

   CHORUS—

   Boot, saddle, to horse, and away!"

Who? My wife Gertrude; that, honest and gay,
Laughs when you talk of surrendering, "Nay!
I've better counselors; what counsel they?

   CHORUS—

   Boot, saddle, to horse, and away!"

                              —BROWNING

b. I should like to rise and go
   Where the golden apples grow;—
   Where below another sky
   Parrot islands anchored lie,
   And, watched by cockatoos and goats,
   Lonely Crusoes building boats;—
   Where in sunshine reaching out
   Eastern cities, miles about,

Are with mosques and minaret
Among sandy gardens set,
And the rich goods from near and far
Hang for sale in the bazaar;—
Where the Great Wall round China goes,
And on one side the desert blows,
And with bell and voice and drum,
Cities on the other hum;—
Where are forests, hot as fire,
Wide as England, tall as a spire,
Full of apes and coconuts
And the negro hunters' huts;—
Where the knotty crocodile
Lies and blinks in the Nile,
And the red flamingo flies
Hunting fish before his eyes. . . .

—STEVENSON

c.   Hear the mellow wedding bells,
      Golden bells!
What a world of happiness their harmony foretells!
  Through the balmy air of night
  How they ring out their delight!
   From the molten-golden notes,
     And all in tune,
   What a liquid ditty floats
To the turtle-dove that listens, while she gloats
     On the moon!
  Oh, from out the sounding cells
What a gush of euphony voluminously wells!
     How it swells!
     How it dwells
  On the Future! how it tells
  Of the rapture that impels
  To the swinging and the ringing
   Of the bells, bells, bells,
Of the bells, bells, bells, bells,
    Bells, bells, bells,—
To the riming and the chiming of the bells!

—POE

d. The following selections in Appendix II will also help you to develop full resonance: Numbers 1, 6, 13, 24, and 26.

5. These exercises emphasize the vocal-quality aspect of resonation. In reading these selections, try to re-create within yourself the broad muscular tensions and relaxations suggested by the material. At the same time, however, try to maintain a condition of selective relaxation throughout the region of your throat. Imaginatively identify yourself with each changing idea and mood. Observe whether your tone color appropriately varies in response to your thinking and feeling.

   a. Here, where the world is quiet,
       Here, where all trouble seems
    Dead winds' and spent waves' riot
       In doubtful dreams of dreams;
    I watch the green field growing
    For reaping folk and sowing,
    For harvest time and mowing,
       A sleepy world of streams.

    I am tired of tears and laughter,
       And men that laugh and weep,
    Of what may come hereafter
       For men that sow to reap:
    I am weary of days and hours,
    Blown buds of barren flowers,
    Desires and dreams and powers
       And everything but sleep.

    Here life has death for neighbor,
       And far from eye or ear
    Wan waves and wet winds labor,
       Weak ships and spirits steer;
    They drive adrift, and whither
    They wot not who make thither;
    But no such winds blow hither,
       And no such things grow here.
            —SWINBURNE

Good for resonance

b. The day is cold, and dark, and dreary;
  It rains, and the wind is never weary;
  The vine still clings to the mouldering wall,
  But at every gust the dead leaves fall,
    And the day is dark and dreary.

  My life is cold, and dark, and dreary;
  It rains, and the wind is never weary;
  My thoughts still cling to the mouldering Past,
  But the hopes of youth fall thick in the blast,
    And the days are dark and dreary.

  Be still, sad heart! and cease repining;
  Behind the clouds is the sun still shining;
  Thy fate is the common fate of all,
  Into each life some rain must fall,
    Some days must be dark and dreary.
                              —LONGFELLOW

c. I do much wonder that one man, seeing how much another man is a
  fool when he dedicates his behaviours to love, will, after he hath laughed
  at such shallow follies in others, become the argument of his own scorn
  by falling in love: and such a man is Claudio. I have known when
  there was no music with him but the drum and the fife; and now had
  he rather hear the tabor and the pipe: I have known when he would
  have walked ten mile a-foot to see a good armour; and now will he lie
  ten nights awake, carving the fashion of a new doublet. He was wont
  to speak plain and to the purpose, like an honest man and a soldier;
  and now he is turned orthography; his words are a very fantastical
  banquet, just so many strange dishes. May I be so converted and see
  with these eyes? I cannot tell; I think not: I will not be sworn but love
  may transform me to an oyster; but I'll take my oath upon it, till he
  have made an oyster of me, he shall never make me such a fool. One
  woman is fair, yet I am well; another virtuous, yet I am well; but till
  all graces be in one woman, one woman shall not come in my grace.
  Rich she shall be, that's certain; wise, or I'll none; virtuous, or I'll
  never cheapen her; mild, or come not near me; noble, or not I for an
  angel; of good discourse, an excellent musician, and her hair shall be
  of what colour it please God.—SHAKESPEARE

d. Prepare a serious extemporaneous speech of about three minutes' duration. Present this in class. Try to generate vigorous physical responses, covert or overt, to your ideas and feelings. Above all, be genuinely concerned with communicating these ideas and feelings to your listeners.

e. Consult the selections in Appendix II for further practice material. Follow your taste in choosing those selections which will best stimulate you to respond with the desired vocal quality.

SUMMARY

Resonance is the product of three physical phenomena: the reflection and concentration of sound in a single direction through open passages; the forced vibration of solid objects in contact with a vibrating body; and the sympathetic vibration of solid bodies or partially enclosed cavities filled with air, in response to a vibrating object tuned to the same frequency. In the human voice, the sound waves which start at the vocal folds pass through the pharyngeal, oral, and nasal cavities. These cavities amplify and modify the fundamental tone and its overtones originally produced at the larynx. The selection of overtones to be resonated varies as the size and shape of the cavities change.

The muscles we use for tone production and resonation are the same muscles which are used for gagging, coughing, sucking, chewing, and swallowing. Some individuals who otherwise are well adjusted have never mastered the small muscular coordinations needed for a good voice. Some of the muscular activities of coughing, chewing, and swallowing have not been eliminated and intrude upon the speech process. Any such intrusion constricts the muscles and narrows the cavities of your throat, mouth, and nose, thus interfering with the desired reflection and amplification of tone.

Your aim in voice production, therefore, should be to relax all the muscles of your throat which are not actually used in the formation and resonation of tone. If you are successful in effecting this type of selective relaxation, and if no organic abnormalities are present, you will produce the best tone of which your individual vocal mechanism is capable, and it will be pleasant to hear.

Vocal quality is the listener's interpretation of resonation. It is the identifying characteristic of an individual's voice. You may describe this personal vocal quality as shrill, metallic, hard, strident, whining; muffled, flat, dull, guttural; oral, nasal, throaty; or round, open, smooth, mellow, and rich.

Physically speaking, however, vocal quality is the complex result of the selective combination of the fundamental and the overtones.

We are also aware of changes in vocal quality when we attempt to communicate meaning and feeling. These particular changes in vocal quality are referred to as *tone color*.

There are several definite faults of vocal quality. Stridency is a resonance fault usually caused by excessive tension in the pharynx and in the muscles of the velum. A harsh, sharp quality results from the prominence given to the higher overtones.

Throatiness is a tonal characteristic produced when the lower part of the pharynx is constricted and when the posterior part of the tongue crowds back into the throat. The tone is often low and muffled, and possesses a guttural quality produced by constriction of the pharyngeal passage.

Nasality is a foghorn quality resulting from the entrapment of the vibrating breath stream in a cavity in which the entrance is substantially larger than the exit, or in which there is a narrow common entrance and exit. The three normal nasal sounds in English speech are M, N, and NG.

Denasality is the lack of nasal resonance—cold-in-the-head speech. Any blockage of the nasal passage, caused by a cold, hay fever, deviated septum, or enlarged adenoids blocking the nasopharynx, may produce this quality.

Vocal quality should be considered in relation to muscular tensions and emotion if it is to be successfully employed in speaking, reading, and acting. You must covertly, if not overtly, engage in general body tensions and relaxations corresponding to the tensions and relaxations of the emotional states involved.

You have now been given information on the process of breathing for speech, phonation, and resonation of the tone. In order to communicate successfully your ideas and feelings, the skills in these processes must be integrated. The following chapter is devoted to this integration.

7

The Integration of the Vocal Skills

Accent is the soul of language; it gives to it both feeling and truth.—
ROUSSEAU

For any activity, the whole is greater than the sum of its parts. Merely putting the parts together is not enough. There must also be an intent and desire to achieve, if the whole activity is to be successfully performed.

The novice pole vaulter is fortunate if his first attempt results in a nine- or ten-foot jump. No matter how hard he tries or how much he wants to go higher, his ceiling is ten feet. Then the track coach begins to analyze the vaulter's form. The coach shows him a better way to hold the pole, the proper distance at which to start his run, the best method to use in taking off from the ground, and the way to handle his body and thrust it over the bar. The vaulter practices and experiments with these vaulting skills and finally works them together so that he goes over the bar set at thirteen feet. The vaulter can achieve this height only if he has the drive to succeed. But this alone is not enough; he must integrate the separate skills into a coordinated whole as well.

In like manner, technical skills alone do not create a responsive voice. Only when the vocal skills are integrated and motivated by your intense desire to communicate and to infuse others with your emotions, can you produce truly effective and communicative vocalization.

THE SKILLS

In previous chapters, you have learned about the skills which you have available for integration. They are the results of the purely physical activities of the vocal mechanism. In Chapter 4, *Breathing for Speech*, two basic skills were discussed, those of loudness and of timing. The relationship between proper breathing and loudness was developed as well as the way in which breathing influences timing, including rate, duration, and pause. The basic concepts of pitch level involved in habitual pitch, optimum pitch, and key, and also the skills concerned with pitch variation for melody, including inflection and step, were presented in Chapter 5. Finally, in Chapter 6, with the consideration of resonance and quality, the skills in the establishment of acceptable quality and the change of quality to communicate meaning were explained. These skills are the tools with which you must work to transmit your ideas to your listener. If they are not clear to you, refer back to those sections of the book in which they are defined.

New Concepts

Before we discuss the integration of these skills for communication, there is a new skill concept which you must understand. This skill has two aspects, energy and projection. These are not the same thing, but are closely related to each other, both psychologically and physically.

Energy

Energy is the basis for projection. Both energy and projection are the results of the same basic physical phenomenon—the increase in the tonicity of the muscles of the whole body. This increased readiness to act affects the muscle tone of the vocal mechanism; the result is the heightened feeling of vitality which is the basis for energy. We often think of energy as applying to individual words—the reinforcement of them so that they become more intense. Sometimes we refer to this as *force,* in contradistinction to mere *loudness.* If the speaker has energy, you will think, "He means what he says!"

To be most effective, however, energy must be controlled. If one touched a match to the gasoline in a can, the gasoline would burn with an explosive flash. The energy of the explosion, uncontrolled, would be wasted. However, if the same gasoline were used in an automobile, under control in the motor, it would drive the car. In the same way, control and direction of vocal energy are necessary if energy is to serve a purpose in communication.

Projection

A speaker who directs his voice with controlled energy is said to be *projecting.* Projection is a difficult concept to define. Psychologically, it depends

You must establish contact.
Talk directly (eye contact)

upon a genuine desire on the part of the speaker to communicate his thoughts and feelings to his hearers. Without this attitude, mechanical adjustments will not make the speaker seem to be projecting. Physically, it depends upon the control of the speaker's bodily activity in response to his desire to communicate. In conversation, discussion, or public speaking, this may take the form of alert posture, responsive facial expression, and eye-to-eye contact with his hearers. On the stage, the orientation may be partly toward the other persons on the stage and partly toward the audience, but the same sense of purposeful activity will be present.

The complex result of these factors emerges in the voice in greater clarity of articulation, more brilliance in resonation, and more efficient use of the breath stream in phonation. For the listener, it seems as if the voice were *aimed* at him. When a mother goes out to call her son to dinner and she does not know just where he is, she will call, "Johnny, Johnny!" with great energy, but will broadcast the call diffusely over the whole neighborhood. However, once she has located Johnny, she projects her call with machine-gun accuracy to Johnny so that he hears her and comes home. If the person vocalizing is projecting, you as the listener will feel, "He is speaking to *me!*"

Projection is related to loudness, but it is not loudness alone, nor does it depend upon loudness. You may have a high degree of loudness and no projection, or very quiet speech with projection. Experiment with loudness, energy, and projection on this statement: "That's a lie, and you're nothing but a dirty liar!" Shout it as loudly as you can, but do not let the words have any meaning, reality, or aim. Now say it at conversational volume with all of the earnestness and conviction you can muster; try to feel the vehemence of the speaker as you aim the statement at someone. Observe that loudness alone does not project the meaning. Experiment with the phrase to see what different levels of energy and projection you can achieve. Notice the differences in muscle tension in your whole body as you do this.

Notice how mere loudness usually results from increased tension in the muscles which control the exhaled breath stream. For energy and projection, there must be the same increase in muscle tension, but this must be in the mechanisms of phonation and resonation as well. As in all of the other vocal skills, the fine balance of tensions and relaxations must be maintained. Otherwise, faults resulting from overtension will appear in breathing, phonation, and resonation.

All of the skills grow out of muscular manipulation of the vocal structures. But no skill results from the action of only a single division of the mechanism; each depends upon the interaction of the structures used in breathing, phonation, and resonation. Your skill in loudness, for example, is dependent upon the integration of the mechanisms of breathing and resonation. Similarly, all of the other skills are derived from the synthesis of the various vocal processes. It is with this synthesis, or integration, that we are concerned in this chapter.

WHAT IS INTEGRATION?

Integration means the synthesis and interaction of all of your vocal skills in the meaningful act of communication. It should be obvious to you by this time that when you speak, your entire vocal equipment, and perhaps your entire body, is utilized. Environmental influences, the past and present state of your health, and all that you have thought and felt affect your control of the vocal skills and your ability to integrate them. Although you may be able to perform and control each of the vocal skills in isolation, as in the exercises given in the various chapters, it is only when you can get them to work together effortlessly to express your meaning that you are integrating.

Vocal communication of meaning and emotion is largely determined by your ability to integrate the expressive elements of voice to satisfy your purpose in speaking. We have already explained voice in terms of the primary skills; these are the basic elements of vocal expression. They are to speaking what the primary colors are to painting. Even as the painter mixes and blends these colors to suit his expressive intention, just so must the speaker mix and blend—integrate—the various aspects of pitch, time, loudness, and tone quality to suit his expressive intention and to meet the intellectual and emotional demands of his material.

Listeners are affected by what they hear and not by good intentions. When you address a listener, you either knowingly or unknowingly engage in several kinds of communication. The words which you utter may carry a denotational, logical message. In addition to this, your personality and manner may reinforce the words spoken—or they may negate the meaning intended. Your voice, too, with all of its melodic and emphatic changes, may animate and strengthen your purpose in communication—or through lack of these expressive changes, your communication may be dull and purposeless and give the lie to your heartfelt intentions as well as to the words selected to express them. Hence, in order to convey ideas to others, there must be the desire to communicate and a mechanism capable of integrating the vocal skills.

HOW MEANING IS ACHIEVED BY INTEGRATION

To achieve meaning through vocalization, you must first understand the total idea of the material you are speaking, reading, or acting. But your own clearness of conception can be conveyed to the listener only by a responsive mechanism. Such a mechanism is one which is capable of performing all the vocal skills necessary for communication and which performs them in unconscious response to your thought processes. This unconscious response should be your ultimate goal; yet at the learning level it may be necessary for you to manipulate the skills consciously in order to be certain that you can perform them and in order to discover their interrelationships.

Using the Skills

In order that you may work on the integration of the vocal skills and analyze your capabilities, the following section includes two types of analysis. The first provides for a thorough understanding of the ideas in the material to be read. The second provides for discovery of the ways in which you can use the skills to express those ideas. The selection which follows, from the Declaration of Independence, is excellent material for analysis. Read it through silently as many times as is necessary to understand the author's purpose, the central idea, the chain of reasoning, and the supporting arguments. Be sure that you know exactly what Jefferson is saying. Answers to the following questions may help you to understand.

1. When did he say it?
2. Why did he say it?
3. Under what circumstances did he say it?
4. To whom did he say it?
5. How was it received and what was its influence?

We hold these truths to be self-evident, that all men are created equal, that they are endowed by their Creator with certain unalienable Rights, that among these are Life, Liberty and the pursuit of Happiness. That to secure these rights, Governments are instituted among Men, deriving their just powers from the consent of the governed. That whenever any Form of Government becomes destructive of these ends, it is the Right of the People to alter or to abolish it, and to institute new Government, laying its foundation on such principles and organizing its powers in such form, as to them shall seem most likely to effect their Safety and Happiness. Prudence, indeed, will dictate that Governments long established should not be changed for light and transient causes; and accordingly all experience hath shown, that mankind are more disposed to suffer, while evils are sufferable, than to right themselves by abolishing the forms to which they are accustomed. But when a long train of abuses and usurpations, pursuing invariably the same Object evinces a design to reduce them under absolute Despotism, it is their right, it is their duty, to throw off such Government, and to provide new Guards for their future security.—JEFFERSON

Your first problem in preparation for reading aloud is to determine the phrasing based on your analysis of meaning.

1. Which words go together to form the meaning groups?
2. Where shall the pauses come to separate those groups?
3. Will the pauses all be of equal length, or will they differ?

Mark what you consider to be the proper phrasing. Then read the passage aloud. Does it sound right? Is the general meaning clear? Can it be read easily in terms of breathing, with loudness sufficient for the classroom audience? If your answer to any of these questions is no, then restudy the phrasing.

You must determine the relative value of the various word groups in terms of the total idea. Answer these questions to assist you in this.

1. Which phrases are the most important and must be pointed up if you are to transmit the idea?
2. Which phrases are relatively unimportant?
3. Which phrases relate most closely to which other phrases; stand parallel to them; are in contrast to them?

How are you going to show the values of the phrases and their relationships? You have all of the vocal tools for this purpose. Will you give emphasis to the most important phrases by increased loudness, greater energy, change in rate, the use of pause, pitch change, quality change, or combinations of these? Will you emphasize all of the important phrases in the same way? What skills will you use to show the relation of parallel or contrasting phrases?

Read the selection aloud again, using the phrasing you have determined, and try the skills on the various phrases to indicate the relative values and relationships. Are the values and relationships clear? Get someone else to listen to you and help judge this. If you are not communicating what you wish, try other ways of doing it. Do not be satisfied with the first pattern you hit upon, unless you are sure that it is the best one.

If each phrasal unit is to be clear, then the meaning and relation of the words in that phrase must be clear. Select a phrase such as, "that they are endowed by their Creator with certain unalienable Rights . . ."

1. Which words communicate the major share of the meaning?

2. Which ones can be subordinated without losing meaning?

3. Which words connect most closely with others; contrast with them; echo them?

You may use the same tools as you had for the phrases to emphasize words and to show their relationships to each other. Put these skills to work in this phrase. Read it aloud. Are the meanings and relationships made clear by the methods used? Are there alternative methods? Try them, and select the most effective ones. Start at the beginning of the paragraph and do the same thing with each phrase. Finally, read the whole selection aloud and judge whether the phrasing is logical and whether phrase and word values and relationships are entirely clear.

Beyond these obvious elements of meaning, there are still more subtle ones for you to communicate.

1. What is the general emotional mood of the selection?

2. What emotional changes are there from word to word, from phrase to phrase?

You have probably worked out the denotative meanings of the words. Now, what associations do they have? What are their connotations? Does the word "equal" have merely the dictionary meaning of "exactly the same"? As it is used here, both in the phrase in which it occurs and as a part of the entire passage, does "equal" have connotations which are much broader than those of the dictionary definition? Many of the words in the selection will have very broad connotations if you stop to think about them. You must hold these broad meanings in mind as you read aloud, if there are to be quality and other changes in vocalization.

Your task is to convey the mood, emotional changes, and word connotations to the listener. While quality changes are particularly important to convey mood, remember that all of the skills contribute. Read the selection aloud, observing your expression of the emotional elements. You should record the passage, using the skills you have selected as being most appropriate. If they do not express your meanings and feelings, record again, making the necessary changes.

Integration

If you have faithfully and accurately carried out the plan for analysis and presentation of the selection from the Declaration of Independence, you will have integrated your vocal skills in the communication of meaning. For the purposes of illustration, our approach to this exercise has been somewhat mechanistic; as the responsiveness of your vocal instrument increases, your conscious analysis of the use of the skills will disappear. Your goal is the development of habitual, spontaneous responses at the performance level. Integration of the skills works in the same way in conversation, public speaking, or acting as it does in reading aloud. After a thorough analysis of the ideas, a person with a fully responsive mechanism and a desire to communicate will integrate the skills automatically to express his meaning.

ANALYSIS OF THE INTEGRATION OF VOCAL SKILLS

Listening

1. Listen to the casual conversation of your friends. Are they communicating their ideas effectively? If so, what vocal skills are they using? Do they use and integrate all of the skills? What faults can you discover in the use of the individual skills and their integration?

2. Listen critically to the performances of your classmates. Does their vocalization suggest a complete grasp of the ideas they are speaking? Do you understand the total idea without difficulty? Is the phrasing clear? Are the meanings and the relation of phrases and of words made explicit? Are the emotional elements and connotative values brought out? Does the total effect concentrate your attention on the idea, or do the techniques employed draw undue attention to themselves?

Self-analysis

1. The analysis of the selection from the Declaration of Independence was, in reality, an exercise in self-analysis. Take another selection with a different type of idea, such as a story or a lyric poem, and follow through the same type of analysis. Answer the questions given in the original exercise.

2. Record the selection you use in the exercise above. Listen critically as you play it back. Is the meaning clear? If not, experiment with different ways of integrating the vocal skills and record again. Get a friend to listen and criticize.

3. Do you hear in your own voice the faults which your instructor and classmates report?

Selections for Self-improvement

The following selections are to be analyzed and practiced in the same way as was the selection from the Declaration of Independence.

a. BOOKS

Books are the treasured wealth of the world and the fit inheritance of generations and nations. Books, the oldest and the best, stand naturally and rightfully on the shelves of every cottage. They have no cause of their own to plead, but while they enlighten and sustain the reader his common sense will not refuse them. Their authors are a natural and irresistible aristocracy in every society, and, more than kings or emperors, exert an influence on mankind. When the illiterate and perhaps scornful trader has earned by enterprise and industry his coveted leisure and independence, and is admitted to the circles of wealth and fashion, he turns inevitably at last to those still higher but yet inaccessible circles of intellect and genius, and is sensible only of the imperfection of his culture and the vanity and insufficiency of all his riches, and further proves his good sense by the pains which he takes to secure for his children that intellectual culture whose want he so keenly feels; and thus it is that he becomes the founder of a family.—THOREAU

b. NATURE

As a fond mother, when the day is o'er
   Leads by the hand her little child to bed, .
   Half willing, half reluctant to be led,
And leave his broken playthings on the floor,
Still gazing at them through the open door,
   Nor wholly reassured and comforted
   By promises of others in their stead,
Which, though more splendid, may not please him more;
So Nature deals with us, and takes away
   Our playthings one by one, and by the hand
     Leads us to rest so gently, that we go
Scarce knowing if we wish to go or stay,
   Being too full of sleep to understand
     How far the unknown transcends the what we know.
                —LONGFELLOW

c. LA GRANDE BRETÊCHE

On the banks of the Loire stands an old brown house, crowned with very high roofs, and so completely isolated that there is nothing near it, not even a fetid tannery or a squalid tavern, such as are commonly seen outside small towns. In front of this house is a garden down to the river, where the box shrubs, formerly clipped close to the walks, now straggle at their own will. A few willows, rooted in the stream, have grown up quickly like an enclosing fence, and half hide the house. The wild plants we call weeds have clothed the bank with their beautiful luxuriance. The fruit-trees, neglected for these ten years past, no longer bear a crop, and their suckers have formed a thicket. The paths, once gravelled, are overgrown with purslane; but, to be accurate, there is no trace of path.—BALZAC

d. OUT UPON IT

Out upon it, I have loved
   Three whole days together!
And am like to love three more,
   If it prove fair weather.

Time shall moult away his wings
   Ere he shall discover
In the whole wide world again
   Such a constant lover.

But the spite on't is, no praise
   Is due at all to me:
Love with me had made no stays,
   Had it any been but she.

Had it any been but she,
   And that very face,
There had been at least ere this
   A dozen dozen in her place.
            —SUCKLING

e. FAREWELL, A LONG FAREWELL

Farewell, a long farewell, to all my greatness!
This is the state of man: To-day he puts forth
The tender leaves of hope, to-morrow blossoms,
And bears his blushing honors thick upon him:
The third day comes a frost, a killing frost;
And—when he thinks, good easy man, full surely
His greatness is a ripening—nips his root;
And then he falls as I do. I have ventured,—
Like little wanton boys that swim on bladders,—
This many summers, in a sea of glory,
But far beyond my depth: my high-blown pride
At length broke under me, and now has left me
Weary and old with service, to the mercy
Of a rude stream that must forever hide me.

—SHAKESPEARE

f. EDUCATION

By the "mud-sill" theory it is assumed that labor and education are incompatible, and any practical combination of them impossible. According to that theory, a blind horse upon a treadmill is a perfect illustration of what a laborer should be—all the better for being blind, that he may not kick understandingly. According to that theory, the education of laborers is not only useless but pernicious and dangerous. In fact, it is, in some sort, deemed a misfortune that laborers should have heads at all. Those same heads are regarded as explosive materials, only to be safely kept in damp places, as far as possible from that peculiar sort of fire which ignites them. A Yankee who could invent a strong-handed man without a head would receive the everlasting gratitude of the "mud-sill" advocates.

But free labor says, "No." Every head should be cultivated and improved by whatever will add to its capacity for performing its charge. In one word, free labor insists on universal education.—LINCOLN

g. WISDOM

But where shall wisdom be found? and where is the place of understanding?

Man knoweth not the price thereof; neither is it found in the land of the living.

The depth saith, It is not in me: and the sea saith, It is not with me.

It cannot be gotten for gold, neither shall silver be weighed for the price thereof.

It cannot be valued with the gold of Ophir, with the precious onyx, or the sapphire.

The gold and the crystal cannot equal it: and the exchange of it shall not be for jewels of fine gold.

No mention shall be made of coral, or of pearls: for the price of wisdom is above rubies.

The topaz of Ethiopia shall not equal it, neither shall it be valued with pure gold.

Whence then cometh wisdom? and where is the place of understanding?

—JOB 28: 12-20

8

Articulation Standards

Speak the speech, I pray you, as I pronounced it to you,—trippingly on the tongue.—SHAKESPEARE

In campaign speeches, occasionally a candidate must speak to a crowd out in the open, in a park or at a railroad station. As you stand on the outer fringe of the group, you hear his voice in the distance, going up and down as he gestures violently, increasing in energy of production as he gives a fine show of enthusiasm. You may be impressed with his delivery and wonder what he is saying. You have heard only *voice*, not *speech*.

The act of speaking is not complete until the listener becomes aware not only of the feelings expressed in voice usage but of the ideas conveyed through the symbols of our language. The articulation of sounds must be coupled with the integration of vocal skills.

Articulation is the process of forming meaningful oral symbols by manipulation of the tongue, lips, jaw, and soft palate. The activity uses the same structures which change the size and shape of the oral cavity for the resonation of tone.

The articulation of sounds, in a larger sense, includes both sound formation and pronunciation, the latter usually being construed as acceptable production of sounds and proper accent of syllables in words. It can also refer to qualities of clearness and distinctness commonly called *enunciation*.

THE IMPORTANCE OF GOOD ARTICULATION

A high-school student was heard to remark one day, "If I ever get elected to the school board, I'm going to fire the math teacher." This sounded like personal prejudice, but actually it was not. "I think any teacher ought to be able to speak the English language so that I can understand him, and he mumbles and runs his words together so that half the time the students don't know what he is saying."

This instructor was not an English or speech teacher, of whom very high standards of articulation should be expected. Yet he was failing in his basic task of communicating his subject matter—not because he did not know mathematics, but because he could not be understood by his hearers.

In marked contrast, a college professor, who must have been told in his youth to speak distinctly, exaggerated his final consonants in such a way that his meaning was obscured by his mannerisms, and he became a subject of mimicry and ridicule by all his students.

These two illustrations point to the basic problems involved in developing standards for good articulation. Articulation is said to be good when the sounds are distinct, accurate, and harmoniously blended into one another. Articulation is no more acceptable when it is overly precise and pedantic than when it lacks clearness and accuracy.

Listening

Careful listening is the first step in the development of good articulation. Unless you have noticeable structural deviations, your present habits of articulation are largely a product of your environment—your home, your associates, your school life. You speak as you have heard others speak. If you wish to improve, you must listen to speakers whose speech is better than your own as well as to those on your own level or below. You must make comparisons between them, to see what the differences are. You should analyze these differences on the basis of the use of the articulatory structures and try to duplicate the movements of the articulators in imitation of what you hear. Through such analyses, you can make any changes in your articulation you wish.

HOW TO SELECT A STANDARD

The pattern of English speech varies widely throughout the world. You are familiar with such broad variations as British and American speech; you are probably aware of the existence of three widely spoken American dialects: Eastern, Southern, and General. Each of these dialects has marked differences within itself. There are also some dialects, confined to narrow geographical limits, which are not readily classifiable into any regional division. The latter, however, are not spoken by educated people, who tend to adopt some form of one of the three main patterns.

Dialects differ from one another primarily in pronunciation, but variations in melody pattern, rhythm, and colloquial vocabulary also exist. Among the British dialects you probably have heard are the familiar "standard British," spoken by British statesmen and other public figures, the Cockney, Lancashire, Scottish, and Irish dialects. In the United States, if you have traveled in the South, you will recognize that differences exist between the pronunciation patterns of Richmond, Virginia, and those of Charleston, South Carolina, or Dallas, Texas, although all three are recognizably Southern. The speech of the educated New Yorker is unlike that of the Bostonian, and neither is quite like that of the resident of the Maine coast. Less marked but nevertheless perceptible differences exist among speech patterns of Indiana, Iowa, and Nebraska. In cosmopolitan areas like New York City or Los Angeles, where those born elsewhere frequently outnumber the natives, the dialects of all areas, including those derived from the influence of foreign languages, are mingled in indescribable confusion.

"If this is the case," you say, "how may I know what is the 'correct' articulation of the words I use?" The answer is to be found in three factors: the area in which you live; your purpose in speaking; and the occasion on which you speak.

The Area in Which You Live

For most of the speaking you do, your standard should be that employed by the educated people of the broad dialect region in which you live. For a large majority of Americans, this dialect is the one we have called General American, some form of which is spoken throughout the United States, except in portions of New England and elsewhere along the Atlantic seaboard, and in the South. Southerners and Easterners, of course, should retain the characteristic features of their own dialects. This does not mean accepting all the local peculiarities of the speech in your immediate area. Franklin Roosevelt's speech, for example, was distinctly Eastern, but was largely free from localisms. Alfred E. Smith's speech, on the other hand, was so highly localized as to be a matter of amusement and even resentment to the radio audience outside New York City. Speech which is acceptable to educated people in any of the three major dialect areas will not be displeasing to discriminating hearers in either of the other regions. You should therefore concentrate on learning clear articulation of speech within your own regional dialect. At the same time, you should learn the main differences between the way you speak and the speech used elsewhere in the English-speaking world.

Your Purpose in Speaking

In a few cases, special dialects are required for special purposes. If you plan to go on the stage, your flexibility as an actor will be to some extent dependent on your ability to adopt the dialect appropriate to the part you are playing. Although the practice is falling into disuse for plays with an American setting, actors still find that they are often called upon to use a modified form of south British dialect, known as stage diction, particularly in Shakespearean, classic, or British plays. The cast of a play which is laid in Scotland would all have to use a Scottish dialect. It would be obviously inappropriate for one member of the family in *Life with Father* to speak General American, another Southern, and a third Eastern. All must speak the same dialect. An actor who cannot hear and readily analyze and adopt a dialect appropriate to his role will not go far.

Radio speech has been stabilized in recent years, with the acceptance of General American dialect, modified somewhat, as the standard of network announcers. Motion pictures also now tend toward the use of modified General American as the standard, after some experimentation with stage diction. Here, of course, as on the stage, special roles may require special dialects.

The Occasion on Which You Speak

Speaking occasions differ in formality. The basic dialect you use should not be affected by these differences, but the degree of precision in your articulation should change. What may be adequate articulation for a casual street-corner conversation, an argument with an umpire, or a bull session will not be precise enough for a formal social occasion or a business interview. Similarly, an even more exacting standard is required of you when you stand before an audience as speaker, reader, or actor. The larger the audience, the greater the number of distractions, the poorer the acoustics of the hall—the greater is the demand upon you for distinct sound production. The advent of public-address systems has made pure lung power less necessary to effective speaking, but it has not reduced in any way the necessity for clear articulation. In some cases, it may actually increase the problem, by accentuation of echoes or by mechanical distortion of the sounds produced.

On the other hand, overprecise speaking may be quite annoying in informal speaking situations, and reading which separates each word from the next, instead of blending sounds in the normal manner of smooth communication, loses effectiveness. Moreover, as we have already noted, unblended speaking or reading aggravates the problem of glottal shock.

THE DICTIONARY AND ARTICULATION STANDARDS

The pronunciations given in carefully edited dictionaries are, for the most part, those of formal speech. Statesmen, leading public speakers, actors, radio personalities, chairmen of university English departments, and other public figures are consulted. Their pronunciation of words is analyzed by the editors of the dictionary. Where conflicts occur, the most commonly used pronunciations are selected and recorded in the dictionary as "standard." The dictionary is therefore an excellent guide to the pronunciation of words in isolation as used by the best educated men in formal speech. However, it does not reflect many of the changes in the articulation pattern which occur in the less formal situations, nor can it show adequately the changes in the pattern induced by the proximity of other words or by the position of words in a sentence. If you rely merely on the list of symbols often given at the bottom of each page, the dictionary does not discriminate between dialects in different parts of the United States, although these differences are dealt with in the more detailed guides to pronunciation given in good dictionaries. One recent dictionary, the sixth edition of Webster's Collegiate Dictionary, eliminates the symbols from the bottom of the page to compel the reader to examine the guide in the introduction.

Unstressed Forms

When the meaning of the phrase modifies the rhythm so that a word or syllable has less prominence than when it is pronounced in isolation, it is called an unstressed form. Within the sentence, monosyllabic articles, conjunctions, and prepositions—such as *and, but, of, for*—are nearly always unstressed. Similarly, auxiliary verbs and other words which serve a secondary function in carrying the meaning of the sentence are usually reduced in importance by pronouncing them in their unstressed forms. Dictionaries recognize some of these variants, but not all, partly because they are so dependent on the context and intent of the speaker that they can be examined only in relation to a specific utterance. The same thing happens to the unaccented syllables of polysyllabic words. Here the dictionary is more helpful, and for the most part reflects the pronunciation of unstressed syllables, if the reader understands the meaning of the diacritical markings. In subsequent pages, as we examine the vowel sounds, we shall note what changes commonly occur in their articulation as they appear in unstressed positions, and shall point out when such changes are acceptable and when they are inappropriate.

Assimilation

In the normal flow of speech, sounds modify the production of surrounding sounds. This modification, known as *assimilation,* may occur when the combination appears within words or at the end of one word and the beginning of another. Assimilation facilitates the movement of the articulatory mechanism in passing from the formation of one sound to that of the next, thus giving smoothness to speech. On the other hand, it may result in the elimination of individual sounds or even whole syllables which are necessary to easy understanding of speech by the hearer. The dangers of faulty assimilation, of course, increase rapidly as the situation becomes more formal, or as the difficulty of hearing is accentuated by the size of the audience and the acoustic properties of the room in which you are speaking.

In our discussion of the sounds of American speech, we shall point out those changes which are normal and acceptable in assimilation, and shall also see some of the more common errors of assimilation which make speech indistinct and unacceptable.

Blending

Closely related to the problem of assimilation is the blending of sounds within a given thought group, without a perceptible break between words. The sounds of speech should flow from one word to another within a phrase in almost exactly the same way that they move from one syllable to another in a long word. There should be no cessation of the stream of speech sounds within a thought group. Blending, of course, involves some assimilation, for the articulation of sounds is always modified in the transition from one articulatory position to another. We treat blending as a separate concept, in order to emphasize to you the necessity of an uninterrupted flow of speech sounds, except where the ideas dictate a pause.

The separation of words results in a pedantic type of speech without any added clearness. Frequently, speakers who keep words moving normally in conversation or public speaking fail to do so when they read aloud. Perhaps you have heard a radio interview read from a script, in which there was a marked contrast in smoothness between the skillful reading of the professional announcer and the faltering manner of other participants, untrained in reading. The disparity may be due in part to timing and melody, but there are also inevitable differences in the skill with which words are blended within the phrase.

You may note the combined effects of stress, assimilation, and blending by taking a short sentence and articulating it in different ways: "I was going because I had heard of his work." First read the sentence slowly, articulating each word independently and with a clear break between words. Then read the sentence at your normal rate, stressing *going, heard,* and *work.* You probably had no break of any kind in the flow of words, and you undoubtedly materially changed the vowel sounds in *was, because, had,* and *of.* The chances are also good that you dropped the H in both *had* and *his.* These changes induced by stress and assimilation would for the most part be fully acceptable in informal speech, but some of them would interfere with clearness in formal platform presentation.

While we shall point out in later sections what some of the stumbling blocks are, in the long run your own common sense must be the guide. You must learn to listen carefully to speakers in all kinds of situations. You must develop sufficient precision to be understood in every situation without forced attention from the listener, but you must not adopt an articulation pattern that calls attention to itself rather than to the subject matter with which you are dealing.

METHODS OF REPRESENTING PRONUNCIATION

Spelling

When written languages were first developed, the symbols used were supposed to represent sounds, and to some extent this original function of the alphabet has persisted. In some languages, alphabetical symbols come much closer to representing sounds than in English. The difficulty in English spelling arises from two chief sources: (1) the diverse origin of English words; (2) the failure of spelling reform to keep pace with changes in pronunciation. Modern English words are derived from virtually every language root, but the most common ones are Anglo-Saxon (of Germanic origin), Norman French, Latin, and Greek. The English spelling of words is generally a direct derivation from the original root, each of which has a somewhat different system of sound symbols. These divergencies have never been reconciled, nor has any systematic spelling reform ever been undertaken to bring them all into a common system.

The resulting inconsistencies are so apparent that it is hardly necessary to point them out. The word *fish* could be spelled GHUTI if we used the GH in *enough,* the U in *busy,* and the TI in *portion.* While it is true that GH and TI never have those sounds in the positions we have given them in our spelling of *fish,* the spelling GHUTI nevertheless points up the absurdity of using those symbols to represent those sounds in any position. We say that in English there are at most six vowels (A, E, I, O, U, and sometimes Y). But in actual use there are fifteen or more vowel sounds. How, then, shall we represent those for which we have no symbol? In normal English spelling, the letter A may represent at least seven different sounds as in: *at, ate, ask, car, many, ball,* and *intricate.* On the other hand, the so-called long E sound may be represented by a number of different letter symbols as in: mach*i*ne, rec*ei*ve, bel*ie*ve, *e*ven, sn*ea*k, l*ee,* and C*ae*sar. The family of words which includes the letter grouping OUGH is another illustration of the inadequacy of our spelling; note the differing pronunciations in d*ough,* b*ough,* en*ough,* thr*ough,* c*ough,* and hicc*ough.* The OES ending in d*oes,* sh*oes,* and fl*oes* is another example of the same difficulty. Moreover, some letters used in spelling do not represent any sound at all in speaking, as the K in *k*nee, the B in com*b,* and the L in ca*l*m. You undoubtedly can list many other examples of the same kind.

Diacritical Marks

Dictionary editors have attempted to solve the problem of representing sounds by respelling words and supplementing the alphabetical symbols with a system of dots and lines known as *diacritical markings.* This is a decided improvement over English spelling as a manner of representing sounds, and for the pronunciation of words in isolation, it is perhaps accurate enough for most uses. Diacritical systems, however, although they are similar, are not uniform. In order to interpret a dictionary pronunciation accurately, you must consult the guide to pronunciation for that particular dictionary. Webster's Collegiate Dictionary, for example, lists sixty-six symbols in the key to pronunciation, whereas the American College Dictionary lists only forty-eight, some of which are quite different from Webster's symbols.

In addition to this, diacritical markings do not distinguish among different dialects, in many cases. The symbol à as it is used in the Webster dictionaries is dependent on your pronunciation of the word *ask.* However, the pronunciation of this word varies from one part of the country to another—from the A in *father,* to the A in *bat.* The symbol à is thus accurate enough to give you the pronunciation of other words in your own dialect, but it is not exact enough to represent the sounds of speech as you hear others produce them. Since the symbol represents a broad range of usage, it cannot represent an exact sound. Precisely the same difficulty is encountered in words marked with the symbol ŏ, since varying interpretations render the symbol ambiguous.

Phonetics

In order to transcribe and study spoken language, scholars have developed phonetic symbols for each sound. Often the alphabet letter can be used to represent a sound. For such sound units, however, as CH, TH, and NG, where there is no single letter to indicate the sounds, or for vowels where the letter stands for a variety of sounds, special symbols had to be created.

By means of such symbols, a written record can be made, for example, of the different ways in which men from the various regions in this country or from foreign countries may say the same word or phrase. Also, by means of phonetics, the listener can record the changes which take place in sounds when they occur together and affect each other's production or when they are stressed or unstressed in the flow of speech.

The use of phonetics, then, permits accuracy in the transcription of speech. The study goes beyond this in providing descriptions of the formation of each sound.

When we say that one phonetic symbol represents each sound in speech, some mention must be made of the *phoneme theory*. A particular sound may have a variety of productions while still maintaining an identity distinct from other sounds. For instance, no two people make a K in exactly the same way, nor will the K's be alike in different positions in such words as *keep*, *basket*, and *duke*. The muscular movements which occur before and after the production of the specific sound affect the immediate formation of that sound.

These variants of one sound are called a *sound family*, or phoneme. If they become too dissimilar to the main and most frequently heard member of the family, they are recognized as the distortions heard in defective speech or as actual substitution of sounds from another phoneme. The distinction between one phoneme and another, ultimately, is always made on the acoustic basis.

METHODS OF CLASSIFYING SOUNDS

Several different methods may be used to classify speech sounds. The distinction most commonly made is between vowels and consonants. This is a somewhat arbitrary distinction, based on the relative importance of the tone and noise components of the sound. When the resonance passages are relatively open, so that the distinctive quality of the sound depends on the shape of the resonator, the sound is called a *vowel*. On the other hand, when the breath stream is stopped, narrowed, or diverted by the articulators in such a way that a considerable noise component is superimposed on the fundamental, the sound is called a *consonant*. The distinction is relative, however. Many consonants contain large tonal components, while most vowels have some noise content.

A second type of distinction which is often made is the positional one— the description of the position and movement of the articulatory organs in the formation of a sound. Thus, vowel sounds may be distinguished from one another by describing the way in which changes in the position of the tongue, lips, and jaw modify the shape of the resonator and its opening, thus determining the quality of the vowel. Similarly, the consonants may be labeled in terms of the point of narrowing or contact between the articulators at which the distinctive characteristics of the sound are produced. Thus, a bilabial sound is one articulated by both lips; a linguadental sound is produced by bringing together the tongue and the teeth; and so on. We use this type of classification in our vowel and consonant charts found in the two following chapters, and in our description of the individual sounds.

A third method of classification is the acoustic method. Consonants may be grouped according to the type of sound which the ear hears. While it is true that these effects are the result of a particular kind of articulatory position, it is convenient to describe them in terms of the acoustic effect alone. Thus, consonant sounds may be voiced or voiceless—that is, made with or without laryngeal tone. They may be nasals, plosives, fricatives, or semivowels. Since numerous articulation problems arise from both similarity in sound and similarity in position, these last two methods of classification may help you to understand your articulation problems.

PHONETICS AS A TOOL FOR IMPROVING ARTICULATION

Ear Training

We have chosen to use the phonetic system of representing sounds primarily because we believe its use to be the best method of making an intensive study of articulation problems. In addition to its great accuracy as a method of representing sounds, the phonetic method makes thorough and precise ear training possible. We have already pointed out that your present method of speaking is a result of imitation of the speech you have heard around you. Now that your speech habits are relatively fixed, however, most of you have stopped listening. You actually do not hear any but the extreme deviations from your own pattern. There is no possibility of your improving your articulation until you again begin to listen to your own speech and compare it with what you want to achieve.

The first step in this process is to learn to recognize sounds in isolation. When you have familiarized yourself with all of the sounds which normally appear in American speech, you should listen to individual words as your instructor pronounces them to you. Some of these pronunciations will not be the ones you would expect from the spelling or even from the diacritical markings given for the word in the dictionary. Nevertheless, you should learn to recognize these deviations and to write them phonetically. When you can do this adequately, you are ready to write phrases, recording the assimilation pattern and changes in the pronunciation of unstressed syllables.

By the time you have mastered this technique, you should be hearing differences in the articulation pattern of people about you, and you should be conscious of the phonetic structure of your own speech. If you over-assimilate, or if you make too great changes in unstressed vowels, you should begin to hear it in your own speech. If you can make a phonographic recording of your speech, you will speed the process of self-analysis.

Modification of the Articulation Pattern

When you are able to hear your own speech and record it phonetically, you are ready to begin any reconstruction which may be needed. By analyzing the phonetic record of your speech, you can discover where clarity is lacking, where vowel or consonant sounds are distorted, and where greater (or in a few cases, less) precision would give it greater force or emphasis. Moreover, by comparing the way in which you produce connected sounds with the phonetic transcript of another voice whose articulation pattern is unmistakably better than your own, you can make a further study of your own problems.

A knowledge of phonetics may thus aid you to improve your speech in two ways. It will serve as a tool for training your ear to hear your own speech and that of people about you. It will furnish a method for objective study of your own speech in relation to the speech of others.

Specialized Uses of Phonetics

If you plan to go on the stage, you will find a knowledge of phonetics an invaluable tool in helping you to master special dialects you may wish to use. Moreover, your ear will be more acute; you will detect differences more readily, and know what adjustments must be made to produce the special sounds called for in the speech you seek to learn.

Teachers can use phonetics as a method of analyzing the sound deficiencies of school children, and in many cases can help students to make the modification they need. Those who make speech correction a career, of course, need a knowledge of phonetics more extensive than we present here.

SUMMARY

Articulation, to be effective, must be clear without being pedantic. The most effective standard for you to choose is that of the educated people of the broad dialect area in which you live. Purely local peculiarities should be eliminated. The preciseness of your articulation may vary with your purpose in speaking and the occasion on which you speak.

Phonetic symbols are valuable tools for improving your articulation, since they are the most accurate means of representing pronunciation. By means of phonetics you can listen to speech analytically. Modification of your present pattern of articulation will occur only when you can hear and analyze deficiencies in your present mode of speaking.

Exercises

LISTENING AND SELF-ANALYSIS

1. Listen carefully to the members of your class. Do all of them speak the same dialect? What differences do you hear? Discover the sectional origin of those whose dialects differ from your own.

2. Do other members of the class speak distinctly at all times? Are some of their sounds omitted or so changed as to make the speech difficult to understand? Do any members of the class fail to blend words, particularly in reading aloud? What effect does this have on the meaning communicated?

3. Listen to the record which you made at the beginning of the course. Is your speech similar to that of other members of the class? Is your articulation clear and easy to understand? Is it overprecise? Do you separate words in reading, where the meaning does not require it? Do you run some words or syllables together, slighting the unaccented parts?

EXERCISES IN THE USE OF THE DICTIONARY

1. Read the sections at the beginning of Webster's Collegiate Dictionary entitled, "A Guide to Pronunciation." As you read Chapters 9 and 10 in this book, compare the Webster guide with the comments on phonetics given in the chapter. Raise questions with the instructor based on your observations.

2. Compare the pronunciation key in Webster's Collegiate Dictionary with that in Harper's American College Dictionary. What differences do you note?

9

The Vowel Sounds in Speech

A visiting lecturer in one of your classes speaks in a sharp, staccato, and monotonous voice. You can understand what he is saying, but his speech disturbs you. Each sound seems to be produced as though it were a bullet from a machine gun. The voice is strident, and the rhythm is so jerky that you are distracted in taking notes on his lecture. The thing which disturbs you in listening to this speaker is the way in which he produces the sounds of the language, especially the vowel sounds.

For all of the vowels, the tone flows relatively freely through the open mouth; hence, changes in duration, loudness, pitch, and quality are more apparent to the listener in the vowel sounds than on the consonants. For the most part, the consonants appear to stop and start the vowels. The vowels give the greatest evidence of your abilities in the use of the vocal skills. In this chapter, notice how the formation of the vowels involves the basic processes of voice production: breathing, phonation, and resonation.

PRINCIPLES OF VOWEL PRODUCTION

In the establishment of standards for acceptable vowel production, you must remember that vowel sounds are unstable, both in their method of articulation and in their acoustic effect. You will be given a description of each vowel as it occurs in isolation. In spoken language, if the vowel is in an emphasized word it will be similar in production to its description in isolation. However, if the vowel occurs in an unstressed word, it may be altered or a different vowel may be used for it. A detailed discussion of the effects of accent and stress on vowel sounds will follow the description of the vowels.

It is well to remember, also, that there is nothing static about the formation of the vowels in connected speech. When you talk, your thoughts are formulated into word groups, or phrases. As each phrase is spoken, the articulatory mechanism moves continuously from the beginning of the phrase to the pause which precedes the next phrase. No sooner is the position for the vowel assumed, than the lips, tongue, and lower jaw move into the position for the next sound. The static description of the vowel, therefore, tends to be misleading.

Any rules, then, which are set down for acceptable vowel production must be flexible. With this in mind, the following suggestions for vowel production are offered.

The vowels must possess:

1. sufficient accuracy to be readily understood;
2. freedom from exaggerated, pedantic production;
3. enough openness for good resonance;
4. sufficient duration, when the vowel is stressed, to allow the changes in pitch, loudness, and quality to be readily discerned;
5. enough unstressing or short production, when the vowel *should* be unstressed, to contribute to an acceptable rhythm pattern for speech.

THE PHONETIC TRANSCRIPTION OF VOWELS

In the preceding chapter, we pointed out that the use of phonetic symbols makes it possible to represent the flow of sounds in any speaking situation. A phonetic symbol represents a group of closely related sounds produced in approximately the same way and having the same acoustic properties for the average ear. The same sound may be articulated in slightly different ways by different persons or in different ways by the same person when it is in different sound combinations. We hear the same sound, EE, as the vowel in the words *bean, seat,* and *tee;* yet the articulatory adjustments for each of the three EE's is slightly different because of the sounds coming before and after each. However, so long as we hear it as one sound in all of these different situations, we consider it to be that sound no matter how it is articulated. As you gain experience in listening to sounds, you will come to recognize slight variations which are the results of positional differences in the articulation of the sound. As long as the different sounds have the same acoustic properties, we consider them to be the same sound and use one phonetic symbol to indicate all of them.

You will learn the phonetic system for vowels more quickly if you will divorce it completely from alphabetic or spelling symbols with which you are familiar. While many of the phonetic symbols are exactly the same as their alphabetic counterparts, they no longer stand for spelled letters, but for sounds alone. Identify them not by giving their alphabetic name, but by pronouncing the sound which they represent. The symbol [u], for example, is not the letter which you pronounce *you*, but a sound. Remember, also, that there are no "silent letters" in phonetics such as frequently occur in spelling. Finally, recall that a symbol stands for one sound and one sound only; it cannot, like a spelling symbol, represent different sounds in different words.

As you study each new symbol, complete a three-way association pattern. Learn the appearance of the symbol; listen as the sound is pronounced by the instructor; produce the sound yourself and observe the articulatory adjustments you make to form it. Now use the sound in connected speech and listen to it. Listen also to other members of your class and to your family and friends, and compare your production of the sound with theirs.

THE MECHANISM FOR THE ARTICULATION OF VOWELS

Like all other phases of the speech process, good vowel articulation involves effective muscle control. The articulators which must be controlled are shown in Figure 12. As differences in the size and shape of the oral and pharyngeal cavities and of the lip opening from the oral cavity determine the vowel produced, the movable articulators which regulate these conditions are the ones which we must consider. These parts are: the walls of the pharynx, the velum, the tongue, the lower jaw, and the lips.

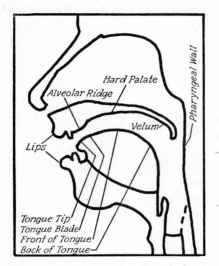

Fig. 12. Diagram showing the articulators in the oral cavity

By far the most active and flexible of these articulators is the tongue. Its complex system of muscles enables it to change its shape and position in the oral cavity in many ways; because of this, it is the most influential factor in determining vowel formation.

In discussing its function in the articulation of vowels, we shall refer to the flexible tip; to the blade, or broad flat part immediately behind the tip; to the front, where the thickest part of the tongue begins; and to the back, where the surface of the tongue curves downward into the pharynx. These parts are shown in Figure 12.

In your own mechanism, locate as many of the vowel articulators as you can. Experiment with the varied movement of which each is capable. When their positions and movements are described in the analysis of a vowel, you will thus be able to duplicate those positions and movements.

THE FORMATION OF VOWELS

In order to produce a vowel, the following four conditions must be present:

1. the vocal folds must be in vibration so that the sound is voiced;

2. the velum must be raised so that the opening into the nasal cavity is closed and the breath stream is directed through the oral cavity;

3. the mouth must be open, with the tongue tip behind the lower front teeth, so that there is a relatively open passageway from the level of the vocal folds through the lips;

4. the movements of the lower jaw, the tongue, and the lips must vary the size, shape, and opening of the oral cavity for each sound.

As you watch in a mirror, form the sound EE as in the word m*e*, then the OO in m*oo*n, and finally the AH in f*a*ther. Notice the differences in mouth opening for each of the three sounds, as suggested in the diagrams in Figure 13. Try them again, and feel the differences in tongue positions as you move from sound to sound. The number of different jaw, lip, and tongue positions and combinations of positions for the production of the vowels is

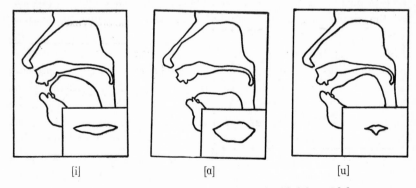

[i]   [ɑ]   [u]

Fig. 13. The positions of the articulators for [i], [ɑ], *and* [u]

infinite. As the positions and tensions of these three parts vary, coupled
with the movements of the walls of the pharynx, the variety of vowels
which we have in General American speech is produced. Fifteen to seventeen
of them are in common American usage. However, as vowels are influenced
in production by the sounds which precede and follow them in connected
speech, there is, in reality, an infinite series based on the slight differences
in the positions of the structures.

The relative instability of the vowels makes it extremely difficult to
classify them accurately into any systematic scheme. They can be distinguished by such differentiating features as the relative openness or close-
ness of the mouth passage and opening, the roundness or spread of the lips,
the general tension or laxness of the functioning muscles, and the length
or shortness of duration of the sound. However, the most satisfactory
scheme of classification for our purposes is that of relative tongue position
in the production of the sound.

In this system, the high point of the tongue in the mouth is used to place
the vowel in relation to the other vowels. Thus, if you will repeat the EE
and AH sounds, and notice the position of the tongue for each, you will find
that the tongue comes much closer to the hard palate for EE than it does for
AH; EE, therefore, is a higher vowel than AH is. While this is a convenient
classification into which all vowels can be fitted, it is only a relative one,
with wide possible individual variation in tongue position for the production of any sound. It must be remembered that in the last analysis the
ear is the judge of the accuracy of the sound, no matter how it is produced.
If you find that you do not produce a vowel with the tongue in the exact
position indicated on the chart, and yet the vowel sounds correct, then do
not worry about the accuracy of your tongue placement. At best, the
position on the chart is relative and indicates approximately the position
for the production of the family of sounds, the phoneme, of that
vowel.

In Figure 14, the commonly used American vowels are arranged according
to the high point of the tongue. The left-hand side of the chart represents
the front of the mouth and the right-hand side the back of it; the top of
the chart represents the hard palate and the bottom the flat surface of the
tongue. As has been suggested, the positions indicated are relative and not
absolute ones. The variations in tongue position from one vowel to another
are relatively slight; they are not actually so broad as they may seem to be
on the diagram. The phonetic symbol and a key word are given for each
sound.

Repeat the key word for each vowel several times, then isolate the vowel and repeat it a number of times until you are sure that you hear it accurately. Try to feel the adjustment of the tongue, jaw, and lips which you make for that sound. After you have tried each sound by itself, try the front vowels and the back vowels in series. As you repeat the front vowels from [i] through [a], notice how the tongue drops as you descend from vowel to vowel; how the jaw moves down for each sound; how the opening for the breath stream becomes larger; how the lips, as the jaw moves down, change from a horizontal spread to a relaxed, open position; and how there is a general relaxation of tension.

Say the back vowels beginning with [u] and moving down to [ɒ]. See again how the tongue drops from sound to sound; how the jaw descends; how the mouth opening becomes larger; how the position of the lips changes from a close rounding to an open position; and how there is greater relaxation. Try the front vowel [i] and then move directly to the back one [u]. Note how the high point of the tongue moves from the front to the back of the mouth as you say these sounds. It is the front of the tongue which rises for the front vowels and the back for the back vowels, not the tip or the blade. (See Figure 12.) If you have difficulty isolating any individual sound, run through the series from top to bottom; from the vowel next above the difficult one, drop the tongue slightly, relax slightly, drop the jaw a little, and increase the size of the mouth opening.

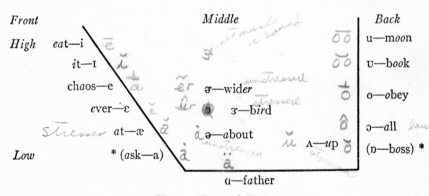

Fig. 14. The vowel diagram

* The sounds [a] and [ɒ] are relatively uncommon in General American speech. Many of you may have difficulty hearing and producing them. However, they are common enough to warrant inclusion in this chart and in the later descriptions.

The middle vowels may be harder for you to duplicate accurately than those produced at the front and back, as the middle ones are less stable in terms of tongue position. Try each of them, and notice that if there is any upward movement of the tongue it is in the middle of the oral cavity. Start with the [ɑ] and move on up through the other sounds to feel this slight movement of the tongue. The [ə] is called the neutral vowel, as the tongue, jaw, and lips are in their most relaxed positions, with the middle of the tongue raised slightly. Try moving from a high front vowel to a middle one; feel how the tongue moves and where its high point is for each. The descriptions of the individual sounds will help you to fix the sound and produce it in various word combinations.

In the following section each vowel is described in detail and examples are given for all of the common combinations of the vowel in American speech. Study the description, produce the vowel in isolation, and notice your production of it in each of the examples. How does your production compare with that indicated? Listen to the sound as others produce it in the example words.

Front Vowels

[i] as in *eat* ē Highest frequency

You raise the front of your tongue high, almost to the hard palate; your jaw is nearly closed, and your lips are spread to a narrow opening; the vocal folds vibrate, and the air is emitted through the mouth. (Since the vocal folds vibrate and the air is emitted through the mouth on all vowels, that feature of production will be omitted from future descriptions.) This sound is usually long, but length varies, depending upon the stress placed on the word or syllable in which it appears. You should avoid undue tension, which will distort production. Care should be used so that there is neither an on-glide nor an off-glide, with [mi] becoming [mɪi] or [miɪ]. Some persons with a Yiddish or south European language background may incorrectly substitute [ɪ] for [i] so that *heat* becomes *hit.*

w*e*	r*ea*p	rec*ei*ve
f*ee*t	bel*ie*ve	mach*i*ne

[ɪ] as in *i*t ĭ

The front of your tongue moves slightly lower and farther back and is more relaxed than it was for [i]; your jaw descends a little, and the lips are less spread. This is a short vowel. This sound is sometimes confused with [i], particularly by persons with a romance-language background, so that *hit* resembles *heat* and *lip* resembles *leap*. You should avoid any drawl which will tend to make the sound a diphthong and change it to [ɪə] as in [ɪət].

s*i*t	b*u*sy	w*o*men
s*y*mbol	v*i*llage	

[e] as in ch*a*os

Your tongue continues to move down and slightly back for this sound; your lips are more relaxed and the jaw is lower than for the previous sound. In other positions, usage varies with the length of the syllable, the emphasis on the syllable, and the association with the sounds which follow it. When [e] is in the final position, the jaw rises slightly as the sound is being produced, and it becomes the diphthong [eɪ] (see page 161 for the diphthong [eɪ]). Try the words listed below. Does your tongue remain stationary in sounding the vowel or does it move in a glide? If there is a slight gliding movement, you are using the diphthong [eɪ] and not the vowel [e]. A fault in production may be nasalization and stridency, especially when there are close nasal consonants as in *same*, *main*, or *name*. With this production, there is excessive tension in the tongue and throat and the velum is partially lowered.

r*a*ke	f*a*te	s*a*me
c*a*pe	d*a*te	

[ɛ] as in *e*ver

The front of your tongue is considerably lower and slightly farther back than for [e]; your lower jaw has dropped, and the lips are more open. This is a short vowel. It is a relatively unstable vowel, and in certain combinations there is a tendency for various other sounds to take its place. In some provincial and careless speech, [ɪ] is frequently substituted for it in *men*, *pen*, *many*, *them*, *yes*, *chest*, and *forget;* it becomes [e] in *egg*, *hair*, *head*, *leg*, *care*, and *bed;* or [ɝ] in *very*, *where*, *merry*, and *America*. These substitutions are substandard General American speech. If you drop the front of your tongue, [æ] may occur as in the dialect variation often spelled "yaas." It, too, can become nasalized, as in *men*. When it is drawled, a diphthong will result with the addition of [ə].

m*e*t	l*e*cture	st*ea*dy
s*e*nd	g*e*t	Th*a*mes
m*a*ny		

[æ] as in *at* ă

You still have a slight elevation in the front of the tongue with a little retraction of it; your jaw moves down a degree as the lips open and tense slightly with some spread. This vowel is short. There is a decided tendency to nasalize this sound into a flat and disagreeable one when there is too great tension in the tongue and a lowering of the velum; this is especially true when it is near a nasal sound, as in *man, hang, damp, map, rang*, or *pan;* or near a plosive sound, [p], [b], [t], [d], [k], or [g], as in *gavel, happy, cat,* and so on. [ɛ], [ʌ], or [ɪ] may be incorrectly substituted for [æ], as in *gather, rather,* or *can.* Here, too, you must use care not to diphthongize the sound into [æə] in words like *had, hand,* or *man.*

cat	hang
man	gas

[a], the intermediate A ȧ

This is an unstable sound and probably does not occur in your speech. It is the sound frequently encountered in stage speech and in some forms of Eastern Seaboard speech in such words as *ask, chance,* and *bath.* However, in General American speech, [æ] is commonly used. For the [a] the front of your tongue will drop down and back slightly and your jaw will be more open than for [æ]. This sound is part way between [æ] and [ɑ]. In British and some American dialects, the [a] words are pronounced with [ɑ]. Contrariwise, in New England and some other sections of the country, the [a] is often substituted for [ɑ], as in *art, department, Harvard,* and *garden.*

dance	class	after
half	aunt	path

BACK VOWELS

[u] as in m*oo*n ōō

The back of your tongue will be tensed and raised nearly to the velum; your lips are rounded and tensed. [u] is generally a long vowel. The lips must be sufficiently rounded on this sound if proper resonance is to be achieved. If the sound is too relaxed, the incorrect [ʊ] may occur as in *room, roof, soon,* or *spoon.* Incorrect diphthongization can take place as [uə] in words like *school* and *pool.*

true	food	shoe
boot	you	rule
flew		

[ʊ] as in b*oo*k o͝o

You will relax the mechanism slightly from the position for [u] and drop the back of the tongue a bit; the jaw drops slightly, and your lip opening is larger. This is a short vowel. Foreigners often confuse [u] with [ʊ] and use a sound resembling [u] in such words as *foot* and *would*. If you unround the lips and shift the tongue toward the middle position, the [ʌ] will occur in *took, look, book, put,* and *pulpit.*

f*oo*t	c*ou*ld	g*oo*d
f*u*ll	b*u*tcher	p*u*t

[o] as in *o*bey ŏ

This sound bears the same relation to [ʊ] as [e] did to [ɪ]. Your tongue will drop slightly and will be less tense than for [ʊ]; your jaw drops, and the lips unround a little. This sound occurs only in the unaccented position. If it is accented, the lips, jaw, and tongue tend to move toward the position for [ʊ], and the diphthong [oʊ] is produced. Check your production of the sound in the words below to see whether it remains stable or is the diphthong. You must use care to keep the lips rounded for the sound. Some persons may relax this sound in the direction of [ʌ] or [ə].

h*o*tel	*o*mit	pr*o*trude
*o*pinion	*o*bedient	

[ɔ] as in *a*ll ɔ̆ *Strongest Sound*

For this sound, you drop the back of the tongue a bit and relax it slightly; your jaw drops a little, and the lips are less tense and are unrounded to an ellipse (they may also protrude). It is a long sound. Incorrectly, the off-glide [ɚ] is at times added to [ɔ] in words like *law, saw,* or *raw* and [ə] may be added to [ɔ] in a word like *water.* (The intrusive ʀ is discussed in detail on page 198.)

t*a*lk	b*ou*ght	l*au*d
cr*a*wl	c*a*ll	fr*au*ght
br*oa*d	g*o*ne	

[ɒ] *know, but leave out*

Like the [a], this is not in common use in General American speech. In British pronunciation, it is used consistently on o words, such as *fog, coffee, god, not, rob,* and *doctor.* For [ɒ], the back of your tongue drops from the [ɔ] position and relaxes a little; the jaw drops slightly, and your lip opening becomes wider and less rounded. The [ɒ] sound is part way between

[ɔ] and [ɑ]. American pronunciation of the o words is completely incon-
sistent; in a few areas the [ɒ] sound is used. In your pronunciation you will
probably use [ɔ] or [ɑ]. For example, how do you pronounce the vowels in
the phrase, "hot dog"?

*o*ffer	l*au*rel
l*o*ss	d*o*ll

MIDDLE VOWELS

[ɑ] as in f*a*ther

Your tongue is low and flat in the mouth, with little tension; the jaw
is lowered slightly from the position of rest, and the lips are unrounded
and wide open. This is the most open vowel sound, and it is long in duration.
The [ɑ] may sound very much like [ɔ] if the tongue is not dropped and
relaxed from the [ɔ] position. This sound takes on an unpleasant quality
if the tip of the tongue is raised. It is susceptible to nasalization when it is
near a nasal sound, as in *calm* or *bomb*. It may also be drawled, with the
addition of the off-glide [ə].

ps*a*l*m*	c*a*lm	sh*ah*
p*a*lm	*a*men	sp*a*
*a*lms		

[ʌ] as in *u*p " vocalized pause "

The middle of your tongue is raised slightly from the position for [ɑ],
and there is a bit more tension in it; your jaw rises a little, and the lips
remain about the same. This is a short vowel. *It never occurs in an unaccented
syllable.* There are many individual variations in tongue position within
the phoneme from person to person.

*u*s	c*o*me	tr*ou*ble
w*o*n	d*oe*s	n*o*thing

[ə] as in *a*bout

In general, for this sound, your tongue will be relaxed with the front
very slightly raised toward the hard palate; the jaw will be in a relaxed
position with the mouth open. This vowel is the unaccented substitute for
most other vowels, and *can occur only in a wholly unaccented syllable or in
an unstressed monosyllable.* It is extremely unstable in production and, while
the high point of the tongue will be in the central area, the exact placement

will vary widely depending upon the stressed vowel for which it is substituted and the sounds surrounding it. The [ə], known as the *schwa* vowel, is in reality a phoneme which contains a number of sounds, all varying slightly in position and sound from one another.

In spelling, the sound can be represented by any vowel symbol, as it is the unstressed form of any vowel sound. When a vowel loses its stress, it may actually lose its identity. For instance, note the difference in the initial sounds in the two words, *able* and *ability*. Although the first sound in *ability* was once the same as that in *able*, the unstressing of the first syllable of *ability* gives an unaccented vowel which can no longer be identified as [eɪ]. If the sound is produced in isolation, it becomes [ʌ], because that happens to be the accented sound near the neutral position; however, the schwa is not merely the unstressed form of [ʌ]. The sound is always short.

telephone	cap*a*ble	comp*a*ny
sof*a*	fam*ou*s	rec*o*gnize
excel*l*ent	evid*e*nce	from here
*a*maze	the boy *a*nd girl	know *o*f him

It is difficult to give clear example words for this sound, as the stress patterns from section to section of the country and from person to person vary so greatly that the sound commonly may be stressed in one area or by one person and unstressed in another area or by another person. Try the following list of words aloud to see whether or not you use the [ə] for any of the vowels. Usage in these words varies widely.

ide*a*	sever*a*l	dist*a*nce
*a*wake	*a*ccount	progr*a*m
hous*e*s	breakf*a*st	diff*i*cult
garl*a*nd	welc*o*me	Apr*i*l
c*o*nnect	*a*lone	terr*i*ble
want*e*d	s*u*ppose	*a*ttention

[ɜ] as in b*ir*d

The front of your tongue will be higher than the back; the tip and blade will be raised from the front of the mouth and curled slightly backward toward the roof of the mouth, without actual contact of the tip with the palate; the jaw is lowered, and the lips are open as for [ə], but there is slightly more tension than for the schwa. This is the vowel used by those persons who do not "drop their ʀ's." The tongue takes the same general

Phoneme — a family of sounds — any sound you recognize as the same one you know —

position as for the consonant R, but instead of gliding from that position to a vowel, holds it, with the resulting "R-colored" vowel sound. *The sound is used only in stressed positions* and is the vocalized form of the spelling forms *-er, -ir, -ear, -our, -or, -ur,* and *-yr.* It varies greatly in position and sound with the section of the country and the speech habits of the individual. You must be careful not to curl the tongue excessively, nor to have too great tension, nor to prolong the [ɝ] unnecessarily. The example words for [ɝ] are listed under [ɜ], the following sound.

[ɜ]

This is the middle vowel used by those who do "drop their R's." It is in common use in parts of New England, New York City, and the South, and in British speech, but not in General American speech. For the [ɜ], the tongue will be in the same general position as for [ɝ], but the tip is held behind the lower front teeth; the jaw and the lips are also in the same general position as for [ɝ]. [ɜ] *occurs only in an accented position and never before another vowel in the same syllable.* It represents the same spelling combinations as does the [ɝ]. If you have difficulty producing the [ɜ], say the sound [ɝ]; then repeat it, holding the tongue tip behind the lower front teeth; the resulting sound will approximate [ɜ]. In an unstressed position, this sound becomes [ə]. In some dialects in the area in and around New York City, [ɜ] is diphthongized into [ɜɪ] or [ʊɪ]; these productions are unacceptable. The comic-strip version [ɔɪ] is sometimes heard, but less commonly than the other two diphthongized forms. Discover which of the two sounds, [ɝ] or [ɜ], you habitually use in the following words.

w*or*d	j*our*ney	m*ur*der
h*ear*d	w*or*ld	m*yrrh*
g*ir*l	att*or*ney	f*ur*
f*er*n	c*olo*nel	

[ɚ] as in weath*er*

Your tongue, lips, and jaw are in the same general position as for [ɝ], but the sound is shorter and more relaxed. This is the unaccented version of [ɝ] and *occurs only in unaccented syllables and unstressed* monosyllables. It is spelled with more than one letter but is a single sound. You must be careful to keep the sound unstressed and neither prolong it nor give it any prominence. Speakers who use the [ɜ] will substitute the [ə] for the [ɚ].

teach*er*	murd*er*	b*ur*lesque

FORMATION OF DIPHTHONGS

A diphthong is a continuous gliding sound in which the articulators move from the position of one vowel to that of another. The sound [ou], in the word *go*, is a combination of the sounds [o] and [ʊ] blended together in a continuous glide so that neither the [o] nor the [ʊ] is a distinct, separate sound. The tongue, jaw, and lips take the position for the [o] and then, as it is sounded, move to the position for the [ʊ] without any cessation of sound. The energy is greatest on the [o] and gradually diminishes as the glide continues to the end of the [ʊ]. The impression then is not of two separate sounds, but of one continuous one. Try the diphthong [ou] in *go*. Say it slowly, prolonging the sound. Feel the movement of the tongue and the lips as they go from the [o] position to that of [ʊ].

Of the five alphabet letters which we have previously been taught to call the "five vowels," four are not pure vowels but diphthongs. Only for the E does the articulatory adjustment remain relatively steady during the production. For A, I, O, and U, a glide activity takes place between two vowel or vowellike sounds, so that the articulatory mechanism moves from one position to another with no cessation of voice; a diphthong results.

There are five main diphthongs. In addition, eight other combinations of various vowels with the unstressed [ɚ] may be classified with the diphthongs, as they have a similar gliding movement in them. All of these are

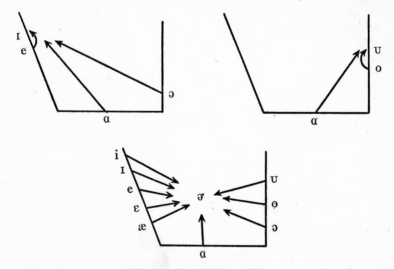

Fig. 15. The diphthong glides

receding diphthongs, that is, combinations of two vowels in which the first sound is stressed and the second unstressed. Thus, the first vowel in each receives stress; as the glide recedes into position for the second, that vowel is much less loud and much less definite in formation.

Figure 15 shows the relationship of the elements in the various diphthongs. The beginning of the glide is indicated by the tail of the arrow; the head points to the final position.

Observation and Listening

Experiment with the production of each of the diphthongs as you did with each of the vowels. Try the sound in isolation; notice the movement as you go from one element to the other. Try the example words, listen for your production, and listen to the way your friends produce them. Descriptions are not given for the diphthongs, as they are made up of vowel sounds which have already been described in detail.

Full Diphthongs

The two vowel elements comprising the full diphthong are so blended together into the glide that both sounds are obscured and become a new sound, called a diphthong.

[aɪ] or [ɑɪ] as in t*i*me

Your tongue starts in the [a] or [ɑ] position and glides to the [ɪ] at the end of the sound. The first element of this sound is sometimes heard as [ɒ] or [ɔ], but these productions are provincialisms to be avoided. When [aɪ] or [ɑɪ] is nasalized in words like *my*, *mine*, or *nine* it is frequently drawled, with unpleasant results. Relative overstress on either of the elements will result in improper production. If there is too much stress on the first element, the second will disappear or become [ə]; this is common in rapid speech and is readily recognizable in Southern speech. Overstress on the second element will result in a syllable division between the elements in the sound, with [i] replacing the [ɪ].

fl*y*	p*ie*	*eye*
ch*i*ld	*ai*sle	ge*y*ser
h*ei*ght	b*uy*	

[ɔɪ] as in b*oy*

You start this sound from the position for [ɔ] and glide to the [ɪ] position. Dialect variations to be avoided include the substitution of [aɪ] or [ɜ] for [ɔɪ] in words like *boil* or *hoist* and *oil* or *joint*. The final element may occur as [i] when the glide goes beyond the position for [ɪ].

h*oi*st	*oi*l	t*oy*
l*oy*al	n*oi*se	v*oi*ce

[ɑʊ] as in s*ou*nd   *most commonly distorted*   *O U (webster)*

Your organs of articulation begin this sound from the position for [ɑ] and glide to the adjustment for [ʊ]. The first element may be properly produced as [ɑ] and improperly given as [æ] or [ɛ]. The latter two substitutions are often nasalized when a nasal sound precedes or follows them. In some cases, a triphthongal production is heard in substandard speech, beginning with [ɛ] or even [ə]. There is a tendency for some speakers to substitute the tense [u] for the more lax [ʊ]. A distorted form of the diphthong heard occasionally uses [æ] and [u].

n*ow*	m*ou*th	l*ou*d
cr*ow*d	d*ou*bt	f*ou*nd

Partial Diphthongs

In partial diphthongs, the glide movement does not begin until a distinct vowel is first heard, followed by a more or less indistinct off-glide or finish.   *Partials* This contrasts with the less definite first element in the full diphthongs and their more distinct off-glide. Frequently, in American speech, these sounds are not diphthongs but vowels, using only the first element of the diphthong. You should analyze your own production of the example words for these two sounds to determine whether you use the diphthong or the vowel when you say them.

[eɪ] as in d*ay*   *deɪ (day)*

The front of your tongue starts in the [e] position and makes an off-glide toward the position for [ɪ]. As the last element of this sound is unstable, it varies greatly from person to person and for the same person from word to word; it may be entirely missing or become [i]. Notice the difference in the sound in the words *cake* and *play*.

gr*ay*	g*a*te	br*ea*k
v*ei*l	f*ai*l	*a*pron

[oʊ] as in g*o*   *O*

Your articulatory position is for the [o] and then assumes the off-glide [ʊ]. Although in General American speech, in accented syllables the sound is rarely produced without some diphthongization, there are many instances where persons use the [o] alone. [u] is an occasional substitute for the final element.

kn*ow*	n*o*te	*oh*
b*oa*t	s*ew*	g*oe*s
d*ou*gh	b*eau*	

Centering Diphthongs

In American speech, there is a group of diphthongs which end in the central position; they are single sounds, although spelled with two letters. In parts of the East and South they end in [ə], and in General American speech in [ɚ]. The final off-glide is unstable, and the exact position of the articulatory organs for it is largely determined by the first part of the diphthong. These diphthongs can be made up of any vowel and the central [ɚ]. They are given here in the General American form.

The most common of the centering diphthongs are:

[ɪɚ] as in *ear*

h*e*re	f*ea*r	w*ei*rd
d*ee*r	f*ie*rce	t*ea*r

[ɛɚ] as in *air*

b*ea*r	p*ai*r	th*e*re
c*a*re	w*ea*r	h*ei*r

[ɑɚ] as in st*ar*

s*e*rgeant	sm*a*rt	st*a*rve

[ɔɚ] or [oɚ] as in *ore*

The use of [ɔɚ] or [oɚ] will depend upon the section of the country or the person speaking. Check your pronunciation of the words listed below to determine whether you use [ɔ] or [o].

d*oor*	c*oa*rse	fl*oor*
c*o*re	t*o*re	*or*

[ʊɚ] as in p*oor*

s*u*re	t*ou*r	m*oor*

A group of rare centering diphthongs which occur infrequently include:

[iɚ] as in w*e're*
[eɚ] as in th*ey're*

Centering Triphthongs

Centering triphthongs are sounds in which a noncentering diphthong ends in an off-glide, either on [ə] or on [ɚ]; in General American speech, the off-glide is [ɚ]. Care must be used in listening for these sounds to be sure that the three sounds occur in one syllable so that a triphthong results. In such words as *fire* and *flour*, the final [ɚ] sound is sometimes pronounced as a separate syllable, resulting in a diphthong plus a vowel, not a triphthong. Check your pronunciation of the example words.

h*ou*r	s*ou*r
h*ire*	m*ayo*r

Exercises

1. Again make use of the recording of your voice. Listen to the way in which you produce the vowel sounds. Are they all clear and correct and still blended into connected speech? Are there any faults present which have been discussed under the various vowel sounds? Transcribe the first fifteen vowel sounds in the recording into phonetic symbols.

2. Write out the vowels in the following sentences phonetically as you *think* you would say them. Then record the sentences and transcribe the vowels phonetically as you actually *do* say them. If it is not possible to record the sentences, have a friend read them to you and transcribe the vowels as he reads. Are there differences between the way you thought you would produce the vowels and the way in which you actually did? What alterations took place in the vowels? Can you explain why they happened?

   a. I must get this paper written tonight.
   b. Do you know where he keeps his books?
   c. Let's see that new movie at the Rex tonight.
   d. It has been three weeks now since I had a letter from him.
   e. There are a lot of reasons for taking a speech course.
   f. The dance is not going to start until after ten.
   g. The assignment for tomorrow will cover chapters nine and eleven.
   h. If you follow the road to the right you will get there.
   i. Several of my friends have television sets in their homes.
   j. I'm really hungry and could surely use a sandwich right now.
   k. Every time I try to pronounce that word I seem to get stuck.
   l. Prices seem to go up, up, and up all of the time.
   m. He changed his major three times in the past year.
   n. Form each sound with care and you will offend no one.
   o. Well, I'm glad that we are through with that part of the book.

THE EFFECTS OF ACCENT AND EMPHASIS
UPON VOWEL SOUNDS

As you listened to your recording, you probably often noticed that two vowels which would have been alike, had they both been in emphasized words, differed materially when one vowel was stressed and the other unstressed. You found that vowels pronounced in isolation were not exactly like those in subordinated words within the running context of speech. Accent and emphasis can effect changes in the articulation of vowels and diphthongs.

When you wish a word to stand out in logical explanation or in emotional expression, you produce it with greater force of utterance and make it longer in duration than the surrounding words. The less meaningful words will then be weakened. Shortness of duration and greater relaxation in the production of the unstressed forms change the articulation of the vowels and sometimes of the consonants in such unstressed forms.

In addition to the sense stress for logical meaning and for emotional expression, the accenting of syllables in the pronunciation of polysyllabic words contributes to the complex stress patterns within the phrases; in turn, it effects changes in the articulation of unaccented syllables within words.

There are two main types of stress: emphasis for meaning and accent for pronunciation. The latter should be examined first. It is more easily recognized, since the changes in articulation of vowels caused by accent are the somewhat consistent product of common usage.

Accent

The accented syllable receives greater distinctness of articulation, greater force, and longer duration than the unaccented. In words of several syllables, there may be a primary and a secondary accent, with the primary receiving greater energy of production. Examples are: *explana'tion* and *distribu'tion.* In our oral language, a strong tendency toward alternate stress contributes to the rhythm of speech.

The vowel in the unaccented syllable, since it is made in a more relaxed manner than if it were in isolation, may become [ɪ], [ə], or [ɚ]. Vowels which were originally the high front [i] in an accented position are more likely to become [ɪ] than [ə] when unaccented.

Notice how a shift in accent in the following paired words changes the production of the vowel when it is unaccented.

analyze	analysis	consultation	consult
application	apply	compact	compáct
comparable	compare	cóntent	contént
declaim	declamation	óbject	objéct
install	installation	pérfect	perféct
drama	dramatic	réfuse	refúse

The prefixes *re-*, *be-*, *de-*, and *pre-* are pronounced [rɪ], [bɪ], [dɪ], and [prɪ] when the premium is placed upon clarity, and [rə], [bə], [də], and [prə] in casual conversation. The ending *-ed* is pronounced [ɪd] by some and [əd] by others in such words as *wanted* and *added*. Endings such as *-ment*, *-ence*, and *-tion* often use the schwa. Listen to the italicized words as the following phrases are spoken and note the vowels in the unaccented syllables.

1. I *receive* . . .
2. He *believed* . . .
3. We *preserved* . . .
4. What *relation* . . .
5. The *attempt* . . .
6. *Pronounce* this . . .
7. *Deliver* this . . .
8. He *becomes* . . .
9. The *interchange* . . .
10. My *interpretation* . . .
11. The *movement* . . .
12. This *evidence* . . .

If the single unaccented syllable is so far weakened that the sounds do not carry or are actually omitted, the listener will have difficulty in understanding what is said. Such speech is called *careless*. When you speak with exceptional rapidity, whole syllables actually seem to be dropped; their energy of production is so weak that they do not carry.

As you listen to another student read the following passage, decide whether he produces the unaccented syllables with too pedantic exactness, whether he weakens them so much that they do not carry, or whether his pronunciation is easily understood.

A little twist to an idea need not rely upon clever wording. We are not all geniuses of the mingled metaphor or the artful analogy. Consider the man who thoughtfully contemplates the lady at the social gathering and murmurs nostalgically, "She must have been beautiful in her younger days." I have a notion that his wife might turn that about in another way. If one dwells with some extra length on *younger*, or mouths over *beautiful*, or comes out with a little uncertainty on *must*, one can do wonders in adding flounces, bows, and ribbons to such a statement or in blending in a corroding acid that will work on the memory at a later date. Of course, the raised eyebrow helps too, but that takes practice.—E. H.

Emphasis

After having listened to a student read the passage above, now criticize it in another way. Did he convey the meaning to you through proper emphasis? Did he give longer duration and greater energy of production to those words which carried the principal meaning? Was there a contrast in the production of these meaningful words and those which served only to connect the parts of the phrase?

To bring about this contrast in emphasis for meaning, the words which you subordinate are made with short duration and little energy, and are sometimes rather indefinite in muscle movement. These unstressed words will consist of weak forms. Just as in the production of unaccented syllables, these words frequently use the short [ɪ], [o], [ə], and [ɚ] as their vowels.

Read the same passage as if each word were of equal value. Have you heard some readers approach this style? Underline the words in each phrase which carry the greatest meaning; as you stress these, analyze what happens to the vowels in the unstressed words.

Here are further examples of changes in articulation of vowels caused by changes in emphasis for meaning. The following sentences will be read aloud to you with the italicized word first stressed and then subordinated and weakened as the word after it is emphasized. Can you write the vowels in the italicized words phonetically?

1. It *was* mine.
2. She *is* annoyed.
3. It *has* happened.
4. They *have* gone.
5. I heard *of* him.
6. He came *from* there.
7. Speak *to* him.
8. I saw *her* house.
9. Send it *for* him.
10. He *had* no choice.
11. It was *the* book.
12. I said, "*A* man."
13. He *and* I will go.
14. I know *his* mother.
15. Go *to* school.
16. She *can* play.

The schwa is used in many of these unstressed words. In some of them, such as *is* and *his*, a shortened [ɪ] is heard, almost as indefinite in formation as the schwa. The words *for* and *her* commonly become [fɚ] and [hɚ] when unstressed.

Here are a few examples of how strong forms are weakened when they are used in unstressed positions in the flow of speech.

[hæz, həz, əz, z]   [hæv, həv, əv, v]
[kæn, kən, kn, kŋ]   [æz, əz, z]
[wɪl, wl, əl, l]   [ðæn, ðən, ðn]
[ʃʊd, ʃəd, ʃd]   [kʊd, kəd, kd]
[ðɛm, ðəm, ðm]   [ɑɚ, ɚ]

In a formal situation where you wish to make the articulation very distinct and easily understood, you may find it advisable not to weaken the forms beyond those presented in the second column. In casual conversation, however, you are likely to use the more extreme, weakened forms. As long as you are readily understood, such usage is not in error.

CARELESS AND FAULTY PRODUCTION OF VOWELS

Careless articulation is usually caused by lack of effort, very rapid speech, or imitation of poor models. The production of vowels may seem faulty to a listener if the speaker happens to come from a different dialect area than his own. Those influences on voice described in Chapter 2 pertain also to articulation.

Vowel sounds may be distorted, omitted, or added in words where they do not belong. In distortion, the sound may be made in an exaggerated way, as when a foreigner says the [i] in *seem*, producing a tense sound with the front of the tongue raised too closely to the hard palate; or he may pronounce [u] with a great protrusion of the lips. Again, one vowel may be substituted for another which is similar. This is actually distortion of production, as in the following examples.

[it iz tru] *for* [ɪt ɪz]   (It is true.)
[aɪ sɔ ət] *for* [ɪt]   (I saw it.)
[haʊ mɪnɪ mɪn] *for* [mɛnɪ mɛn]   (How many men?)
[dɪd i gɪt ɪt] *for* [gɛt ɪt]   (Did he get it?)
[hɛz i gɔn] *for* [hæz]   (Has he gone?)
[ɛsk ɪm] *for* [æsk]   (Ask him.)
[maɪ kɔɚ] *for* [kɑɚ]   (My car)
[maɪ buk] *for* [bʊk]   (My book)

Vowels may be diphthongized, when a person adds a schwa after a "pure" vowel, as in these examples.

[ə bɛəd] *for* [bɛd]   (A bed)
[ə mæən] *for* [mæn]   (A man)
[aɪ fiə wɛəl] *for* [fil wɛl]   (I feel well.)
[maɪ haʊəs] *for* [haʊs]   (My house)
[gəoʊ] *for* [goʊ]   (Go)

The final half of the diphthong may be weakened, as is often true in Southern speech.

[haᵁ faᶦn] *for* [haʊ faɪn]   (How fine)
[ə laᵁd saᵁnd] *for* [laʊd saʊnd]   (A loud sound)
[ple] *for* [pleɪ]   (Play) *Not necessarily a fault.*

Vowels may be omitted when a "telescoped" version of a word is given, with one or more syllables slurred over.

[prɑbli] *for* [prɑbəbli]   (probably)
[kʌmpni] *for* [kʌmpəni]   (company)
[præps] *for* [pɚhæps]   (perhaps)

A vowel may be added where it does not belong, as in the following words.

[æθələtɪk] *for* [æθletɪk]   (athletic)
[tʊwɔɚd] *for* [tɔɚd]   (toward)
[ʌmbɚɛlə] *for* [ʌmbrɛlə]   (umbrella)

The distortion is, of course, the common fault. It is so common in casual conversation that it is scarcely noticed. If you carry slurred speech into a situation where your speech will be judged as uneducated or slovenly, then the careless speech can be damaging to your social and vocational future.

Listening and Analysis

If errors of carelessness are called to your attention, begin to list words and phrases in which they occur. Analyze what you do, the possible reasons for your errors, and begin to listen to and correct yourself in conversation. Practice the words in phrases with the correct vowel sounds; combine them into meaningful sentences. Listen to other speakers produce these sound combinations. Become a critical judge of others and of yourself.

The same suggestions hold true if you are of foreign-language background. Ask someone to criticize your production of single words, listen as he repeats them so that he may be a model for you, then reproduce what you have heard; use the words in meaningful contexts.

SUMMARY

Vowels give the greatest evidence of your use of the vocal skills involved in breathing, phonation, and resonation. Because they are unstable in their method of articulation and their acoustic effect, and because they are not static in formation, the rules for their production must be flexible. In spite of slight differences in formation, if a sound has the acoustic properties of a certain vowel, we consider it to be that vowel. The articulators with which we are concerned in vowel formation are: the walls of the pharynx, the velum, the tongue, the lower jaw, and the lips.

When you produce a vowel, the following conditions must be present: (1) the vocal folds must vibrate, (2) the velum must be raised against the back wall of the pharynx, (3) there must be a relatively open passageway from the vocal folds through the lips, and (4) the movements of the articulators must vary the size and shape of the oral cavity and its opening for each sound. The vowels in General American speech may be divided roughly into front, middle, and back, according to the highest point which the tongue reaches in producing the sound.

A diphthong is a continuous gliding sound in which the articulators move from the position for one vowel to that for another. There are five main diphthongs, three full and two partial, as well as a group of eight centering diphthongs ending in [ɚ].

Although the vowels and diphthongs have been presented as if they were static units produced in isolation, in the flow of actual speech they vary greatly according to the stress given them. There are two major types of stress: emphasis for meaning and accent for pronunciation. When you stress a syllable, you give it greater energy of production and make it longer than the surrounding sound units. The unemphasized words and unaccented syllables are weakened, that is, they become short and somewhat indefinite in formation. The vowels in these syllables change from the strong forms used in stressing; they usually become the short [ɪ], [o], [ə], and [ɚ] vowels.

This stressing and unstressing of syllables contributes to the rhythm of your speech. But even more important, it allows you to point out, by means of your vocal changes, the words which carry the main ideas and to sub-ordinate those which only connect the ideas.

In careless and faulty vowel production, the vowels may be distorted, diphthongized, omitted, or added where they do not belong. This distortion in casual conversation is often scarcely noticed. But if you wish to be clearly understood for professional or social reasons, you must produce the vowel sounds with clarity. You should be versatile enough to adjust your articulation to the demands of the immediate situation.

10

The Consonant Sounds in Speech

Frequently a student registers for a voice-training course because his speech has been criticized as difficult to understand. Someone has told him that he is slurring some of his sounds, particularly the consonants. The conclusion that poor consonant production is the major speech fault is often exaggerated by grade- and high-school teachers who belabor their pupils with pedantic drills and make learning dull by unnatural repetition of word lists.

Actually, such an approach separates a part from the whole. The faulty production of consonants must be examined as a dynamic aspect of the entire vocal process. If phonation and resonation are not effective, if muscle movements are cramped and awkward, if breathing cannot be controlled, improvement of articulation alone will not make you an acceptable speaker. Articulation is no more important than skilled timing, or interest-arousing melody, or pleasing quality. Yet while all of the aspects of speech share in producing the effect upon the listener, without accuracy of consonant production other skills may be wasted, for the speaker cannot be understood.

PRINCIPLES OF CONSONANT PRODUCTION

The adjective *clear* is often applied to good production of consonants, but this does not imply absolute uniformity of formation. Just as the vowels vary slightly from word to word and from person to person, the consonants, too, are influenced by neighboring sounds and by emphases in the running context of speech. There are, for instance, small differences in the way T is produced in *time, letter, sit, went,* and *just,* or in the unstressed word *to* and the emphasized *tell;* all of these, however, are recognizable as belonging to the T family, or phoneme.

171

In describing vowels, we have shown that these sounds are characterized by varying and somewhat indefinite degrees of openness of the mouth. To produce consonants, the breath stream is stopped momentarily at a particular place in the mouth, or made to flow through a narrow passageway, or diverted through the nose for nasal sounds. The positions for the articulation of consonants are therefore much more definite than those for vowels.

Consonants, therefore, even if they do vary slightly in oral context, must be clean cut in action, with quick and rather definite movements. Clarity, then, means accuracy in direction of muscle movement and in place of production, so that the consonant may be easily recognized. Smoothness of production of the whole meaningful phrase is achieved by the blending of these easily recognizable individual consonants and their accompanying vowels into a steadily moving pattern of sounds. Clarity and smoothness of articulation permit logical understanding of the language symbols.

Think of accuracy of production as a relative concept. Speech requires amazing agility in continuous muscle movement. Even as one sound is being produced, your mechanism is in the process of starting the next, so that the forward flow of sounds will not be broken. The articulation process involves dynamic movement rather than a series of static positions. The sounds must be clearly recognized by the listener, but pedantic accuracy must not interfere with a steady forward movement through the articulated phrase.

Before we describe the consonants, notice how blending of sounds for smoothness may be achieved:

1. If two consonants are similar in their place of production, the movements for both are made only once. For instance, as you say "had two," the tongue tip is raised once, and thus the words are blended together.

2. If the consonants sound alike, as for instance the nasal quality of M, N, and NG, or the frictional traits of F, S, and TH, no break occurs between them. In the phrase, "if some," the friction sound of the F continues into S.

3. When sounds spoken in sequence are made in different parts of the mouth, the mechanism starts the second even as the first is being formed. While you are making the B in *black*, the tongue tip starts up for the L.

4. When two sounds coming together are closely related in place of production but are acoustically quite different, one will change or be assimilated in favor of the other. For example, observe how the T is made with the tongue tip against the teeth when you say "at the."

After we have presented the individual consonants, we shall examine these four rules of blending and assimilation in greater detail.

THE PHONETIC TRANSCRIPTION OF CONSONANTS

In phonetics, as we have pointed out, each sound is represented by a single symbol. Such is not the case in written English. Since ours is not a phonetic language, we will need additional symbols for such consonant sounds as TH, SH, and NG. Notice also that the written letters X and Q are actually combinations of consonant sounds, while C is an ambiguous symbol. For most of the consonants, however, the alphabet letter identifies the spoken sound.

THE MECHANISM FOR THE ARTICULATION OF CONSONANTS

The parts of the articulatory mechanism have been shown in Figure 12. The movable parts for both vowel and consonant production are the jaw, lips, tongue, and velum. In producing consonants, the lips may move toward or away from each other; they can protrude or extend horizontally; or the lower lip may touch the upper teeth. The tongue can approach or touch the teeth, the alveolar ridge, the palate, or the velum. The velum can be raised against the back wall of the pharynx or lowered to permit an opening into the nasal cavity. All of these movements serve the primary purposes of chewing, sucking, and swallowing; we have learned to use them also to form the sounds of our language.

THE FORMATION OF CONSONANTS

Unlike the vowels, consonants may be either voiced or unvoiced. Many of them can be studied in pairs. The two sounds [k] and [g], for example, are articulated in the same way in the mouth, but for the voiceless [k] the vocal folds are at rest, while for the [g] the folds vibrate, and vocalization is heard. You can feel the difference between voiceless and voiced forms by placing the finger tips against the thyroid cartilage while you produce the paired sounds of [s] and [z]. (Do not say "ess" and "zee"; produce the consonant alone without the accompanying vowel.)

In the descriptions of the consonant sounds which follow, the first classification in each group is an acoustic one—a term which describes what the listener hears as *plosive, nasal,* and so on. The individual sounds are then described in terms of position of the articulators. In the accompanying consonant table (Figure 16), the vertical classification is the acoustic one; the horizontal organization is positional, following the articulatory positions from front to back.

Fig. 16. Consonant Chart *

	Bilabial	Labio-dental	Lingua-dental	Lingua-alveolar	Lingua-palatal	Lingua-velar	Glottal
Nasals	m			n		ŋ	
Plosives	p b			t d		k g	
Fricatives		f v	θ ð	s z	ʃ ʒ		h
Semivowels	w			l	r j		

handwritten annotations: "Two Lips" above Bilabial; "Tongue" above Lingua-dental; "Hard Palate" under Lingua-palatal; "Soft Palate" under Lingua-velar; "Mouth" at left margin

* Symbols at left of each column are voiceless; those at right are voiced.

NASAL CONSONANTS

All except three sounds in American speech are resonated and articulated primarily in the oral cavity, and the presence of noticeable nasality is regarded as a vocal fault. Three sounds, however, are primarily dependent upon nasal resonance. In the production of each of these sounds, the exit through the oral cavity is blocked in some manner, the velum is lowered, and the vocalized breath stream passes into the nasal cavity and out through the nares. All three sounds resemble vowels in that they are often given sustained tone and may stand alone in syllabic form as in *sudden* [sʌdn]. Aside from the position of the velum, the placement of the articulators for the three nasals [m], [n], and [ŋ] corresponds to the positions for the plosives [b], [d], and [g].

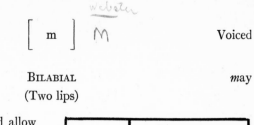

[**m**] M   Voiced

BILABIAL   *m*ay

(Two lips)

Close the lips lightly and allow the vocalized sound to come out through the nose. The teeth are slightly separated, and the tongue is in a relaxed position. Compare this position with that for [p] and [b] in the section dealing with plosives.

When the [m] appears in connected speech, the tongue assumes the position for the vowel which comes before or after the nasal sound.

Faulty production: excessive pressure so that the flow of speech is interrupted; denasalization when the nasal passageway is blocked either temporarily or by some chronic condition (if this occurs, a [b] is substituted); insufficient duration.

Common Combinations

*sm*all

fi*lm*, hu*mp*, fa*rm*

Tongue Gum ridge

LINGUA-ALVEOLAR

no

(Tongue tip, gum ridge)

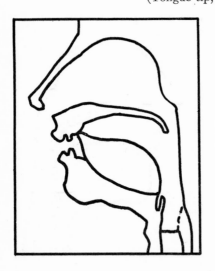

Raise the tip of the tongue to make contact with the alveolar ridge behind the upper front teeth; the sides of the tongue touch the inner edges of the teeth. Hold this oral closure, and allow the vocalized sound to pass out the nose. Compare this position with that for [t] and [d] in the section on plosives.

This sound is longer in duration when combined with vowels or with continuant consonants than when it is combined with plosives: mi*n*ing, da*n*ce, as compared to re*nt*.

Final [n] is often syllabic: butto*n*, sudd*en*, oft*en*.

Faulty production: denasalization when the nasal passageway is blocked ([d] is substituted); weak production in final position; substitution of [m] when the [n] occurs before or after [p], [b], or [m], as in ha*pp*en, gover*nm*ent.

Common Combinations

s*n*ow

re*n*t, la*n*d, tur*n*, o*n*ce, lu*nch*

[ŋ] *ng*ŋŋ Voiced

LINGUAVELAR ri*ng*
(Tongue back, soft palate)

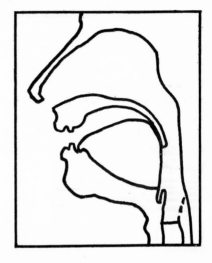

Raise the back part of the tongue so that a light contact is made with the soft palate; the air passageway through the mouth is thus closed. As you hold this closure, allow the vocalized breath to escape through the nose. The tongue tip remains behind the lower front teeth. The size of your mouth opening varies with the vowel which precedes the [ŋ]. Compare this position with that for [k] and [g] in the section on plosives.

When the suffixes *-ing* and *-er* are added to words ending in [ŋ], this sound usually maintains its identity and no [g] is added after it: si*ng*er, ri*ng*ing. (Stro*ng*er, lo*ng*er, and you*ng*er are typical exceptions to this rule.) Usage varies widely on other words in which NG, NK, or NC appear. Note the varying pronunciation on the following words: I*n*ca, i*n*come, a*ng*er, ba*n*k, to*ng*ue, ju*n*ction, li*ng*er, si*ng*le, ca*n*ker, co*n*crete, co*n*cord, co*ng*regation. In most words of this type, the [g] or [k] is pronounced, following an [ŋ], but prefixes ending in N tend to maintain the identity of the [n], particularly if the syllable is stressed. No [g] or [k] should be inserted between words, when the first word ends in [ŋ].

Faulty production: substitution of [n] in the *-ing* ending; denasalization when nasal passageway is blocked ([g] is substituted); insufficient duration; addition of [k] or [g], particularly if the sound which follows is a vowel: Lo*ng* Island [lɔŋg aɪlənd].

Common Combinations

stre*ngth*, belo*ng*ed, ra*nk*, a*ng*le

PLOSIVE CONSONANTS

As we have already noted, the articulatory positions for the production of plosive consonants correspond to those for the nasals, with the exception of the position of the soft palate. In the plosive group, the velum is raised and the entrance into the nasal cavity closed. Thus, instead of breath flowing continuously into the nasal cavity, pressure is built up behind the point of blockage at the lips, alveolar ridge, or velum. When the tongue is suddenly dropped, or the lips opened, the air pressure is released and a slight explosive sound is heard. This is most noticeable in the voiceless forms in the initial position of a stressed syllable. Here the explosion takes the form of a slight sound of escaping breath or aspiration before the succeeding vowel sound is heard. The voiced forms are not ordinarily aspirated, but the sudden release of pressure still produces the plosive effect from which the name of this group is derived.

Voiceless   [p *and* b]   Voiced

*p*ay   *Oral* BILABIAL   *b*ay
(Two lips)

Close the lips lightly. Your breath mounts up in pressure behind the lips and escapes explosively when the closure is released. Your lower jaw may also move down when the release occurs.

You can hear the slight aspirate explosion most readily when a vowel follows the initial [p] in a stressed syllable. The explosive phase is greatly modified or even eliminated when [p] is combined with another consonant, or in the final position. [b] is not ordinarily aspirated. If a nasal sound follows [p] or [b], the plosive phase is directed through the nasal passage: kee*p m*oving, o*bn*oxious.

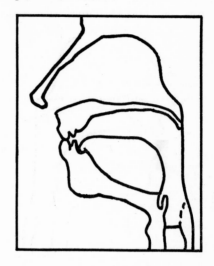

Faulty production: lower lip against edges of upper teeth; excessive pressure so that explosion calls attention to itself; pressure so light that a friction sound results.

Unvoicing in final position.

Common Combinations

*p*lace, *p*ride, *sp*end   *bl*ue, *br*ight
he*lp*, har*p*, ga*sp*, prom*pt*, lum*p*   bu*lb*, her*b*

Voiceless $\begin{bmatrix} \text{t} & \textit{and} & \text{d} \end{bmatrix}$ Voiced

*t*ime *d*ime

(Tongue tip, gum ridge)

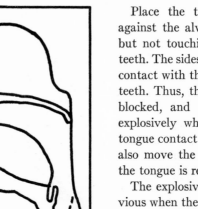

Place the tip of your tongue against the alveolar ridge, behind but not touching the upper front teeth. The sides of the tongue make contact with the inner edges of the teeth. Thus, the air passageway is blocked, and the breath escapes explosively when you release the tongue contact suddenly. You may also move the lower jaw down as the tongue is released.

The explosive phase is most obvious when the [t] or [d] is followed by a vowel. When a consonant follows or when [t] or [d] is final, the explosion is modified or even eliminated. If the succeeding sound is nasal, the explosion of breath escapes through the nose: ea*t n*o, ha*d m*ore. If the succeeding consonant is an L, the tongue tip remains up and the breath explodes around the sides of the tongue: li*ttl*e, can*dl*e. If the [t] or [d] is followed by TH, the tongue tip touches the inside of the upper teeth: wen*t th*is, ha*d th*at.

Faulty production: tongue tip pressing against inner and lower edges of the upper teeth (dental production); excessive pressure with too obvious explosion; pressure too light for the sound to be identified; omission in final position when in combination with other consonants: ju*s*t, ke*p*t, ol*d*, se*n*d.

Excessive explosion in medial position: en*t*er*t*ain, a*tt*ribu*t*ed; substitution of [d]: liber*t*y [lɪbɚdɪ]; substitution of glottal stop in medial position: bo*tt*le, bu*tt*er.

Unvoicing in final position: rente*d*, ol*d*.

Common Combinations

*t*ree, *tw*ice, *st*op	*dr*y, *dw*arf
hear*t*, we*p*t, we*n*t, we*s*t	la*n*d, ol*d*, ya*r*d
bo*tt*le	la*dl*e

$$\begin{bmatrix} \text{t} & and & \text{d} \\ & continued & \end{bmatrix}$$

In past tenses ending in *-ed*, the final sound is pronounced [t] if the sound before it is voiceless, [d] if the sound before it is voiced: ho*pp*ed, ro*bb*ed, wan*ted*.

Voiceless $$\begin{bmatrix} \text{k} & and & \text{g} \end{bmatrix}$$ Voiced

*c*ome

LINGUAVELAR

*g*o

*k*eep

(Tongue back, soft palate)

Raise the back part of the tongue so that a light contact is made with the velum. This shuts off the air passageway, and pressure is built up. The breath escapes explosively when you suddenly lower the tongue. The tongue tip remains behind the lower front teeth.

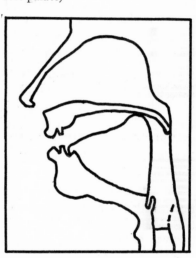

You hear the aspiration when the [k] occurs before a vowel. In the [g], the aspiration is greatly reduced or eliminated entirely. If the sounds are in final position, the tongue relaxes and little or no explosion occurs. If a nasal sound follows, the explosion is emitted nasally: ma*k*e more, fra*gm*ent.

Faulty production: excessive pressure so that the explosion is obvious; pressure so light that friction results; guttural production.

Unvoicing in final position.

Common Combinations

*c*lass, *c*ream, *qu*een, s*ch*ool
mi*lk*, lar*k*, tas*k*, fo*x*, pa*ct*
e*x*cuse

*g*lass, *g*reen
an*g*le, bur*g*
e*x*act

Note that the letter x may be pronounced [ks] or [gz].

Assimilation Faults Involving Nasal and Plosive Consonants

We have noted in connection with each of the plosive and nasal consonants certain problems in faulty production. Some of these problems result directly from the similarity in tongue position between the plosive and its parallel nasal sound. When a number of sounds having a similar articulatory position are in close proximity to each other, you may have a tendency to telescope the sounds and even to omit entire syllables. This is particularly true of the alveolar sounds [t], [d], and [n]. The *-ted* and *-ded* syllables and the various NT combinations cause particular difficulty. In 1940, when Wendell Willkie was running for *President of the United States*, he continually reduced this nine-syllable phrase in his speeches to four or five syllables: [prɛz djunaɪdə steɪs]. You may hear his pronunciation of this phrase in the Columbia album, *I Can Hear It Now*, Volume I.

The common addition of [g] to [ŋ] is, of course, a European heritage from language backgrounds such as Spanish, Hungarian, Italian, or Yiddish. However, the fact that [ŋ], [k], and [g] are made in the same articulatory position makes this error difficult to eradicate. In addition, speakers having this fault often rationalize it by pointing to the NG spelling of words in this category. Teachers sometimes give it additional support by urging their students who substitute [n] for [ŋ] not to drop their G's. This is a worthy aim, but an unphonetic way of expressing it, since [ŋ] is not two sounds, but one.

The substitution of one nasal for another is due to general similarity in the acoustic effect of the three sounds. Since it is somewhat easier to articulate [m] than [n], and [n] than [ŋ], speakers often take the path of least resistance, particularly in words where the articulators have previously been in the easier position. Corruptions of the words *something, happen, running,* and similar words are facilitated by these circumstances.

Exercises

1. Listen to a recording of your speech. Do you make any of the errors discussed in the description of the nasal and plosive sounds? Does your speech differ in the articulation of these sounds from that of your associates?

2. Listen to the following sentences as your instructor reads them to you. What articulation problems do you notice? Indicate errors by underlining them on the phonetic transcript. Do you make any of these errors?

a. [gʌvəmən ʌv ðə pipl]
b. [junaɪd wi stæn// dɪvaɪd wi fɔl]
c. [hi wəz goɪŋg əweɪ wɪð ʌs]
d. [aɪ sɔ ə mæn lɛnθən ə roʊp]
e. [ɪts bɛʔɚ tʊ hæv lɪbɚdɪ ðn sleɪvɚrɪ]
f. [ɪts gʊnə hæpm mʌndɪ]

3. Read the following sentences for clear articulation of nasals and plosives, but do not fail to blend words within the phrase.

a. The accident dented the fender on my late-model car.
b. Today I'm going to get off at the Atlantic Avenue subway station.
c. The chairman of the subcommittee kept mentioning the October deadline.
d. The thug robbed the nightclub, but obtained only an empty bead purse.
e. At midnight the workmen witnessed the robbery.
f. He tiptoed through the dark night in the rain.
g. The six leaders exhorted the crowd to exert their maximum effort.
h. I saw him running away and looking up the street as he ran.
i. Seeing him coming toward me, I started singing a song to attract his attention.

4. Practice reading the following selections in Appendix II, paying particular attention to nasal and plosive sounds: Numbers 2, 3, 14, 27, and 29.

FRICATIVE CONSONANTS

There are nine generally recognized American fricative consonant sounds. These are [f], [v]; [θ], [ð]; [s], [z]; [ʃ], [ʒ]; and [h]. These sounds are formed by narrowing the mouth passageway at some point and in such a manner that the breath stream is partially obstructed. The air forced through this restricted opening produces a friction sound.

Voiceless $\Big[$ f   *and*   v $\Big]$ Voiced

*f*eel   LABIODENTAL   *v*eal
(Lower lip, upper teeth)

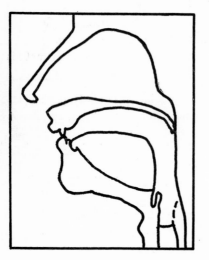

Raise your lower lip gently against the edges of your upper front teeth. The audible friction of continuous breath being forced between your lip and teeth produces the [f] sound. When, to this breath stream, you add the vibration of your vocal folds, the [v] sound is produced.

Faulty production: exaggerated position of lower lip, either protruding or drawn back too far; excessive pressure of the lip against the teeth so that the breath is almost or entirely stopped and a plosive sound is made; bilabial production occurring in some forms of foreign speech.

Common Combinations

*f*lower, *f*ree, s*ph*ere   twel*v*e, star*v*e
di*phth*eria, di*phth*ong
sel*f*, sur*f*, le*f*t, fi*fth*

Voiceless   [θ   *and*   ð]   Voiced

*th*ink   LINGUADENTAL   *th*em
                          (Tongue tip between teeth)

Protrude your flattened tongue tip slightly between your teeth so that the underside of the tip rests against the lower teeth and the upper side makes very light contact with the inner edges of the upper teeth. Direct the breath stream in a continuous flow over the center of your tongue and between your teeth. This will produce the [θ] sound. When vocal vibration is added, the voiced [ð] will result.

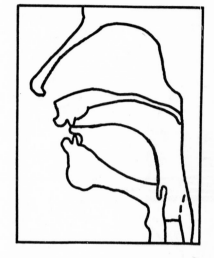

The TH sounds are the only ones which require the tongue to move forward in the mouth and touch the front teeth.

When the TH is encountered at the beginning of nouns, verbs, and adjectives, it usually represents the voiceless [θ] sound, as in *thimble, think,* and *thin.* However, the initial TH occurring in the article *the* and in pronouns, conjunctions, and adverbs, such as *they, than,* and *then,* generally represents the voiced sound. In the medial position, there is no consistent rule you can follow. In the final position, voiced [ð] is usually indicated by the addition of E to TH, as in *bathe.*

Faulty production: excessive protrusion; excessive pressure of the tongue against the edges or inside surfaces of the teeth so that a plosive sound results (dental [t] or [d]), often heard among speakers influenced by a foreign background; actual substitution of the [t] or [d] sound with the tongue tip on the alveolar ridge; substitution of the [s] or [z] sound, also traceable to foreign influence; use of the lower lip instead of the tongue tip between the teeth so that the [f] or [v] sound is substituted, as in infantile speech.

Common Combinations

*th*ree, *th*wart   mou*th*s, ba*thed*
fif*th,* wid*th*
heal*th,* stren*gth*

Voiceless $\begin{bmatrix} \text{s} & \textit{and} & \text{z} \end{bmatrix}$ Voiced

*s*oon LINGUA-ALVEOLAR *z*oo
(Tongue tip or blade, gum ridge)

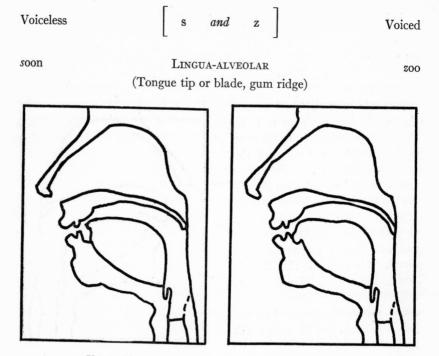

Up position   *Down position*

There are two main positions for the production of [s] and [z], both of which are satisfactory and which sound alike.

For either the up or the down position of these sibilants, bring your teeth almost together in a natural bite and draw your lips back slightly. If the up position is habitual, you will find that you arch your tongue toward the alveolar ridge with the sides of the tongue pressed against the inner edges of your upper teeth to a point of contact with your upper gums while maintaining a small, ditchlike groove along the middle of your tongue. With the tongue tip raised toward the alveolar ridge, but free from any actual contact with it, a narrow stream of breath is forced along this center groove and out through the small aperture formed by the grooved tongue tip held close to the alveolar ridge. This breath stream passing over the cutting edge of your front teeth makes the hissing, unvoiced [s] sound. When vocal vibration is added, the voiced [z] sound results.

In the down position, you place the tongue tip against your lower gums and press it forward against your lower front teeth. The tongue blade moves up toward your alveolar ridge. The tongue is grooved in much the same manner as it was in the up position, and the breath stream is forced down the middle of this groove and out over the cutting edges of your front teeth. You will notice that the opening for the escape of the breath stream in both the up and the down positions will be approximately a quarter of an inch behind your upper front teeth.

It should be noted that an essential factor in the production of these sounds is the direction of a narrow stream of breath over the cutting edges of the lower front teeth. Consequently, if there is any irregularity present in the formation of your dental structure, it will be advisable for you to experiment with different compensatory tongue positions in order to succeed in effecting the desired sounds.

It should also be noted that opinion has been expressed preferring the up position when the [s] is made in conjunction with the alveolar sounds [l], [n], and [t] in such words as *slow, snow,* and *stay.* The economy of action involved is apparent. When the [s] is made in the up position, the tongue tip is in immediate readiness for the ensuing lingua-alveolar sounds. If, on the other hand, the down position is employed for the production of the [s] sound when it is encountered in the consonant combinations [sl], [sn], and [st], an unpleasant whistling sound frequently results when the tongue tip performs the double action required in moving rapidly from the lower gum to the alveolar ridge.

This same school of thought presents the above-mentioned principle of economy of action as its reason for preferring the down position for the production of the [s] and [z] sounds when they are made in conjunction with all vowel sounds. The basic vowel position, with the tongue tip against the lower front teeth and barely touching the lower gums, is also recommended for the [s] sound when it occurs in the consonant combinations [sk], [sm], [sp], [skw], and [sw], in such words as *school, scamp, small, spell, squaw,* and *sweet.* With the tongue tip thus well against the lower front teeth on the [s] sound, it already is in position for adjoining vowel sounds. This position is likely to eliminate the sharp, whistling sibilant frequently produced by the double action involved when the tongue tip leaves the alveolar ridge and thrusts down against the lower front teeth.

However, it must be pointedly stated that use of either the up or the down position is largely a matter of personal preference. An acoustically satisfactory [s] or [z] sound can be articulated in either position. You should carefully examine your own performance in executing these sounds. If the sound you now make is acoustically satisfactory, you should make no change in your manner of producing it. If it is faulty, however, you may well experiment with the alternate position in order to improve its quality.

$$\begin{bmatrix} \text{s} \quad and \quad \text{z} \\ continued \end{bmatrix}$$

Faulty production: occurring in any one of the three more general types of *lisping*—(1) protrusion, or central lisp, in which the tongue tip thrusts out over the edges of the upper front teeth or presses against them in such fashion that the [θ] sound becomes substituted for the [s]; this fault is generally encountered in the speech of children, but it should be added that in infantile speech, any one of the fricative sounds may be exchanged or substituted for another (*ice* may be pronounced [aɪf], [aɪθ], or [aɪʃ]); (2) lateral lisp, in which the tongue tip makes a closure at the center of the alveolar ridge or the upper front teeth and the breath is forced to escape over one or both lateral edges of the tongue; excess saliva may be present during emission of this sound; (3) whistling, or dominant [s], due to overprolongation or excessive muscular tension, the tongue tip or blade being held tightly against the palate or alveolar ridge so that the opening for the breath stream is very small.

The whistling, or prolonged sibilant, is more common than the other two lisping faults. If you have been told that your speech is marked by this sharp, hissing [s]—a serious handicap in radio or stage work—use a mirror to study its production. Often the tongue tip or the blade is held too tensely against the alveolar ridge so that the opening through which your breath escapes is smaller than required. Also, the tongue may be raised toward a place on your palate farther back than necessary. With your raised tongue held in slightly different positions, listen carefully and judge the sounds produced. Experiment. Try greater relaxation of the muscles of the front of your tongue, with a larger opening between the tongue and your alveolar ridge, so that you produce a soft, somewhat slurred sound. Shorten the duration of this sound. Careful listening and trial-and-error practice will indicate the best position. Now use words with [s] in a final position; prolong the vowel sounds in these words, but shorten the final sibilant. Next, place these words within a phrase so that the final [s] is followed by a succeeding word, as in *glass of water, I will miss you.*

A fault encountered in the use of the [z] sound is unvoicing in the final position, so that such words as *was* become [wəs], as in [hi wəs əwei].

Foreign students should note that s is often used to designate the sound of [z] in English spelling. A final s is pronounced as [z] when the preceding sound is voiced, as in such words as *buds, dogs, plums, runs, graves, hills, cars,* and *brothers.* It is also pronounced as [z] in the final position when the schwa vowel sound [ə] comes between it and the preceding sounds with sibilant qualities, such as [s], [z], sH [ʃ], zH [ʒ], cH [tʃ], and J [dʒ], in such words as *passes, wishes, matches,* and *bridges.*

Voiceless $\qquad\qquad \begin{bmatrix} \text{s} \quad and \quad \text{z} \\ continued \end{bmatrix} \qquad\qquad$ Voiced

Common Combinations

*s*pool, *sm*ile, *st*ay, *sw*ell, *sph*ere, *sn*ake, *sk*ate, *sl*eep, *spl*it, *spr*ing, *str*eet, *scr*eam
bo*x*, cla*sp*, la*st*, ta*sk*

In final position, the [z] combines with any voiced consonant except those with sibilant qualities noted above.

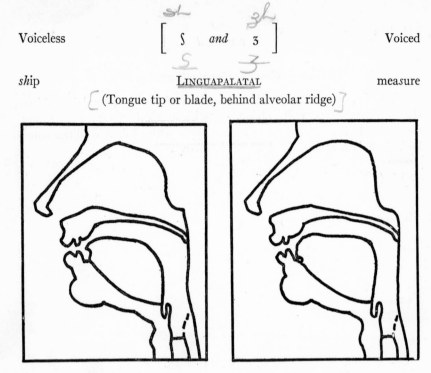

Up position   *Down position*

The [s] is a narrow-breath-stream sound, whereas the [ʃ] and [ʒ] are broad-breath-stream sounds. With your tongue tip flattened, in either the up or the down position, the sides of your tongue should touch the inner edges of your upper teeth. The teeth should be nearly closed. A fairly wide passageway is thus formed down the mid-line of your tongue. The broadened breath stream is directed through this passageway and out a wide but shallow opening made by the grooved tip or blade of your tongue raised toward the back of your alveolar ridge. Your lips may be slightly rounded and protruded. The sound thus produced is the voiceless [ʃ]. When vocal-fold vibration is added, the voiced [ʒ] results. The latter sound may be spelled with s, z, or G, as in *measure, azure* and *garage*.

These sounds differ from the narrow fricatives [s] and [z] in that the opening for the breath is wider and farther back on the hard palate and the lips are rounded. Note that [ʃ] and [ʒ] are not combinations of [s] or [z] with [h], but are single sound units.

Faulty production: protrusion lisp; lateral lisp; excessive tension, so that

$$\left[\begin{array}{cc} \int & \text{and} \quad 3 \\ & \text{continued} \end{array}\right]$$

the sound is prolonged and accompanied by undue friction; substitutions of [s] or [z].

Unvoicing.

Common Combinations

*sh*rill
wi*shed*

Notice the use of these two sounds in the affricate combinations described on page 192.

*More   but also
voiced*

Voiceless

$$\left[\begin{array}{c} h \end{array}\right]$$

*h*ow   GLOTTAL

To produce the [h], the glottis, or opening between the vocal folds, is partially closed, but not enough to produce vocal-fold vibration. The articulatory mechanism assumes the position for the vowel sound which is to follow the [h], and the escaping breath produces a slight, breathy friction before the vowel is vocalized.

Faulty production: omission in foreign accent or in careless speech (however, when [h] is the initial sound in an unaccented word in the middle of a phrase, it may be slighted or even omitted without being considered faulty); velar friction in some types of foreign accent.

Affricates *plosive + fricative*

The two affricates used in English, although they combine movements for plosive and fricative sounds, function as independent sound units. For [tʃ] and [dʒ], the tongue forms a momentary block for the breath as in the plosive; then the breath is exploded while the articulatory mechanism assumes the position for the fricative.

Voiceless   [tʃ   *and*   dʒ   ]   Voiced

*ch*urch   Combination of Lingua-alveolar Plosives and   *j*udge
                    Linguapalatal Fricatives

To produce the [tʃ], the approximate position and movements for the [t] are rapidly followed by those for [ʃ]. The tongue tip is held in contact with the alveolar ridge, the body of the tongue assumes the arched position for the [ʃ], the tongue tip releases suddenly, and the breath is exploded between tongue and palate in the opening characteristic of the [ʃ].

In producing [dʒ], the same action occurs, but since voice accompanies this activity, the [d] is quickly followed by [ʒ].

Faulty production: substitution of [ʃ] and [ʒ]; exaggerated explosion or protrusion. If [ʃ] and [ʒ] are faulty in the individual's speech, these sounds will also be distorted. [dʒ] is commonly unvoiced.

Common Combinations

lu*nch*, bu*tcher*, mar*ched*   ra*nge*, bi*lge*, ju*dged*

Articulation Faults Involving Fricative and Affricative Sounds

Many of the articulatory faults in the production of fricatives can be traced to the similarity in sound between some of these consonants. For instance, listen to another person produce [f], [s], [ʃ], and [θ] with his hand cupped over his mouth. When you cannot see the movements of the structures, the difference between the characteristic friction sounds may be difficult to hear. Children who do not watch the lips often say [fɪŋk] or [sɪŋk] for [θɪŋk]; [su] for [ʃu]; [sʌnɪ] for [fʌnɪ], and so forth. Foreigners who do not have the TH in their language may substitute [s] and [z] for [θ] and [ð].

Other faults may be due to the similarity in position between two consonants. The tongue has only a little way to move from the [s] position to produce the protrusion lisp which sounds like [θ]: [si] changes to [θi]. A reverse tendency brings the tongue back from the position for [θ] and [ð] and the speaker substitutes the plosives [t] and [d]. In this substitution, the [t] and [d] are usually articulated with the tongue pressed against the upper teeth (dental production): [tɪŋk] for [θɪŋk] and [brʌdɚ] for [brʌðɚ].

The s combines with many consonants. Probably the most difficult blends for some people are those which require a very small movement from the position of [s] to the alveolar consonant following: [stim], [slip], [sniz]. It is especially hard to return to the position of the [s] and [z] again: [poʊsts], [goʊsts], [pɛnslz], [lɛsnz]. A well-known stumbling block is the word *statistics* [stətɪstɪks]. The addition of [s] or [z] to [θ] or [ð] may also be difficult: [bɝθs], [pæðz].

The voiced fricatives and the voiced affricate are frequently unvoiced by foreigners. In rapid, somewhat careless speech, this unvoicing is common. Make up conversational sentences for the following words to see if you unvoice the italicized consonants when you speak rapidly: glo*v*es, bro*th*er, doe*s*, gara*g*e, villa*g*e.

Often you hear a very noisy production of fricatives. Since there are so many of these sounds in our language, particularly [s] and [z], any extra pressure of breath as it escapes through the small passageways, or any prolongation of the friction sound, affects most of the words spoken. The characteristic sputtering and hissing of this type of speech is accentuated if the [t] and [d] sounds are produced in a dental position.

When these sounds are used in the running context of speech, you must guard against substitution of one fricative for another, faulty placement, unvoicing of normally voiced fricatives, and extreme tension in production.

Exercises

1. As you listen to a record of your own speech, do you discover any deviations from the average in your production of fricative and affricate sounds?

2. Listen to the following sentences as your instructor reads them to you. What differences in articulation do you notice?

a. [hæf ju ɛfɚ hɝt əf ɪm]
b. [aɪ tɪŋk dət i sɔ mi goʊ deɚ]
c. [zeɪ seɪ zeɚ ɪs sʌmsɪŋ rɔŋ]
d. [dəs i noʊ ɪt wəs hɪs]

   e. [aɪ fɔt væt wəz maɪ mʌvɚ]
   f. [aɪ θɔ hɚ itɪn aɪθkwim]
   g. [i wəz rɒɪt ɪɚ]
   h. [ðə ʃɪkns ræn tə ðə ɛtʃ əf ðə roʊt]
   i. [pʊtʃɚ bægɪtʃ ɪnə gɚɑtʃ]
   j. [aɪ kwɛsʃn ɪz sɛns ə jumɚ]

3. Read the following sentences for clear articulation of the fricatives and affricates. Be certain to blend words within the phrase.

   a. Diphthongs are combinations of vowel sounds spoken in a continuous glide.
   b. He severed his connection with the Western Insurance Company.
   c. The author faithfully presented the social conditions existing in both the Northern and Southern sections of this country.
   d. In spite of the excitement surging around him, he clasped his hands and gazed out at the distant sea.
   e. A pleasant voice and good speech are significant factors in successful business and social relationships.
   f. Quartz, otherwise known as silicon dioxide, is one of our commonest minerals.
   g. His unusual treasures were housed in a luxurious mansion.
   h. Though he lived in humble surroundings, he felt no humility.
   i. The true humorist views humanity with kindly and sympathetic amusement.
   j. True Christian virtue transcends church attendance.
   k. He righteously chose to ignore the question.
   l. The judge was subjected to savage jibes and jeers.
   m. Fifteen telephone posts were installed against the protests of the local residents.
   n. We hold these truths to be self-evident.

SEMIVOWELS

There are certain sounds which are similar to vowels, in that they are produced with the mouth in a relatively open position; they also possess strong resonance characteristics with a minimum of friction.

The first two consonants in this classification, [w] and [j], are characterized by the gliding movement of the tongue, lips, and lower jaw from one position to another. If the articulatory mechanism were held in the initial position for [w] and [j], you would hear [u] and [i]. The glide into the position for the vowel which follows these consonants identifies the sound to the listener. Notice the movement of the lips and jaw in going from [w] to [ɔ] in the word *walk;* on the other hand, the glide is not strong between the words *you ought.* Similarly, notice the difference in movement of tongue and jaw, first as you articulate *yes,* and then as you speak the two words *he entered.*

The vowel R's [ɝ] and [ɚ] have already been presented (see pages 157–158). The consonant differs from the vowel in two important ways—in the presence of greater friction and in the characteristic glide movement of the semivowel. For the vowels [ɝ] and [ɚ], there is no glide; the position is held as the sound is produced.

$$\left[\quad w \quad \right] \text{ɯ}$$ Voiced

BILABIAL   *water*

Round and protrude the lips and raise the back of the tongue as if you were going to produce the vowel [u]. As the tone begins, quickly move the lips and tongue into the position for the vowel which follows.

Faulty production: exaggerated movement of the lips; substitution of [v] in foreign accent; overrelaxation of the lips so that the movement is not apparent.

Common Combinations

*tw*elve, *dw*ell, *thw*art, *sw*im, *qu*een, ang*u*ish

GLOTTAL FRICATIVE APPROACH TO [w]

[hw], probably used in American speech more extensively than the voice-less [ʍ], appears in such words as *why, when, where.* With the lips in the rounded position for [w], the friction sound of the [h] accompanies the glide movement of the lips. The blowing of the breath stream against the lips can easily be felt.

Faulty production: in rapid conversation or in careless speech, [w] is often substituted for [hw]. When clear articulation is required, although the sub-stitution is widely used, it is still considered better to say [hwɑt] than [wɑt], [hwɪtʃ] than [wɪtʃ], [hwaɪ] than [waɪ], and so forth.

$$\left[\quad j \quad \right] \qquad \qquad \text{Voiced}$$

LINGUAPALATAL   *yes*

Raise the tongue in a position close to that assumed for the vowel [i]; as voice is produced, your tongue quickly glides into the position for the vowel following. The lips spread slightly at the start of the sound.

In English spelling, when y appears at the beginning of a syllable it is pronounced [j]. The i in conjunction with a vowel is pronounced [j], with the glide activity apparent: on*ion*, famil*iar*, sav*ior*.

The [j] occurs commonly with the long vowel [u] to form a combination which is similar to a diphthong. In its initial position, as in *use, union, uvula,* the glide movement is strong.

The use of the combination [ju] is not consistent in American speech. Following consonants which do not make use of the front of the tongue, the [j] is used. Examples: *pupil, beauty, cute, argue, few, view, music, human.* After consonants which do employ the front of the tongue, [ju] is used when a premium is placed upon exactness or "niceness" of articulation. In casual speech, its use will depend upon the early environment and education of the speaker. Frequently, a very brief [ɪ] is inserted before [u] instead of the strong glide of [j]. In this usage, the combination of sounds actually becomes a diphthong. Some speakers use the [u] alone. Words like the following may be heard with [ju], [ɪu], or [u]: *student, tune, duty, assume, suit, resume, enthusiasm, new, lucid.*

Faulty production: a pronounced friction sound.

LINGUAPALATAL *r*ed

There are many variations in the formation of the consonant [r]. Most of you will raise the broadened tongue tip toward the palate just in back of the alveolar ridge, start the vocalization for the sound, and then, with a gliding movement, change the position of the tongue and lips to that of the vowel which follows the [r]. Others will retract the tongue tip from the lower front teeth but elevate the tip very little. Some, as they start the sound, will curl the tip back toward the hard palate.

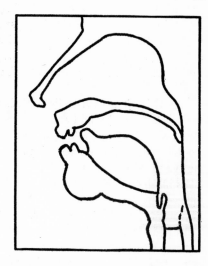

A slight friction often accompanies the production. This, plus the glide movement, makes the sound recognizable as a consonant. If the starting position were held, the vowel [ɝ] would be heard instead. The variations for the production of this vowel have already been discussed on pages 157–158.

When the letter R occurs at the end of a word or before a final consonant, the consonantal glide is not present. The sound is either the accented [ɝ], as in [fɝ], [nɝs], or the unaccented [ɚ], as in [wɪntɚ]. In some localities, where the R is not sounded in final position, these words will be pronounced without the R coloring: [fɜ], [wɪntə]. The letter R following a vowel is heard as the receding half of a centering diphthong: [fɪɚ], [kɛɚ], [mɔɚ], [kɑɚ], [pʊɚ] (see page 162).

Certain recognizable variations in the production of this consonant need description so that you may analyze what you hear in the speech of those around you.

The trilled R requires a tense tongue with the tip hitting the alveolar ridge repeatedly. It occurs in several foreign languages and in Scottish and Irish dialects. To produce the British single-tapped R, the tongue tip touches the ridge once, much as in the production of [d]. Listen to the British pronunciation of *sorry, cherish*. The extreme retroflex R, such as is sometimes heard in pronounced Middle Western dialect, is made by curling the tongue tip back upon itself. This position muffles the sound by changing the resonance. Often the ʀ can be retroflex in position without sounding faulty. The back of the tongue may also be raised to produce a variety of ʀ. The German and Russian uvular ʀ is made with the back of the tongue raised toward the end of the soft palate, in such a way that the air stream causes the uvula to flutter. The Germans also use a back-tongue ʀ accompanied by definite friction.

The [r] is often used to link words together when the first word ends in the vowel [ɝ] or [ɚ] and the next word begins with a vowel: [fɝ r ɪz lɔŋ], [ðɛɚ r ɑɚ tu]. If the linking [r] is too strongly stressed, so that the second word sounds as if it started with an ʀ, the production is usually considered faulty. In certain sections of the country, where the final ʀ is pronounced [ɜ] as in *fur* [fɜ], [ə] as in *butter* [bʌtə], or omitted as in *far* [fɑ], the vowel is followed by a linking [r] to permit an easy transition to the vowel in the next word: [fɜ r ɪz lɔŋ], [ðɛ r ɑə].

An [r] is sometimes inserted between two words when the first ends with a vowel and the second begins with a vowel. The use of this intrusive [r] seems to facilitate movement from one vowel to the next. In Eastern Seaboard speech, such phrases as these may be heard: [ən aɪdɪə rəv hɪz], [əmɛrɪkə rɪz fri], [ðə sofə rɪz maɪn]. Notice, in producing these phrases, how the final schwa itself may be influenced, often becoming the [ɚ]. In General American speech, the intrusive [r] is considered a fault. In some cases, speakers use [ɚ] at the end of single words where it has no actual function: *law* [lɔɚ], *piano* [pɪænɚ].

Faulty production: substitution of [w] in lalling or infantile speech; excessive friction; muffled retroflex ʀ; foreign ʀ; insertion of [ə] or [ɚ] when [r] is combined with other consonants, as in *tree* [təri], *pray* [pəreɪ].

Common Combinations

*p*ride, *b*ring, *tr*y, *dr*eam, *cr*y, *gr*een, *thr*ee, *shr*ink, *spr*ing, *str*eet

LINGUA-ALVEOLAR   *leap*, schoo*l*

Hold the tip of the tongue lightly against the center of the alveolar ridge. The voiced breath flows out over the relaxed sides of the tongue. The lips and back of the tongue assume the position of the vowel which follows or precedes [l].

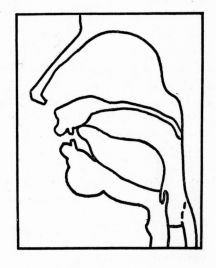

The [l] sounds like a vowel because of its resonance. While the tongue tip remains on the ridge for the various sounds of [l], the body and back of the tongue take a vowel position. When [l] occurs in initial position or after an initial consonant, as in the words *lead, blue, play,* it is said to be *clear;* the position of the front of the tongue resembles that of [i]. When it occurs in final position or before a final consonant, as in *all, bulk, field,* it is called *dark;* the position of the back of the tongue is raised in a position resembling [u]. Occasionally, a foreigner, when learning American speech, will use the clear or the dark [l] in all words.

Final [l], after a consonant, will be syllabic, that is, the [l] can form a syllable by itself without an accompanying vowel. Examples: *apple, bottle, able, uncle, little, castle.* The insertion of a schwa before this [l] is considered faulty.

Faulty production: substitution of [w] or [j] in baby talk; omission in final position; retroflex with tongue tip turned back on itself; dental [l], with the tongue pressed against the teeth as it occurs in some foreign languages; tip held against lower front teeth and sound produced with blade of tongue and accompanying friction noises and nasalization. When [l] is combined with an initial consonant, the schwa vowel should not be inserted: *blue* [bəlu], *place* [pəleɪs].

Common Combinations

*p*lace, *b*lue, *c*lean, *g*lass, *f*ly, *s*leep, fi*l*m, he*l*p, bu*l*b, me*l*t, he*l*d, si*l*k, she*l*f, twe*l*ve, hea*lth*, fa*l*se.

Articulation Faults Involving the Semivowel Sounds

The fact that the four semivowels are similar to vowels in acoustic effect and in position may account for some of the errors in their production. When we refer to the omission of final ʀ's, we mean that the schwa has been substituted for the final [ɚ], so that even the ʀ coloring of the vowel has disappeared. In rapid speech or baby talk, [l] is sometimes not completed; the tongue tip does not contact the alveolar ridge. We then hear substitutions of [ə] or even [ʊ] for the [l]: [pæs ðə sɔət], [aɪ fiə gʊd], [mɔə mɪʊk]. The [l] in final position is often omitted, so that the preceding vowel alone is heard: [kɔ] for [kɔl], [ɔ əv əm] for [ɔl əv ðəm].

Another error involving [l] is the insertion of the schwa before the final [l]: [fiəl], [puəl], [ʃeəl]. The articulatory mechanism does not move into the [l] position fast enough; since vocalization continues, we hear the [ə] as the movement takes place.

Since [r] and [l] both require complex muscle activity, children may substitute the easier semivowels which sound somewhat like [r] and [l]. Hence the child may say [wɛd dwɛs] or [aɪjaɪk ɪt], [jɛwoʊ] or [jɛɪmboʊ]. If a person has used this lalling speech in childhood, he may still have little glide movement for these sounds and therefore give weak productions difficult to recognize. The tongue then needs to become more vigorous in movement. The speaker may need the practice provided in actual speech correction.

Extreme tension of production for any of these four semivowels will result in excessive friction. With [r] and [l], the tongue may also be retracted so that the sounds have a muffled quality.

These consonants are strongly influenced by the speech models in the speaker's environment. You can easily recognize regional differences in their articulation. They can only be said to be faulty if they attract attention to themselves or if they interfere with communication.

Exercises

1. As you listen to a record of your own speech, can you recognize any deviation from the average in the production of your semivowels?

2. Listen to the following sentences as your instructor reads them. What differences do you notice?

   a. [wɛn ɪz ðə wɛðɚ gʌnə wɔɚm ʌp]
   b. [jɛs ðə stjudənts wɪl əsjum ɔl rɪspɑnsɪbɪlɪtɪ]
   c. [si tʊk pwaɪd ɪn ɚ wɛd dwɛs]
   d. [aɪ riəlɪ fiəl bɛtɚ]

e. [waɪ dɪd i seɪ ɪt wz ɔ raɪt]

f. [pəliz gɪv mi ə bəlu wʌn]

g. [aɪ hæd noʊ aɪdiɚ hi kəd pleɪ ðə pɪænɚ]

h. [ə lɪtə hɛəp wəd bɨ əpwɪʃɪetəd]

3. Read the following sentences for clear articulation of the semivowel sounds. Blend the sounds within the phrases.

a. Is he able to present a clean bill of health?

b. Twelve men reduced the castle to a pile of rubble.

c. He tried to follow his dream of building a great empire.

d. I feel that it is humanly impossible to complete the whole volume.

e. All right, I will file the will when he calls me.

f. I would rather read a railroad timetable than his erudite verse.

g. The long light shakes
Across the lakes,
And the wild cataract leaps in glory.
—TENNYSON

h. Helen, thy beauty is to me
Like those Nicaean barks of yore,
That gently, o'er the perfumed sea,
The weary, wayworn wanderer bore. . . .
—POE

THE BLENDING AND ASSIMILATION OF SOUNDS IN SPEECH

If you have always lived in the United States and do not have a serious speech defect, you will probably be able to produce all the consonants as they have been described. As the sounds are grouped into words and the words into communicative phrases, however, their production may change in the running oral context. In order that the words within the phrase may flow together smoothly, there must be a steady movement from one sound to the next, both within words and between words. You have heard people speak as if each word were a single dropped pebble. If you repeat the following sentence with short breaks between words, you may recognize this meaningless mannerism: "As they told Tom the news, they all watched his face."

After you have read the staccato production, read the first phrase as a unit. Notice the forward movement of the tongue from [z] to [ð] between the first two words, *as they;* the economy of one contact of tongue tip to gum ridge between *told* and *Tom;* the beginning of the [ð] even as the [m] is formed, between the words, *Tom the.* Observe further how the [w] starts while the tongue tip is up for [l] between the words, *all watched;* [z] blends into [f] with continuing friction sound between *his* and *face.*

Thus the processes of blending and assimilation have made the continuing movement of the articulated phrase smooth and easy to produce.

Simple rules for the blending of sounds have been presented at the beginning of this chapter. Now that you have studied the individual sounds in detail, you may examine with greater understanding the joining and modification of these sounds in oral communication.

Two tendencies are at war in articulation: one, the inclination to give the easiest production of the sound with the least muscular effort; and the other, the attempt to achieve pedantic accuracy in the mistaken belief that it is necessary for clarity. For the most readily accepted speech, you should discover for yourself the middle way—enough assimilation and blending between words for smoothness in production, and sufficient clarity for immediate comprehension in the specific speech situation. With the nature of the speaking situation in mind, you can understand that some situations require an emphasis on clearness of production, and others, more casual in nature, permit more extensive assimilation of sounds.

When two consonants occur together in the flow of sounds within a phrase or within single words, one may bring about a change in the other in order to simplify the transition between the two. Such a change occurred in *as they*, with the [ð] affecting the formation of the [z]. This modification is called *assimilation.* If the first sound influences the second, this is called *progressive assimilation;* if the second modifies the first, the assimilation is *regressive;* or each may influence the other in *mutual* assimilation. If we were very exact in describing what occurs, we could contend that such modifications always take place. However, your discrimination may not be acute enough to perceive this.

If sounds are similar enough, they blend readily, with little or no change in articulatory position, as between the words *told Tom.* In the case of *all watched*, the smooth blending of [l] and [w] is brought about for these very dissimilar sounds by beginning the movement for the second even as the first consonant is made.

The suggestions for blending and assimilation presented earlier can now be amplified in some detail.

1. *If the sounds are similar in place of production,* the movements which characterize the sounds are made only once.

 a. When two like or similar plosives occur together, hold the first for its normal duration and release on the second member of the pair.

[aɪ hæd taɪm]   [wi it tədeɪ]

[ə bæk geɪt]   [ə mæd dɔg]

[maɪ tɑp bʊk]   [aɪ beɪk kʊkiz]

 b. When two similar continuants occur together, if the sounds are the same, give a single prolonged production, with this qualification: in fricative continuants, it is desirable to diminish the energy of the first consonant of the group.

[wi ɔl laɪk hɪm]   [ɪts hæf fʊl]

[ɪn noʊ taɪm]   [wi boθ θɪŋk soʊ]

[wi mɪs sʌm əv ðɛm]

If the two continuants are voiceless and voiced counterparts, a gradual voicing or unvoicing begins while the one production is made.

[boθ ðiz bɔɪz]   [æz sun əz aɪ kæn]

[wi hæv fɔɚ]

 c. When a plosive is followed by a continuant similar in place of production, the plosive is stopped in its usual position but released into the position for the continuant.

[drɪŋk tæp wɒtɚ]   [hi həd lɔŋd fɚ ðɪs]

[æt sʌm dans]   [ə lɪtl bɔɪ]

 d. When a continuant is followed by a plosive similar in placement, the position for the continuant acts as a starting point for the plosive.

[æz tə ðɪs fækt]   [ðɪs ɪz hɪz dɔg]

[ən ɔl taɪm haɪ]

2. *If the sounds are similar in auditory character* (fricative, plosive, nasal, etc.) but not in placement, there is no break between them.

a. When two plosives occur together, the formation of the first is made, but only the second is exploded.

[ə næpkɪn]   [gʊd baɪ]

[ə rʌbdɑʊn]   [æt kæmp]

b. When two fricatives occur together, the friction sound is continuous.

[æz ʃi θɔt əv sʌmθɪŋ]

[ðeɪ boθ si ðɪs]

c. When two nasals occur together, the nasalization is continuous.

[ɒn maɪ weɪ]   [ðə taɪm nɛvɚ kʌmz]

[lɛts sɪŋ mɔɚ]

d. When two semivowels occur together, there is no break.

[ɔl raɪt]

[sɛl wʌn əv ðəm]

3. *If the sounds occur in different regions of the mouth and are similar in auditory character,* the mechanism gets ready for the production of the second or even starts it as the first is still being produced.

[ə glæs]   [braɪt]

[klaɪm ʌp]   [twaɪn]

[blu]   [sɪŋ laɪk ə bɝd]

4. *Neighboring unlike sounds are assimilated frequently,* so that one sound changes its placement or its voicing to be more like the other sound.

a. When two sounds are unlike in place of production, one may modify the other so that the transition is easy.

[æt ðə stɔɚ]   [ə hæf bæk]

[ɔl ðə taɪm]   [tu ɑbvɪəs]

[ɪn ðə hɑʊs]

This same tendency to make sounds more compatible is present in certain words whose pronunciation has long been accepted.

[bæŋk]   [pɪktʃɚ]   [soldʒɚ]

[æŋgɚ]   [neɪtʃɚ]   [prodʌkʃən]

Within many words or combinations between words, assimilation is used in conversational, casual speech, but not in formal speech.

[ɛdʒʊkeɪʃən]	or	[ɛdjukeɪʃən]
[aɪ gɛs ʃu wɪl]	or	[aɪ gɛs ju wɪl]
[wont ʃu go]	or	[wont ju go]
[æz ʒu si]	or	[æz ju si]

These combinations of sounds should not be so extremely assimilated that careless forms are used, with certain consonants slurred over or omitted, as in such phrases as: [lɛmi si], [aɚntʃə goɪn], [wʌtʃə gɑt], [gʊnə goʊ]. For instance, a quick and weak [tʃ] connects *don't you* in casual speech. If this is exploded with force or if the [t] is omitted, the phrase sounds careless.

b. When two sounds are unlike in voicing, one may modify the other so that both are either voiced or unvoiced. In established usage, the final s in plurals or present tenses tends to assume the voiced or unvoiced character of the sound which precedes it.

[tʌbz—tɑps]	[gɜˑlz]
[roʊdz—hæts]	[drimz]
[dɔgz—keɪks]	[loʊnz]
[lɪvz—skɪfs]	[kɑɚz]

The ending *-ed* is voiced or unvoiced depending upon the sound which precedes it.

[rʌbd—stɑpt]	[lɪvd—læft]
[tægd—kɪkt]	[geɪzd—gɛst]

c. When two sounds are unlike in the direction of the breath stream, one may modify the other. If a nasal follows a plosive, the explosion is emitted through the nose.

[sʌdn]	[pɑɚk nɪɚ]
[bʌtn]	[æt maɪ haʊs]

These modifications of articulation to bring about smooth juncture and blending are advocated to do away with pedantic preciseness in speech. When the modifications become so extreme that quick comprehension is disturbed, then speech is careless and faulty.

CARELESS AND FAULTY PRODUCTION OF CONSONANTS

The same causes which contribute to the faulty production of vowels also affect consonants: little energy in production, rapid speech, or imitation of poor models. More basic reasons for indistinct articulation will lie in differences in physical structure, the environment, and the personality of the speaker.

Consonants may be distorted, omitted, or so weak that they are difficult to hear. One consonant may actually be substituted for another or be added to a word where it should not appear. Substitution and weak or slurred production are the most common faults in careless speech.

In extreme assimilation, any of these faults may be apparent. The same rules which operate to facilitate the blending of sounds are now so over-worked that one or more of the consonants loses its identity. Sometimes the extreme assimilation may occur on unaccented words within a phrase; if the words themselves are not necessary to meaning, the carelessness does not interfere with communication. But if the fault occurs on the stressed words, the poor articulation is then obvious and disturbing to the listener.

Phrases such as the following may be understood by someone who knows you well, but will not be understood with ease if you use them in speaking across a room or in talking to several people. Listeners who are strangers to you may also make unflattering judgments of your speech and education.

[aɪm gʌnə tɛl jə sʌmpm]	I'm going to tell you something.
[ɪ smaɪ prɑbm]	It's my problem.
[hɑ dʒɚ gɪt əweɪ]	How did you get away?
[don tʃə si]	Don't you see?
[waɪn tʃə tɛl əm]	Why didn't you tell them?
[hi dɪnt gɪmi ɪz bʊk]	He didn't give me his book.
[opm ðə dɔɚ wɛn naɪ nɑk]	Open the door when I knock.
[aɪ dɪnt rɛkənaɪz ðə kwɛʃn]	I didn't recognize the question.

Endings of words may be slurred or the final consonant omitted all together.

[hi toʊl mi]	He told me.
[ðə wɝl ɪz raʊn]	The world is round.
[ðə gretəs mæn]	The greatest man.
[dʒɪs wʌn]	Just one.
[wi wɛn əweɪ]	We went away.
[aɪm gʌnə goʊ]	I'm going to go.

[gɪmi ə bʊk]   Give me a book.
[sɔɚtə bæd]   Sort of bad.
[kaɪnə naɪs]   Kind of nice.
[enɪθɪn goʊz]   Anything goes.

Another common fault is the unvoicing of voiced consonants.

[maɪ bægɪtʃ]   My baggage.
[ðə dʒʌtʃ sɛt soʊ]   The judge said so.
[hi ɪs hɪɚ]   He is here.
[dəs hi noʊ]   Does he know?
[ɔɚgənɪseɪʃn]   Organization.
[ðɪs dɔk kʌms hɪɚ]   This dog comes here.
[aɪ hæf tə goʊ hoʊm]   I have to go home.

The unvoiced consonants are sometimes mistakenly voiced.

[lɪbɚdi]   liberty   [lɛdʒɪsledʒɚ]   legislature
[rɛdʒɪzdɚ]   register   [mʌldɪplaɪ]   multiply

Some speakers will consistently substitute one consonant for another. Some of these are foreignisms.

[goʊɪn hoʊm]   Going home.
[wɑt dəz i min]   What does he mean?
[aɪ tɪŋk dæts maɪ bʊk]   I think that's my book.
[doʊz ɚ maɪn]   Those are mine.

Sometimes in careless speech, particularly when the second word starts with a vowel, the consonant at the end of the first word is omitted and used to start the second. Occasionally the result is ludicrous, if the words so joined receive great emphasis. This is a frequently used comedy device on radio and television.

[ɪt wə zɔfəl]   It was awful.
[aɪ hævə naɪdɪə fɚ ə nʌðɚ pleɪ]   I have an idea for another play.
[aɪm nɑ tɪntrəstəd ə tɔl]   I'm not interested at all.
[aɪ wʌnt sə maɪs]   I want some ice.
[wi wə leɪm tə pliz]   We will aim to please.
[hi ɪzn teɪbl tə goʊ]   He isn't able to go.
[aɪ nid sə mɛɚ]   I need some air.

You hear such phrases every day in the speech around you. As you begin to listen to faulty production, you will formulate your judgment as to when and where such speech is acceptable. There are times when careless speech will produce an unfavorable effect upon your listeners.

Specific classifications of errors are known as *articulatory defects*. For instance, any speaker who produces the sibilants [s], [z], [ʃ], and [ʒ], in an atypical way, so that the sounds call attention to themselves, is called a *lisper*. Those who cannot move the tongue tip with accuracy and agility, in such sounds as [r], [l], and sometimes [t], [d], and [n], are said to have a *lalling* defect. The classification of *foreign accent* refers, of course, to distortions and substitutions of consonants and vowels, but also includes a rhythm pattern distinctly different from General American speech.

Some speakers will make all the plosives with great pressure and the fricatives with such small openings that the friction sound is obvious. For some personal reason, these tense speakers, with their staccato, barking speech, are overarticulating. You cannot listen to them with any feeling of ease. According to our definitions, this articulation is faulty, even though each sound is made "correctly."

If listeners have difficulty understanding you, you may have a habit of muffling your articulation. This is probably due to the muscular tension which results in smallness of movement of the oral structures. This habit may have been brought about by extreme self-consciousness or a desire to hide some physical difference, such as protruding teeth or thick lips. Both articulation and voice quality are affected in muffled speech, since the tense lips and tight jaw distort sounds and the small mouth opening masks the tone. Practice of greater openness of mouth and more relaxation of jaw, coupled with exercises for resonance, will help to break the habit.

Listening and Self-analysis

1. In listening to a public lecture or a speech on the radio, or in unobtrusive eavesdropping in a restaurant or bus, try to analyze the articulation of many varied speakers. Is their production of sounds careless, precise, muffled, or adequately clear? Can you analyze with some accuracy the ways in which these people combine sounds in meaningful speech? Write out some of their statements. How does their articulation differ from your own?

2. Listen to records made by actors and professional readers, and to recordings taken of political speakers. Note specific ways in which their articulation differs from yours.

3. Again listen to your original recording; note good blending and assimilation; pick out any signs of carelessness.

4. After you have made your final recording, compare the clarity of articulation with that of the first record.

Exercises for Improvement

1. Choose one of the selections from Appendix II. Read this aloud to a classmate, and then listen while he reads. Mark on the passage the words which are pronounced inaccurately and which you and your classmate pronounce differently. Note also any sounds which are produced in a faulty manner, or slurred, or spoken with exaggerated preciseness.

2. If you have specific articulatory faults, read again the material in Chapters 9 and 10 describing the sounds on which you have difficulty. Make lists of words and phrases containing these sounds in various combinations. Use them in conversational sentences in practice. Try also to introduce them into casual conversation with your friends.

3. Read the selection which you have prepared to the class. Do your classmates and the instructor think you have improved on articulation?

SUMMARY

A definition of good articulation must include reference to both accuracy of production of sounds and smooth blending of the consonants into a continuous flow of speech. The concept of uniformity of production of consonants, either in the speech of one person or from one speaker to another, is misleading. What is usually thought of as a single consonant will vary in its position, voicing, and duration under the influence of other consonants within the phrase, of the variations in stress, and, of course, with the different articulatory structures of different speakers. But if the consonant is readily recognizable and does not differ enough from the average to call attention to itself, it can be considered accurate.

Consonants differ from vowels in that the breath stream is blocked, narrowed, or diverted through the nose rather than flowing through the wide-open mouth. Also, all vowels are voiced, while consonants are both voiced and voiceless.

Many of the consonants occur in voiced and voiceless pairs. These pairs, such as [g] and [k], are made in the same position in the mouth; for the first, the vocal folds vibrate, and for the second, no vibration is present.

Consonants may be classified according to their acoustic quality. There are three nasals in our language, [m], [n], and [ŋ]. The opening through the mouth is blocked, and the vocalized breath stream passes through the nose.

A plosive is characterized by the closure at lips, tongue, and alveolar ridge, or tongue and velum, the building up of air pressure behind this blockade, and the sudden or explosive release of the air. For the fricatives, the breath stream is made to flow through a narrow opening between lips and teeth, tongue tip and teeth, tongue and palate, or half-closed vocal folds. A friction sound results. The semivowels are similar to vowels in their openness and their resonance characteristics, but they also require pronounced gliding movements.

The consonants can also be described in terms of the position of the articulators. For example, the bilabial [p] requires the contact of the two lips.

When sounds are combined into words in running oral context, each may affect the production of neighboring sounds. Thus the smooth, steady movement of the articulators can be maintained by simplifying the transition between sounds by means of blending and assimilation. If sounds occurring together are alike in their place of production, only the movement for one is made. If they are similar in acoustic effect, there is no break between the sounds. Often, while producing sounds made in different parts of the mouth, the mechanism starts the production of the second even as the first is being made. One sound can also change the production of another to make the two more similar. These processes aid smooth transition.

When assimilation or modification of sounds is extreme, so that consonants are omitted or slurred or one is substituted for another, careless and faulty articulation will tend to interfere with the speaker's communication. The goal in practicing to attain good articulation is not pedantic preciseness, but the use of sounds which can be easily understood and which fit smoothly into the pattern of communicative speech. Accuracy or clearness of articulation should be suited to the needs of the present speaking situation, and thus may vary. The quick understanding of the language symbols by the immediate listeners is the basis of judgment of articulation.

11

What Next?

When you started this course, you were instructed to make a recording of your voice. From time to time you have been asked to listen to this record, and to analyze it to determine what problems you have had and what skills you could use more effectively. You should now make a new recording, using the same reading materials and a similar informal talk or interview.

SELF-ANALYSIS

When you have made your final disk recording, play both sides. Write a comparison of the records, answering two fundamental questions:
1. How have you improved?
2. What still remains to be done?

In order to make an intelligent and orderly analysis, recall the four questions asked of you in Chapter 1:
1. Can you be heard by the listener?
2. Can you be understood by the listener?
3. Is your voice pleasant to listen to?
4. Is your voice flexible enough to convey the shades of meaning and of feeling which you intend?

When these questions were first asked, you did not have enough background to interpret them fully; now, however, you should fill in additional questions under each of the four headings from the knowledge you have gained in the reading of the book. You will find material developing the first question in Chapter 4. Chapters 9 and 10, together with the material in Chapter 4 on timing, will help you to work out subdivisions of the second question. The sections in Chapters 5 and 6 on melody and quality and on faults of phonation and resonance will be of value in clarifying the implications of the third question. Throughout Chapters 4 to 7 you will find materials to assist you in developing the fourth question.

Write an outline, or a series of questions, showing the criteria for criticism under each of the four headings. Applying these standards, write an analysis and comparison of the two records you have made.

When you have completed this analysis, you are ready to begin your final oral assignment. Keeping in mind all the factors which you noted in your analysis, prepare a short extemporaneous talk for the class, and couple it with the reading of a brief selection of poetry or prose. The two parts should be related to each other and form an integrated whole. Try to make specific improvements on factors in which you were weak in your final recording.

While the other students are presenting their final speeches and readings in class, test your ability at listening and analysis by writing short criticisms or marking comments on a criticism chart prepared on the basis of the four questions discussed earlier.

STUMBLING BLOCKS

Even though you have made substantial progress in improving your speech during the past few months, you will not retain your new habits unless you really wish to. You will recall that in Chapter 2 we pointed out how environmental and emotional factors have influenced your habits of speech. Of course these influences did not stop when you enrolled in this course. Perhaps even while you have been trying to improve your voice, some of these factors have been preventing or aiding you in developing skills.

At any rate, it is certain that in the future many of you will be confronted by conditions which may tend to upset the new habits you have acquired. Perhaps you will face an emotional crisis, which will disturb the quality of your voice. Or you may be thrown temporarily into an environment in which good articulation is of little value for social prestige. If you want to retain good speech habits, you must recognize these stumbling blocks, and guard against them.

AFTER THIS CLASS

Your continued improvement is now *your* responsibility. The learning of new techniques under the stimulation of group work in a class may not ensure permanent improvement, even under favorable conditions. Since one semester is not sufficient time to fix new habits, we suggest that you continue to give conscious attention to your voice.

1. Listen frequently to the varied aspects of vocal production and articulation of your friends, your family, your professors, and the professional speakers whom you hear in the movies and on radio and television.

2. Listen to yourself in daily speaking situations in your classes. If you give oral reports, participate in discussion, or read aloud in other classes, these situations will present opportunities for you to judge the effectiveness of your speech.

3. Recall frequently the criticisms of your classmates and instructor. These once helped you to establish goals of improvement; do they continue to operate as motivating forces?

4. Read aloud to yourself, occasionally. Do you sound interesting? Can you still vary timing, melody, and quality for fine shades in meaning?

5. Try consciously to bring in the new habits of vocal skills and clear articulation as you argue, discuss, question, and describe in daily conversation.

Eventually, the skills you have sought to establish will no longer have to be practiced consciously but will occur automatically.

Other courses will help you in your plans for continued improvement. Perhaps you will enroll in a class in public speaking, oral interpretation, radio speaking, or acting. The need for continued practice in vocal skill in any of these courses is obvious.

In psychology courses, consider the relationship between voice and personality. If you are training to become a teacher, study the influence of good and bad speech upon teaching procedures. When you read literature, notice how often stylistic devices are better understood when the passage is read aloud. In studying foreign languages, notice how your ability to reproduce alien sounds is aided by your understanding of the nature of the articulatory mechanism.

You will forget much of the technical material in this book. It was presented to you only to provide a sound basis for your improvement. What we hope you will not lose is your critical ability and your belief that speech skills are a strong personal asset to you, both socially and professionally.

Perhaps our objectives will be reached in a measure when someone says to you, "You talk a little differently than you used to. I think you sound more sure of yourself—as if you enjoyed speaking—as if you were confident that you're good at it. What have you been doing?" Then you will realize with some satisfaction that your endeavor to improve your speech is beginning to take effect.

APPENDIX I

Recording Devices

There are three kinds of recording equipment suitable for use in voice courses, each of which can be made to serve a specific purpose in voice training. Disk-recording devices are best adapted to permanent recordings, which may be used for comparison of achievement at the beginning and at the end of the course. Magnetic recorders of the wire or tape variety are best for classroom exercises. For practice rooms or the instructor's office, steel-tape recorders of the one-minute voice-mirror type are the most useful.

DISK RECORDERS

While some companies make a portable disk recorder, good machines are usually too bulky and heavy to be moved about for classroom use. Moreover, they easily get out of adjustment from the jar of constant moving. Most effective results will be obtained from disk-recording apparatus if it is permanently installed and all recordings made in one place. Preferably, this should be an acoustically treated room, large enough to allow normal public-speaking methods to be used.

Each student should record one side of a ten- or twelve-inch record at the beginning of the course, and the other side at the end of the course, for comparison. The first part of each side should record an informal interview between the operator and the student. The latter should sit before the microphone and answer questions about his name, his sectional origin, the date of the recording, and why he is taking the course. At the second recording, he may be asked what benefits he thinks he has derived from the course. In the second part of the record, the student should stand before the microphone, as if he were facing an audience, and read a short passage of informal prose. The third part of the record should show his voice as it sounds in extemporaneous speaking.

The student should listen to the initial record after it is made, making such preliminary analysis as he can at this point in his development. He should use the record again as a point of reference in learning each new skill throughout the term. When the final recording has been made, both the student and the instructor should make comparisons between the two and project a plan for further improvement along lines indicated by their analysis.

WIRE AND TAPE RECORDERS

The recent development of magnetic wire and tape recorders has given teachers and students of voice an indispensable classroom tool. These instruments are more flexible for use with a group of students than are the disk machines, and they are usually lighter and easier to handle. Moreover, it is easier for the amateur to make an acceptable recording with them than with disk machines. In addition, they are inexpensive to operate, since the wire or tape can be used many times over without destroying its fidelity. However, magnetic recorders are not well adapted to individual, permanent recordings for comparison at the end of the term. Both types of machines are therefore needed.

The instructor should bring the wire or tape recorder to class often enough so that students may hear themselves as they actually sound when reading or speaking to others. Samplings may be taken of speeches or readings without the students' knowing which portions are being recorded. The recordings may then be played back for discussion and analysis by the class. Frequently, students are able to hear even the voices of other students more objectively through recordings than in the original, and their acuity in self-analysis is correspondingly improved.

VOICE MIRRORS

Machines of the voice-mirror type contain an endless steel tape; those most suitable for use in vocal training have tapes which take from one to three minutes to pass through the recording head. At the end of that time, the process is repeated, the preceding minute being erased as the new recording is made. Most such machines have a control providing for three operating positions—record, hold, repeat. It is thus possible to make a recording, play it back, discuss it with the student, and play it again.

Since these machines are virtually foolproof in operation, they are ideal for installation in students' practice rooms or in instructors' offices, where they may be used by many different people. There are no complicated adjustments to make, and nothing to get out of alignment or require attention during the making of the recording. An individual student can make very rapid progress working by himself with one of these machines, once he knows what to listen for as he hears the recording played back.

While wire or tape recorders may also be used in the office or practice room, the voice-mirror type of machine is superior in this situation, just as the other two types of machines are particularly well adapted to their special uses. A well-equipped voice laboratory needs all three types of equipment.

APPENDIX II

Selections for Practice

HOW TO USE READING SELECTIONS

The reading selections presented here are an integral part of the text. Although they are given apart from the main body of information and exercises, they are meaningful only if interpreted in terms of the concepts given earlier. For that reason, throughout the body of the book, you have been referred to specific selections in this appendix to help you in learning particular skills. Of course, the authors of these selections did not intend to have them used in this way, and in reading them you cannot treat them as abstract exercises without any relationship to the context and original intent of the author. We have selected them for this book because we believe that without adequate control of the particular skills to which we have related them, you cannot give the selections the meaning and emotional expression which the authors intended. If you understand these skills and know how to use them, you can call them into play in support of the meanings and feelings which the authors had in mind. Yet, unless you react to those meanings and emotions, your manipulation of the mechanical elements will give a mechanical result.

Moreover, it is not the sole purpose of this course to train you as a good reader. You should also learn to transfer all of the skills of good voice usage to informal speech and to platform speaking. Particularly in the prose selections, therefore, you should identify yourself with the concepts and the type of motivation out of which the author derived his idea and language. You should create from your own experience a pattern of thought and feeling which will make his words vital to you. In this way you will hasten the transition to the informal and extempore speaking situations.

In order to help you correlate the intent of the author with the skills

you wish to learn, each selection has been furnished with a brief introduction, in which are noted the special meanings and feelings to be observed
and the special skills of voice usage which can be practiced in bringing out
these factors.

READING SELECTIONS

1. Dover Beach

The setting of this poem is the coast of England, at night, looking toward the
French coast, but it might be anywhere—a pier on Chicago's north shore, Catalina
Island, Long Island looking toward the Connecticut shore, the beach at Biloxi.
You should visualize your own setting, and try to think the ageless philosophy
and emotions which the author intended.

The mood of the poem is particularly well adapted to the use of a deliberate
rate, with many long sounds, although one or two places suggest a definite change
of pace. The last stanza needs a quality change to indicate the shift from the
reflective concepts to the warmth of personal emotions. A modification of the
resonance traits of the voice is needed to reflect this change.

> The sea is calm to-night.
> The tide is full, the moon lies fair
> Upon the straits;—on the French coast the light
> Gleams and is gone; the cliffs of England stand,
> Glimmering and vast, out in the tranquil bay.
> Come to the window, sweet is the night-air!
> Only, from the long line of spray
> Where the sea meets the moon-blanch'd sand,
> Listen! you hear the grating roar
> Of pebbles which the waves draw back, and fling,
> At their return, up the high strand,
> Begin, and cease; and then again begin,
> With tremulous cadence slow; and bring
> The eternal note of sadness in.
>
> Sophocles, long ago,
> Heard it on the Aegean, and it brought
> Into his mind the turbid ebb and flow
> Of human misery; we
> Find also in the sound a thought,
> Hearing it by this distant northern sea.

The Sea of Faith
Was once, too, at the full, and round earth's shore
Lay like the folds of a bright girdle furl'd;
But now I only hear
Its melancholy, long, withdrawing roar,
Retreating, to the breath
Of the night-wind, down the vast edges drear
And naked shingles of the world.

Ah, love, let us be true
To one another! for the world, which seems
To lie before us like a land of dreams,
So various, so beautiful, so new,
Hath really neither joy, nor love, nor light,
Nor certitude, nor peace, nor help for pain;
And we are here as on a darkling plain,
Swept with confused alarms of struggle and flight,
Where ignorant armies clash by night.

—MATTHEW ARNOLD

2. BEAT! BEAT! DRUMS!

This poem was written during the Civil War, but like any powerful piece of writing, it applies equally to any war crisis of any people or nation. Consider your own feelings and those of your family during World War II, and reflect through them the passionate irony of Whitman's poem.

You cannot read this selection with the interpretation it demands unless you feel a tremendous surge of energy in your body as you read. The articulation must be sharply defined—almost explosive. The breath stream must be under complete control and driven from strong actions of the abdominal muscles. The strong, vibrant tone needed to reflect the passionate feelings of the poem can be secured in this way.

Beat! beat! drums!—blow! bugles! blow!
Through the windows—through the doors—burst like a ruthless force,
Into the solemn church, and scatter the congregation,
Into the school where the scholar is studying;
Leave not the bridegroom quiet—no happiness must he have now with
    his bride,
Nor the peaceful farmer any peace, plowing his field or gathering his grain,
So fierce you whirr and pound you drums—so shrill you bugles blow.

Beat! beat! drums!—blow! bugles! blow!
Over the traffic of the cities—over the rumble of the wheels in the streets;
Are beds prepared for sleepers at night in the houses? no sleepers must
    sleep in those beds,
No bargainers' bargains by day—no brokers or speculators—would they
    continue?
Would the talkers be talking? would the singer attempt to sing?
Would the lawyer rise in the court to state his case before the judge?
Then rattle quicker, heavier drums—you bugles wilder blow.

Beat! beat! drums!—blow! bugles! blow!
Make no parley—stop for no expostulation,
Mind not the timid—mind not the weeper or prayer,
Mind not the old man beseeching the young man,
Let not the child's voice be heard, nor the mother's entreaties,
Make even the trestles to shake the dead where they lie awaiting the hearses,
So strong you thump, O terrible drums—so loud you bugles blow.

                  —WALT WHITMAN

3. I Hear America Singing

As the title suggests, this selection is buoyant and joyous in mood. The melody
and time changes which it evokes should suggest, but not imitate, those of the
songs described in the context.

I hear America singing, the varied carols I hear,
Those mechanics, each one singing his as it should be blithe and strong,
The carpenter singing his as he measures his plank or beam,
The mason singing his as he makes ready for work, or leaves off work,
The boatman singing what belongs to him in his boat, the deckhand singing
    on the steamboat deck,
The shoemaker singing as he sits on his bench, the hatter singing as he
    stands,
The wood-cutter's song, the playboy's on his way in the morning, or at
    noon intermission or at sundown,
The delicious singing of the mother, or of the young wife at work, or of the
    girl sewing or washing,
Each singing what belongs to him or her and to none else,
The day what belongs to the day—at night the party of young fellows,
    robust, friendly,
Singing with open mouths their strong melodious songs.

                  —WALT WHITMAN

4. THE PASSING OF ARTHUR

This selection records the solemn but hopeful approach to death by a believer in immortality. The rate is slow, with many long sounds. There are no abrupt melody changes, although the melody is not monotonous.

And slowly answer'd Arthur from the barge:
"The old order changeth, yielding place to new,
And God fulfils Himself in many ways,
Lest one good custom should corrupt the world.
Comfort thyself: what comfort is in me?
I have lived my life, and that which I have done
May He within Himself make pure! but thou,
If thou shouldst never see my face again,
Pray for my soul. More things are wrought by prayer
Than this world dreams of. Wherefore, let thy voice
Rise like a fountain for me night and day.
For what are men better than sheep or goats
That nourish a blind life within the brain,
If, knowing God, they lift not hands of prayer
Both for themselves and those who call them friend?
For so the whole round earth is every way
Bound by gold chains about the feet of God.
But now farewell. I am going a long way
With these thou seest—if indeed I go—
(For all my mind is clouded with a doubt)
To the island-valley of Avilion;
Where falls not hail, or rain, or any snow,
Nor ever wind blows loudly; but it lies
Deep-meadow'd, happy, fair with orchard-lawns
And bowery hollows crown'd with summer sea,
Where I will heal me of my grievous wound."

—ALFRED TENNYSON

5. OZYMANDIAS OF EGYPT

The picture suggested by this selection might be set in any of the ancient lands of the Middle East, or in any area where there is a dead and forgotten civilization. But its real message is a warning to contemporary rulers that their days are numbered and their works are soon to be forgotten.

As in most sonnets, a change in rate, melody, and quality is essential to show the change in mood midway in the poem. There are really three moods to interpret—descriptive, boasting, philosophical. Experiment with changes in timing, energy, and quality to bring out these shifts in mood. The entire selection, however, demands a full and resonant tone to convey the vastness of the desert and the scope of a great idea.

> I met a traveller from an antique land
> Who said: "Two vast and trunkless legs of stone
> Stand in the desert. Near them, on the sand,
> Half sunk, a shatter'd visage lies, whose frown,
> And wrinkled lip, and sneer of cold command,
> Tell that its sculptor well those passions read
> Which yet survive, stamp'd on these lifeless things,
> The hand that mock'd them and the heart that fed;
> And on the pedestal these words appear:
> 'My name is Ozymandias, king of kings:
> Look on my works, ye Mighty, and despair!'
> Nothing beside remains. Round the decay
> Of that colossal wreck, boundless and bare
> The lone and level sands stretch far away."
>
> —PERCY BYSSHE SHELLEY

6. COMPOSED UPON WESTMINSTER BRIDGE

Look out upon your own city in the early morning on a bright spring day. Get the feeling of peace and strength which Wordsworth reflects in this poem.

This selection adapts itself well to a moderate rate and a quiet strength which comes from firm but not loud tones. Keep the phrases moving; make adequate use of pause and duration to point the ideas. Feel the moods of the poem and reflect them through changes in the quality of your voice.

> Earth has not anything to show more fair:
> Dull would he be of soul who could pass by
> A sight so touching in its majesty:

This City now doth like a garment wear
The beauty of the morning; silent, bare,
Ships, towers, domes, theatres, and temples lie
Open unto the fields, and to the sky;
All bright and glittering in the smokeless air.
Never did sun more beautifully steep
In his first splendour valley, rock, or hill;
Ne'er saw I, never felt, a calm so deep!
The river glideth at his own sweet will:
Dear God! the very houses seem asleep;
And all that mighty heart is lying still!

—WILLIAM WORDSWORTH

7. SONNET XXIX

As in other sonnets, the mood of this poem changes in the ninth line. Visualize these moods by thinking first of your blackest troubles and then of the satisfying and redeeming qualities of friendship and love.

These concepts may be reflected, in reading, by a change in the pattern of melody and timing in the two parts of the poem. In the first part, the rate may well be moderately slow, varying as the mood changes. In the second part, the rate may increase and the melody be more varied. A quality change may be introduced in the last two lines, along with a new rate and inflectional pattern. Experiment with these elements until you can produce the mood you feel.

When in disgrace with fortune and men's eyes
I all alone beweep my outcast state,
And trouble deaf heaven with my bootless cries,
And look upon myself, and curse my fate,
Wishing me like to one more rich in hope,
Featur'd like him, like him with friends possess'd,
Desiring this man's art, and that man's scope,
With what I most enjoy contented least;
Yet in these thoughts myself almost despising,
Haply I think on thee,—and then my state,
Like to the lark at break of day arising
From sullen earth, sings hymns at Heaven's gate;
   For thy sweet love remember'd such wealth brings
   That then I scorn to change my state with kings.

—WILLIAM SHAKESPEARE

8. The Night Has Been Long

If you have ever attended a Gilbert and Sullivan opera, you are aware of the fact that there is little depth in the lyrics. They tell a story, but the emotions are purposely shallow, and the music gets most of its interest from changes in tempo. Yet in spite of the fast rate at which many of the lyrics are sung, a good Gilbert and Sullivan singer can always be understood, and never gasps for breath in the wrong place. In this selection, the story is an amusing one, and you should enjoy it as you read, but you need not expect to evoke great emotional response.

The selection should be studied carefully for the most effective places to pause for breath. The rate should be quite fast, with some prolongation of picture words and an occasional slowing down of a phrase, without breaking its rhythm, where you think the humor can be heightened. The articulation must be very precise, but the movement of the phrase must not be broken.

When you're lying awake with a dismal headache, and repose is tabooed
    by anxiety,
I conceive you may use any language you choose to indulge in without
    impropriety,
For your brain is on fire—the bedclothes conspire of usual slumber to
    plunder you:
First your counterpane goes and uncovers your toes, and your sheet slips
    demurely from under you;
Then the blanketing tickles—you feel like mixed pickles, so terribly sharp
    is the pricking;
And you're hot and you're cross, and you tumble and toss till there's
    nothing 'twixt you and the ticking;
Then your bedclothes all creep to the floor in a heap, and you pick 'em up
    all in a tangle;
Next your pillow resigns and politely declines to remain at its usual
    angle.
Well, you get some repose in the form of a doze, with hot eyeballs and
    head ever-aching;
But your slumber teems with such horrible dreams that you'd very much
    better be waking.
You're a regular wreck, with a crick in your neck,
And no wonder you snore, for your head's on the floor,
And you're needles and pins from your soles to your shins,
And your flesh is a-creep, for your left leg's asleep, . . .

And some fluff in your lung, and a feverish tongue,
And a thirst that's intense, and a general sense
That you haven't been sleeping in clover.
But the darkness has past, and it's daylight at last,
And the night has been long—ditto, ditto, my song—
And thank goodness, they're both of them over!

—W. S. GILBERT

9. WHY SO PALE AND WAN, FOND LOVER?

You have probably met the young man in this poem; if you have, you should be able to reflect the poet's amused impatience with his subject.

You will get good results in reading the poem by pitching the three stanzas in different keys. The greatest variety in melody and timing should come on the last stanza. This is a good selection for practice in clear production of vowels and in articulating the glide consonants, particularly [w] and [hw].

Why so pale and wan, fond lover?
    Prithee, why so pale?
Will, when looking well can't move her,
    Looking ill prevail?
    Prithee, why so pale?

Why so dull and mute, young sinner?
    Prithee, why so mute?
Will, when speaking well can't win her,
    Saying nothing do't?
    Prithee, why so mute?

Quit, quit for shame! This will not move:
    This cannot take her.
If of herself she will not love,
    Nothing can make her:
    The devil take her!

—SIR JOHN SUCKLING

10. COME LIVE WITH ME AND BE MY LOVE

If you are a city dweller, the images of this poem will be foreign to you; if you are from the farm, they may seem completely unrealistic. But a young man in love is seldom realistic, and you do not have to live in the country to share with him his desire to give his loved one the best of everything. Re-create the mood.

The movement of the poem is light. It is adapted to the upper middle key of your voice. The articulation should be clear and crisp, but should not call attention to itself.

Come live with me, and be my love;
And we will all the pleasures prove
That hills and valleys, dales and fields,
Woods, or steepy mountain yields.

And we will sit upon the rocks,
Seeing the shepherds feed their flocks
By shallow rivers, to whose falls
Melodious birds sing madrigals.

And I will make thee beds of roses,
And a thousand fragrant posies;
A cap of flowers, and a kirtle
Embroidered all with leaves of myrtle;

A gown made of the finest wool
Which from our pretty lambs we pull;
Fair-lined slippers for the cold,
With buckles of the purest gold;

A belt of straw and ivy-buds,
With coral clasps and amber studs;
An if these pleasures may thee move,
Come live with me, and be my love.

The shepherd-swains shall dance and sing
For thy delight each May morning;
If these delights thy mind may move,
Then live with me, and be my love.

—CHRISTOPHER MARLOWE

11. PSALMS

In these two selections, the psalmist deals with themes of great elevation of thought, drawing his inspiration from the grandeur of nature—the mountains and the stars. In each psalm, picture to yourself the natural setting which inspired the writer, and react as he did to the philosophical implications of the scene.

The primary tools for effective reading of these passages are sustained tone, limited range of melody, relatively slow rate, and frequent use of long duration to point up the important ideas. Careful phrasing for both breath control and meaning is essential.

a. Psalm 121

I will lift up mine eyes unto the hills, from whence cometh my help.
My help cometh from the Lord, which made heaven and earth.
He will not suffer thy foot to be moved: he that keepeth thee will not
    slumber.
Behold, he that keepeth Israel shall neither slumber nor sleep.
The Lord is thy keeper: the Lord is thy shade upon thy right hand.
The sun shall not smite thee by day, nor the moon by night.
The Lord shall preserve thee from all evil: he shall preserve thy soul.
The Lord shall preserve thy going out and thy coming in from this time
    forth, and even for evermore.

b. Psalm 8

When I consider thy heavens, the work of thy fingers, the moon and the
    stars, which thou hast ordained;
What is man, that thou art mindful of him? and the son of man, that thou
    visitest him?
For thou hast made him a little lower than the angels, and hast crowned
    him with glory and honour.

12. CHILDE HAROLD'S PILGRIMAGE

These four stanzas are selections from a long poem by Byron. The first two stanzas picture the ball given for the officers of the allied forces on the night before the Battle of Waterloo. Try to imagine a gay party where all of the dancers realize that a battle is about to be fought and are half-listening for the opening guns.

The last two stanzas are a rhapsody on nature. One must appreciate the grandeur of nature both on land and at sea to understand fully Byron's feelings in this section.

All four of the stanzas contain phrasing problems to which you must pay attention. The first two stanzas must have energy without excessive volume, and require much variety of melody to depict the scene. In the last line of the first stanza and in the last four lines of the second, there are changes which must be reflected vocally.

The last two stanzas, particularly the fourth, must be read at a slow rate, with much attention to duration. At the same time, you must achieve subdued and sustained power in both stanzas.

a. Canto III

XXI

There was a sound of revelry by night,
And Belgium's capital had gather'd then
Her Beauty and her Chivalry, and bright
The lamps shown o'er fair women and brave men;
A thousand hearts beat happily; and when
Music arose with its voluptuous swell,
Soft eyes look'd love to eyes which spake again,
And all went merry as a marriage bell;
But hush! hark! a deep sound strikes like a rising knell!

XXII

Did ye not hear it?—No; 'twas but the wind,
Or the car rattling o'er the stony street;
On with the dance! let joy be unconfined;
No sleep till morn, when Youth and Pleasure meet
To chase the glowing Hours with flying feet—
But hark!—that heavy sound breaks in once more,
As if the clouds its echo would repeat;
And nearer, clearer, deadlier than before!
Arm! Arm! it is—it is—the cannon's opening roar!

b. Canto IV

CLXXVIII

There is a pleasure in the pathless woods,
There is a rapture on the lonely shore,
There is society, where none intrudes,
By the deep Sea, and music in its roar:

I love not Man the less, but Nature more,
From these our interviews, in which I steal
From all I may be, or have been before,
To mingle with the Universe, and feel
What I can ne'er express, yet cannot all conceal.

CLXXIX

Roll on, thou deep and dark blue Ocean—roll!
Ten thousand fleets sweep over thee in vain;
Man marks the earth with ruin—his control
Stops with the shore; upon the watery plain
The wrecks are all thy deed, nor doth remain
A shadow of man's ravage, save his own,
When, for a moment, like a drop of rain,
He sinks into thy depths with bubbling groan,
Without a grave, unknell'd, uncoffin'd, and unknown.

—LORD BYRON

13. The Lunatic, the Lover, and the Poet

In the following lines from Shakespeare's *A Midsummer Night's Dream*, the noble Duke Theseus talks about the powerful influence that imagination has upon our thoughts. With particular reference to the three types of men mentioned, he implies that many of us, carried away by our imaginations, may become the victims of our own fancies. Read the speech with these thoughts in mind.

You will find that this selection lends itself to the development of vocal quality. Try to suggest with your voice the qualities of the ideas and images expressed. Also, pay careful attention to phrasing, pauses, and the changes in melody necessary in order to communicate the intended meaning.

Lovers and madmen have such seething brains,
Such shaping fantasies, that apprehend
More than cool reason ever comprehends.
The lunatic, the lover, and the poet,
Are of imagination all compact:
One sees more devils than vast hell can hold,
That is, the madman; the lover, all as frantic,
Sees Helen's beauty in a brow of Egypt:
The poet's eye, in a fine frenzy rolling,
Doth glance from heaven to earth, from earth to heaven;

And, as imagination bodies forth
The forms of things unknown, the poet's pen
Turns them to shapes, and gives to airy nothing
A local habitation and a name.
Such tricks hath strong imagination,
That, if it would but apprehend some joy,
It comprehends some bringer of that joy;
Or in the night, imagining some fear,
How easy is a bush supposed a bear!

—WILLIAM SHAKESPEARE

14. MARCHING ALONG

This selection from Robert Browning's *Cavalier Tunes* is a swaggering marching song sung by loyal supporters of King Charles I. It praises the King and his Cavaliers while contemptuously deriding the Puritans and their leaders.

In reading this aloud, you will find that the swinging rhythm is conducive to freedom of tone. In practicing, be sure that you observe the phrasal pauses and see that you have ample breath support for sustained, resonant tones.

Kentish Sir Byng stood for his King,
Bidding the crop-headed Parliament swing;
And, pressing a troop unable to stoop
And see the rogues flourish and honest folk droop,
Marched them along, fifty-score strong,
Great-hearted gentlemen, singing this song.

God for King Charles! Pym and such carles
To the Devil that prompts 'em their treasonous parles!
Cavaliers, up! Lips from the cup,
Hands from the pasty, nor bite take nor sup
Till you're—

CHORUS—
Marching along, fifty-score strong,
Great-hearted gentlemen, singing this song.

Hampden to hell, and his obsequies' knell.
Serve Hazelrig, Fiennes, and young Harry as well!
England, good cheer! Rupert is near!
Kentish and loyalists, keep we not here,

CHORUS—
Marching along, fifty-score strong,
Great-hearted gentlemen, singing this song?

Then, God for King Charles! Pym and his snarls
To the Devil that pricks on such pestilent carles!
Hold by the right, you double your might;
So, onward to Nottingham, fresh for the fight,

CHORUS—
March we along, fifty-score strong,
Great-hearted gentlemen, singing this song!
—ROBERT BROWNING

15. ONCE MORE UNTO THE BREACH, DEAR FRIENDS

In this speech from Shakespeare's *Henry V*, the King addresses his soldiers before attacking a French town. One cannot read this speech without being inspired by Henry's pride in his men and his country, and by his driving will to triumph over the French. Read it aloud with feelings of pride and challenge. Follow Shakespeare's own advice, beginning with the sixth line, "Then imitate the action of the tiger," and continuing to the middle of the seventeenth line. Shakespeare was of the opinion that physical states form the foundation of spiritual qualities. In a similar manner, by engaging your body in the physical tensions and relaxations corresponding to the emotional tensions and relaxations involved, appropriate vocal qualities will be aroused. Allow your emotions to color your voice.

In addition, this selection adapts itself to changes in rate, melody, and energy, as well as to projection and strength of tone.

Once more unto the breach, dear friends, once more;
Or close the wall up with our English dead!
In peace there's nothing so becomes a man
As modest stillness and humility:
But when the blast of war blows in our ears,
Then imitate the action of the tiger;
Stiffen the sinews, summon up the blood,
Disguise fair nature with hard-favored rage;
Then lend the eye a terrible aspect;
Let it pry through the portage of the head
Like the brass cannon; let the brow o'erwhelm it
As fearfully as doth a galled rock
O'erhang and jutty his confounded base,
Swill'd with the wild and wasteful ocean.

Now set the teeth and stretch the nostril wide,
Hold hard the breath, and bend up every spirit
To his full height! On, on, you noblest English,
Whose blood is fet from fathers of war-proof!
Fathers that, like so many Alexanders,
Have in these parts from morn till even fought,
And sheathed their swords for lack of argument.
Dishonour not your mothers; now attest
That those whom you call'd fathers did beget you.
Be copy now to men of grosser blood,
And teach them how to war. And you, good yeomen,
Whose limbs were made in England, show us here
The mettle of your pasture; let us swear
That you are worth your breeding; which I doubt not;
For there is none of you so mean and base
That hath not noble lustre in your eyes.
I see you stand like greyhounds in the slips,
Straining upon the start. The game's afoot:
Follow your spirit; and upon this charge
Cry 'God for Harry, England, and Saint George!'

—WILLIAM SHAKESPEARE

16. HAMLET'S ADVICE TO THE PLAYERS

Hamlet is giving advice to the strolling players who are to perform in the court. He is warning them against ham acting. The speech is straightforward and direct. As you read aloud, visualize the acting faults which Hamlet is describing. There may be some allusions which you will have to look up in reference books.

Watch your phrasing in this selection. Also, it is particularly important that the articulation be clear and precise. Strive for variety of melody and distinct changes in vocal quality as the different acting traits are presented. Watch to see where the rate can be varied in relation to the changes in idea.

Speak the speech, I pray you, as I pronounced it to you,—trippingly on the tongue; but if you mouth it, as many of your players do, I had as lief the town-crier spoke my lines. Nor do not saw the air too much with your hand, thus; but use all gently: for in the very torrent, tempest, and, as I may say, whirlwind of your passion, you must acquire and beget a temperance, that may give it smoothness. O! it offends me to the soul to hear a robustious periwig-pated fellow tear a passion to tatters, to very rags, to split the ears of the groundlings, who, for the most part, are capable of nothing but inexplicable dumb-shows and noise; I would have such a fellow whipped for o'er-doing Termagant; it out-Herods Herod; pray you, avoid it.

Be not too tame neither, but let your own discretion be your tutor: suit the action to the word, the word to the action; with this special observance, that you o'erstep not the modesty of nature; for anything so overdone is from the purpose of playing, whose end, both at the first and now, was and is, to hold, as 'twere, the mirror up to nature; to show virtue her own feature, scorn her own image, and the very age and body of the time his form and pressure. Now, this overdone, or come tardy off, though it make the unskilful laugh, cannot but make the judicious grieve; the censure of the which one must in your allowance o'erweigh a whole theater of others. O! there be players that I have seen play, and heard others praise, and that highly, not to speak it profanely, that, having neither the accent of Christians nor the gait of Christian, pagan, nor man, have so strutted and bellowed, that I have thought some of nature's journeymen had made men, and not made them well,—they imitated humanity so abominably.
—WILLIAM SHAKESPEARE

17. THE HUMANITY OF THE SLAVE

This excerpt is from a speech given by Lincoln in Peoria, Illinois, on October 16, 1854. He is addressing the citizens of the South, asking them to question the concept of slaves as property. Lincoln had a direct, conversational style of speaking which is evident in this selection. Try to picture the excitement of political debate and the burning issues involved in the slavery controversy before you try to read the selection.

You have a problem of energy and directness in reading this material. The questions are pointed and the statements positive and assertive. You must keep the underlying vocal energy all through the reading. See that the phrasing is clear and that there is a variety of melody. You will find that the ideas build toward a climax of energy and positiveness without unnecessary loudness.

You have among you a sneaking individual of the class of native tyrants known as the *slave-dealer*. He watches your necessities, and crawls up to buy your slave at a speculating price. If you cannot help it, you sell to him; but if you can help it, you drive him from your door. You despise him utterly; you do not recognize him as a friend, or even as an honest man. . . . If you are obliged to deal with him, you try to get through the job without so much as touching him. . . . Now, why is this? You do not so treat the man who deals in cotton, corn, or tobacco.

And yet again. There are in the United States and Territories . . . over four hundred and thirty thousand free blacks. At five hundred dollars per head, they are worth over two hundred millions of dollars. How comes this vast amount of property to be running about without owners? We do not see free horses or free cattle running at large. How is this? All these free blacks are the descendents of slaves, or have been slaves themselves; and they would be slaves now but for something that has operated on their white owners, inducing them at vast pecuniary sacrifice to liberate them. What is that something? Is there any mistaking it? In all these cases it is your sense of justice and human sympathy continually telling you that the poor negro has some natural right to himself,—that those who deny it and make mere merchandise of him deserve kickings, contempt, and death.

And now why will you ask us to deny the humanity of the slave, and estimate him as only the equal of the hog?—ABRAHAM LINCOLN

18. A House Divided

This selection is the introduction to the speech Lincoln gave on his nomination to the Senate in 1858. The controversy between the North and the South over slavery was acute. Lincoln basically was opposing the extension of slavery. His statement here is a direct and straightforward analysis of the problem as he saw it.

You must be careful to work out the phrasing and the interrelationships of the parts of the idea if you are to read this passage effectively. It requires energy and proper emphasis on both words and phrases. You must be sure to get variety of all of the vocal elements if the ideas are to be clear and the reading free from monotony.

If we could first know where we are, and whither we are tending, we could better judge what to do, and how to do it. We are now far into the fifth year since a policy was initiated with the avowed object and confident promise of putting an end to slavery agitation. Under the operation of that policy, that agitation has not only not ceased, but has constantly augmented. In my opinion it will not cease until a crisis shall have been reached and passed. "A house divided against itself cannot stand." I believe that this government cannot endure permanently, half slave and half free. I do not expect the Union to be dissolved,—I do not expect the house to fall; but I do expect it will cease to be.divided. It will become all one thing, or all the other. Either the opponents of slavery will arrest the further spread of it, and place it where the public mind shall rest in the belief that it is in the course of ultimate extinction; or its advocates will push it forward till it shall become alike lawful in all the States, old as well as new, North as well as South.—ABRAHAM LINCOLN

19. The Crime against Kansas

Sumner was one of the earliest and most fiery Senatorial advocates of the abolition of slavery. This speech was against the extension of slavery into the Nebraska Territory, which included Kansas. Sumner was quick to use invective in his speaking. For the violent attacks on the South contained in this speech, he was severely cane whipped by Preston Brooks of South Carolina.

The basic problem in this selection is one of energy and force. Be sure that you are communicating the urgency and positiveness of the speaker. Analyze the excerpt, and see how it builds to a climax. Be sure that you vary the energy as is necessary. At the same time, there should be variety of rate and melody. See that your repeated reading of the word "swindle" does not become monotonous.

Sir, the Nebraska Bill was in every respect a swindle. It was a swindle of the North by the South. On the part of those who had already completely enjoyed their share of the Missouri Compromise, it was a swindle of those whose share was yet absolutely untouched; and the plea of unconstitutionality set up—like the plea of usury after the borrowed money has been enjoyed—did not make it less a swindle. Urged as a bill of peace, it was a swindle of the whole country. Urged as opening the doors to slave-masters with their slaves, it was a swindle of popular sovereignty in its asserted doctrine. Urged as sanctioning popular sovereignty, it was a swindle of slave-masters in their asserted rights. It was a swindle of a broad territory, thus cheated of protection against slavery. It was a swindle of a great cause, early espoused by Washington, Franklin, and Jefferson, surrounded by the best fathers of the Republic. Sir, it was a swindle of God-given, inalienable rights. Turn it over, look at it on all sides, and it is everywhere a swindle; and, if the word I now employ has not the authority of classical usage, it has, on this occasion, the indubitable authority of fitness. No other word will adequately express the mingled meanness and wickedness of the cheat.—CHARLES SUMNER

20. A Poor Relation

Lamb is trying to picture a poor relation in a series of different ways. Try to visualize how such a person who has become a pest might appear. Then see how Lamb has described him. See if you can get the feeling of each of the different descriptive phrases. What is Lamb's basic reaction to such persons?

This selection presents two problems, one in phrasing and the other in variety of melody and rate. Because the selection is a series of short phrases, it may easily become monotonous. Each phrase must differ from the others in melody pattern to bring out the diverse reactions. How will quality contribute to the establishment of Lamb's basic attitude?

A poor relation is the most irrelevant thing in nature—a piece of impertinent correspondency—an odious approximation—a haunting conscience—a preposterous shadow, lengthening in the noontide of our prosperity—an unwelcome remembrancer—a perpetually recurring mortification—a drain on your purse—a more intolerable dun upon your pride—a drawback upon success—a rebuke to your rising—a stain in your blood—a blot on your 'scutcheon—a rent in your garment—a death's head at your banquet—a lion in your path—a frog in your chamber—a fly in your ointment—a mote in your eye—a triumph to your enemy, an apology to your friends—the one thing not needful—the hail in harvest—the ounce of sour in a pound of sweet.—CHARLES LAMB

21. TWO YEARS BEFORE THE MAST

In 1840, Dana made a voyage as a seaman from Boston to the west coast of North America. This description is a part of the record which young Dana made of the trip. Imagine that you are standing on the deck of an old sailing ship in the fog. Out of the fog come the sounds which the author describes to you.

You must pay particular attention to your time pattern, including rate, duration, and pause, in reading this selection. Phrasing may be a problem for you unless you analyze it carefully before you read. There must be some subtle changes in melody and quality to bring out the meaning.

Towards morning the wind went down, and during the whole forenoon we lay tossing about in a dead calm, and in the midst of a thick fog. . . .

The calm of the morning reminds me of a scene . . . which I remember from its being the first time that I had heard the near breathing of whales. It was on the night that we passed between the Faulkland Islands and Staten Land. We had the watch from twelve to four, and, coming upon the deck, found the little brig lying perfectly still, enclosed in a thick fog, and the sea as smooth as though oil had been poured upon it; yet now and then a long, low swell rolling under its surface, slightly lifting the vessel, but without breaking the glassy smoothness of the water. We were surrounded far and near by shoals of sluggish whales and grampuses, which the fog prevented our seeing, rising slowly to the surface, or perhaps lying out at length, heaving out those lazy, deep, and long-drawn breathings which give such an impression of supineness and strength. Some of the watch were asleep, and the others were quiet, so that there was nothing to break the illusion, and I stood leaning over the bulwarks, listening to the slow breathings of the mighty creatures,—now one breaking the water just alongside, whose black body I almost fancied that I could see through the fog; and again another, which I could just hear in the distance,—until the low and regular swell seemed like the heaving of the ocean's mighty bosom to the sound of its own heavy and long-drawn respirations.—RICHARD HENRY DANA

22. LIFE ON THE MISSISSIPPI

Mark Twain had a gift for telling interesting stories in a simple, direct manner. In these two excerpts from *Life on the Mississippi,* he has captured the flavor of life in a small Missouri town on the Mississippi in the middle of the nineteenth century. Try to visualize the two characters he is describing and to feel the author's attitudes toward them. Try to tell each of the stories as though you had observed the characters in them.

In both of these selections, you must strive to get variety of melody if you are to picture these two persons fully. The phrasing must be carefully worked out in both, to achieve the conversational quality of Twain's style. The second excerpt presents a problem in energy, especially in the quotation from the mate. Work for an easy, conversational directness in both selections.

a. By and by one of our boys went away. He was not heard of for a long time. At last he turned up as apprentice engineer or "striker" on a steamboat. This thing shook the bottom out of all my Sunday-school teachings. That boy had been notoriously worldly, and I just the reverse; yet he was exalted to this eminence, and I left in obscurity and misery. There was nothing generous about this fellow in his greatness. . . . Whenever his boat was laid up he would come home and swell around the town in his blackest and greasiest clothes, so that nobody could help remembering that he was a steamboatman; and he used all sorts of steamboat technicalities in his talk, as if he were so used to them that he forgot common people could not understand them. . . . This fellow had money, too, and hair-oil. Also an ignorant silver watch and a showy brass watch-chain. . . . If ever a youth was cordially admired and hated by his comrades, this one was. . . . When his boat blew up at last, it diffused a tranquil contentment among us such as we had not known for months. But when he came home the next week, alive, renowned, and appeared in church all battered up and bandaged, a shining hero, stared at and wondered at by everybody, it seemed to us that the partiality of Providence for an undeserving reptile had reached a point where it was open to criticism.

b. I was sorry I hated the mate so, because it was not in (young) human nature not to admire him. He was huge and muscular, his face was bearded and whiskered all over; he had a red woman and a blue woman tattooed on his right arm . . . ; and in the matter of profanity he was sublime. . . . When he gave even the simplest order, he discharged it like a blast of lightning, and sent a long, reverberating peal of profanity thundering after it. I could not help contrasting the way in which the average landsman would give an order with the mate's way of doing it. If the landsman should wish the gangplank moved a foot farther forward, he would probably say: "James, or William, one of you push that plank forward, please"; but put the mate in his place, and he would roar out: "Here, now, start that gangplank for'ard! Lively, now! *What*'re you about! Snatch it! *snatch* it! There! there! Aft again! aft again! Don't you hear me? Dash it to dash! are you going to *sleep* over it! '*Vast* heaving. 'Vast heaving, I tell you! Going to heave it clear astern? WHERE're you going with that barrel! *for'ard* with it 'fore I make you swallow it, you dash-dash-dash-*dashed* split between a tired mud-turtle and a crippled hearse-horse!"

I wished I could talk like that.—MARK TWAIN

23. THE FALL OF THE HOUSE OF USHER

Poe is noted for the gloomy, melancholy moods which he created in his writing. This selection is an excellent example of such a mood created by the description of the landscape and the reactions it arouses. The story to which this is an introduction is a tale of horror such as only Poe could write. Try to picture a dark day in winter as you read.

The over-all rate of this reading is slow. In it, you must pay particular attention to duration and pause; if you allow the rate to be too fast you will not communicate the mood. Because of the slow rate, phrasing for breathing may present a problem. See what you can do with quality to set the emotional mood which Poe is trying to establish. Be sure that there is melody variety, as well.

During the whole of a dull, dark, and soundless day in the autumn of the year, when the clouds hung oppressively low in the heavens, I had been passing alone, on horseback, through a singularly dreary tract of country; and at length found myself, as the shades of the evening drew on, within view of the melancholy House of Usher. I know not how it was—but, with the first glimpse of the building, a sense of insufferable gloom pervaded my spirit. I say insufferable; for the feeling was unrelieved by any of that half-pleasurable, because poetic, sentiment with which the mind usually receives even the sternest natural images of the desolate or terrible. I looked upon the scene before me—upon the mere house, and the simple landscape features of the domain, upon the bleak walls, upon the vacant eye-like windows, upon a few rank sedges, and upon a few white trunks of decayed trees—with an utter depression of soul which I can compare to no earthly sensation more properly than to the after-dream of the reveller upon opium: the bitter lapse into everyday life, the hideous dropping off of the veil. There was an iciness, a sinking, a sickening of the heart, an unredeemed dreariness of thought which no goading of the imagination could torture into aught of the sublime. What was it—I paused to think—what was it that so unnerved me in the contemplation of the House of Usher?—EDGAR ALLAN POE

24. THE NEW SOUTH

Henry Grady came north from Georgia, in 1886, to deliver the speech from which this sample is taken. The speech was given before the New England Society of New York. Grady created a sensational effect in this effort to bring about understanding between North and South. Remember that he was giving the speech before a basically hostile audience in an era when the Civil War was still being fought in words. You must try to see the picture which he is painting for his audience before you try to read the selection aloud.

You have a difficult phrasing problem in this selection. See that there is variety and contrast in melody, quality, and energy between the two contrasting sections. If you study the selection, you will find that variety and contrast of time pattern are called for. Remember that these paragraphs are part of a speech.

Let me picture to you the footsore Confederate soldier, as, buttoning up in his faded gray jacket the parole which was to bear testimony to his children of his fidelity and faith, he turned his face southward from Appomattox in April, 1865. Think of him as—ragged, half-starved, heavyhearted, enfeebled by want and wounds, having fought to exhaustion—he surrenders his gun, wrings the hands of his comrades in silence, and lifting his tear-stained and pallid face for the last time to the graves that dot the old Virginia hills, pulls his gray cap over his brow and begins the slow and painful journey. What does he find—let me ask you who went to your homes eager to find, in the welcome you had justly earned, full payment for four years' sacrifice—what does he find, when, having followed the battle-stained cross against overwhelming odds, dreading death not half so much as surrender, he reaches the home he left so prosperous and beautiful? He finds his house in ruins, his farm devastated, his slaves free, his stock killed, his barns empty, his trade destroyed, his money worthless; his social system, feudal in its magnificence, swept away; his people without law or legal status; his comrades slain, and the burdens of others heavy on his shoulders. Crushed by defeat, his very traditions gone; without money,

credit, employment, material, or training; and besides all this, confronted
with the gravest problem that ever met human intelligence—the establishment of a status for the vast body of his liberated slaves.

What does he do—this hero in gray . . . ? Does he sit down in sullenness
and despair? Not for a day. Surely God, who had stripped him of his prosperity, inspired him in his adversity. As ruin was never before so overwhelming, never was restoration swifter. The soldier stepped from the
trenches into the furrow; horses that had charged Federal guns marched
before the plough; and the fields that ran red with human blood in April
were green with the harvest in June.—HENRY W. GRADY

25. THE FIFTY-YARD DASH *

This whimsical selection offers you an opportunity to relive some of your own
childhood experiences—your mental victories and actual defeats. Recapture them
and project yourself into the language of the author.

The selection is particularly well adapted to changes in rate and melody and to
the use of pause. Since the language is colloquial, some of the characteristic assimi-
lations of informal speech may be used, but the articulation should be clear.

That spring Longfellow School announced that a track meet was to be
held, one school to compete against another; *everybody* to participate.

Here, I believed, was my chance. In my opinion I would be first in every
event.

Somehow or other, however, continuous meditation on the theme of
athletics had the effect of growing into a fury of anticipation that continued
all day and all night, so that before the day of the track meet I had run
the fifty-yard dash any number of hundreds of times, had jumped the
running broad jump, the standing broad jump, and the high jump, and in
each event had made my competitors look like weaklings.

This tremendous inner activity, which was strictly Yoga, changed on
the day of the track meet into fever.

The time came at last for me and three other athletes . . . to go to
our marks, get set, and go; and I did, in a blind rush of speed which I knew
had never before occurred in the history of athletics.

It seemed to me that never before had any living man moved so swiftly.
Within myself I ran the fifty yards fifty times before I so much as opened

* William Saroyan, *My Name Is Aram*, New York: Harcourt, Brace and Company, Inc., 1940. (By permission.)

my eyes to find out how far back I had left the other runners. I was very much amazed at what I saw.

Three boys were four yards ahead of me and going away.

It was incredible. It was unbelievable, but it was obviously the truth. There ought to be some mistake, but there wasn't. There they were, ahead of me, going away.

Well, it simply meant that I would have to overtake them, with my eyes open, and win the race. This I proceeded to do. They continued, incredibly, however, to go away, in spite of my intention. I became irritated and decided to put them in their places for the impertinence, and began releasing all the mysterious vital forces within myself that I had. Somehow or other, however, not even this seemed to bring me any closer to them and I felt that in some strange way I was being betrayed. If so, I decided, I would shame my betrayer by winning the race in spite of the betrayal, and once again I threw fresh life and energy into my running. There wasn't a great distance still to do, but I knew I would be able to do it.

Then I knew I wouldn't.

The race was over.

I was last, by ten yards.

—WILLIAM SAROYAN

26. AARON BURR

In reading this selection, try to visualize the person whom you know who most resembles Clark's portrait of Burr. React in your own way to each of the qualities, good or bad, portrayed in the successive phrases of the second paragraph. Try to reflect your feelings in your voice.

This selection needs careful phrasing and the use of pause. Both the individual short phrases and the selection as a whole need to be read in such a way as to produce a cumulative effect. Experiment with changes in pitch and rate to contribute to this effect.

To fill a long felt want, the lawyers have invented the phrase "moral insanity"; the incurable defect in Burr's make-up was "moral idiocy," so to speak: that is to say he was constitutionally and utterly void of moral principles and wholly incapable of discerning or appreciating it in others. Morally, he was totally color-blind.

Whether outstripping all his fellows at Princeton; deliberately scouting the religion of his fathers; fighting valiantly as a soldier of the Revolution; making love to all women, bewitching many and marrying a widow older than himself; standing proudly at the head of the New York Bar; filling the great offices of Attorney-General, Senator of the United States, and Vice-President; remaining silent and motionless when a word or motion would have made him President; killing Alexander Hamilton in a duel; fleeing in disguise a fugitive from justice; dreaming of an empire, himself the emperor; plotting the ruin and dismemberment of his country; on trial for his life on a charge of high treason; a vagabond in Europe, to-day dancing with ladies of the blood royal, to-morrow starving in a garret; stealing back muffled incognito to his native land; cut by his old acquaintances, repulsed by his quondam friends; at the age of nearly fourscore wedding Madame Jumel against her will; carrying for forty years a load of obloquy sufficient to have damned half the world; at last on the banks of the River Styx cracking jokes with the grim Ferryman himself;—anywhere, everywhere, in all places, at all times, and under all circumstances, he is the same: bland, bold, brilliant, amiable, seductive, plausible . . . ; and utterly without trace of conscience.—CHAMP CLARK

27. THE VALUE OF DISSENSION

Someone has said that a dictatorship is like a fine steamer. It rides the waves easily and the passengers are comfortable in their staterooms; but when it strikes the rocks, it goes down and all are lost. Democracy, on the other hand, is like a raft. All of the passengers continually have wet feet, but it stays afloat. In the following selection, written in 1817 as a speech in defense of a man charged with sedition, Lord Jeffrey deals with a problem as contemporary as tomorrow morning. Since the issue is perennial, each of us must meet it for ourselves. Remember the criticisms of Congressional wranglings you have heard or read, and reply to them in the words of Jeffrey.

This selection provides an excellent opportunity for using changes in rate and pitch, coupled with proper use of pause, to put phrases in meaningful relationship to each other. The logical structure of the speech is clear, but subordination of some phrases and forceful emphasis of others are needed to carry the ideas to the listener. The type of analysis suggested in Chapter 7 will help you to decide how to read this selection.

There is a dissension known to this country, and known to all free countries, and to them only, which, however terrible it may appear to the sons of habitual slavery, or the minions of arbitrary power, or the contented and envied possessors of present influence, is of that wholesome nature that on it the life and health of the Constitution ultimately depend. It is not a frightful commotion, but a healthful exercise, not an exhausting fever, but a natural movement indicating and maintaining that vigour unimpaired.

In a free country, where the principles of Government are well understood, and the laws well administered, parties will ever be found opposed to parties. . . . This dissension is the life and heart and spirit of our Constitution; and true policy should promote discussion on those great points on which discussion must always be keen, and, in some degree, stormy and violent, because it is on them that the liberty, the prosperity, and happiness of the nation depend, and to them that all men of spirit, ingenuity, and talents have devoted their whole lives. . . . If this dissension were prevented, liberty would be extinguished. That very hostility which appears to excite so much apprehension is the parent of public prosperity, and of all the advantages in a free state for which it is worth while to contend.—LORD FRANCIS JEFFREY

28. THE COURT OF NATURE—MAN VS. WOMAN

Look about you on campus on a spring day and you will find plenty of inspiration for reading this mock-serious selection from *The Autocrat of the Breakfast Table*. Note the way in which the author uses the ponderous terminology of the law to deal with a light, almost frivolous, theme. Enjoy this tongue-in-cheek attitude as you read.

Adapt the rate, duration, and frequency of pause to the ponderous language. Experiment with levels of loudness and with melody pattern to determine what methods best reflect the mood and language of the selection.

Sir, all men love all women. That is the *prima-facie* aspect of the case. The Court of Nature assumes the law to be, that all men do so; and the individual man is bound to show cause why he does not love any particular woman. A man, says one of my old black-letter law-books, may show divers good reasons, as thus: He hath not seen the person named in the indictment; she is of tender age, or the reverse of that; she hath certain personal disqualifications,—as, for instance, she . . . hath an ill-favored countenance; or, his capacity of loving being limited, his affections are engrossed by a previous comer; and so of other conditions. Not the less is it true that he is bound by duty and inclined by nature to love each and every woman. Therefore it is that each woman virtually summons every man to show cause why he doth not love her. This is not by written document, or direct speech, for the most part, but by certain signs of silk, gold, and other materials, which say to all men,—Look on me and love, as in duty bound. Then the man pleadeth his special incapacity, whatsoever that may be,— as, for instance, impecuniosity, or that he hath one or many wives in his household, or that he is of mean figure, or small capacity; of which reasons it may be noted, that the first is, according to late decisions, of chiefest authority.—So far the old law-book. But there is a note from an older authority, saying that every woman doth also love each and every man, except there be some good reason to the contrary; and a very observing friend of mine, a young unmarried clergyman, tells me, that, so far as his experience goes, he has reason to think the ancient author had fact to justify his statement.—OLIVER WENDELL HOLMES

29. THE FORCE OF CONVERSATION

Dr. Holmes has caught, in this selection from *The Autocrat of the Breakfast Table*, a factor in our thinking and writing which all of us have experienced. What is the value of a conference with your instructor? Why do you like to study with others? What happens to your thinking in a bull session? Let Dr. Holmes speak for you as you re-create these experiences.

The selection is particularly well adapted to the use of pause and variations in duration, melody, and quality. Try to reflect changes in meaning and imagery by the use of these vocal factors.

Besides, there is another thing about this talking, which you forget. It shapes our thoughts for us;—the waves of conversation roll them as the surf rolls the pebbles on the shore. Let me modify the image a little. I rough out my thoughts in talk as an artist models in clay. Spoken language is so plastic,—you can pat and coax, and spread and shave, and rub out, and fill up, and stick on so easily, when you work that soft material, that there is nothing like it for modelling. Out of it come the shapes which you turn into marble or bronze in your immortal books, if you happen to write such. Or, to use another illustration, writing or printing is like shooting with a rifle; you may hit your reader's mind, or miss it;—but talking is like playing at a mark with the pipe of an engine; if it is within reach, and you have time enough, you can't help hitting it.—OLIVER WENDELL HOLMES

Index

Exercises for improvement, loudness
and meaning, 44–46
melody, 85–89
nasality and denasality, 111–112
open throat, 105–106
pitch, 77–78
relaxation, 69–70
steadiness of tone, 38–40
timing, 52–55
tone placement, 106–108
vocal faults, 69–74
vocal quality, 109
and meaning, 113–120
(*See also* Listening exercises)
Exhalation (expiration), 32–36, 41

F

Fall of the House of Usher, The, 239–240
False vocal folds, 61
Farewell, a Long Farewell, 132
Fatigue and illness, 13, 22
Fauces, isthmus of, 94
pillars of, 94
Fifty-Yard Dash, The, 241–242
Flatness of voice, 112
Flexibility, 7
Force of Conversation, The, 245
Forced vibration, 27–28, 98
Frequency, 25
Fricative consonants, 174, 184–186
Friends, influence of, 15–16
Fundamental tone, 26

G

General American speech, 135–137
Gilbert, W. S., 225–226
Glide, 81, 82
Glottal consonant, 174, 191
Glottal shock, 67
exercises, 71–72
Glottis, 61–64, 66, 89, 90
Grady, Henry W., 240–241
Gray, Thomas, 115

H

Habit, 2–3
Habitual pitch, 74–75, 80, 81, 123
Hamlet's Advice to the Players, 233–234
Hard palate, 93, 148, 173
Harshness, 65, 67
exercises, 72–73
Hawthorne, Nathaniel, 63
Hearing loss, 13
Herrick, Robert, 88
High-frequency deafness, 6–7
Hoarseness, 65, 68
exercises, 73–74
Holmes, Oliver Wendell, 87, 88, 244–245
Home influence, 14–15
House Divided, A, 235
Humanity of the Slave, The, 234–235
Hyoid bone, 59, 60, 62

I

I Can Hear It Now, record album, 10, 109
I Hear America Singing, 221
Illness, effect of, 13
Imitation, 14
Improvement in speech skill, methods of continuing, 211–213
plan for, 8–9
Inflection, 81–82, 123
circumflex, 82, 84
falling, 82, 84
rising, 82, 84
Ingersoll, Robert, 55
Inhalation (inspiration), 32, 33, 35, 41, 50
Integration, 122–133
defined, 125
and meaning, 126–129
Intonation, 82
Intrusive R, 198

J

Jefferson, Thomas, 127
Jeffrey, Francis (Lord), 243–244